March 19, 2007

Rob:

Keep up the good work and thanks for your support.

Mike

Superbrands®

CANADA

AN INSIGHT INTO MANY OF CANADA'S STRONGEST AND MOST TRUSTED BRANDS

VOLUME I

Superbrands Canada®

Publisher
Richard E. Brown

Associate Publisher
David Seaberg

Carl Meyer
Managing Director
America's Greatest Brands

Managing Editor
Christina Pochmursky

Design Director
Jack Huber

Copyeditor
Bob Land

Cover Photograph
Shaun Lowe

Published by
Superbrands Canada Inc.
15 Zorra Street
Toronto, Ontario M8Z 4Z6

Telephone (416) 259-9631
Facsimile (416) 259-9634
Email r.brown@vicbrownmedia.com
www.superbrandscanada.com

Special thanks to Stephen Smith, Luke Johnson, Bill Colgrave,
Richard Thomas, Peter Ledbetter, Mark Farrer-Brown, Ben
Redmond, Eamonn Sadler, Pete McCutchen, Rob Manfredi,
Alan Middleton, Rick Padulo, Garry Lee, Bob Kincaide,
Monica Ruffo, David Leonard, Edward Gould, Rob Guenette,
David Dunne, Ann Brown, Katrin Adler, Vanessa Dylyn.

Additional thanks to:
Peter Choy, Ming Lee, and World Print Ltd., Brian Forman of
Forman & Forman, Nelly Torossian and Premier Quality Printing

ISBN 0-9781656-0-8

Superbrands®
CANADA

AN INSIGHT INTO MANY OF CANADA'S STRONGEST AND MOST TRUSTED BRANDS
VOLUME I

This book is dedicated to the men and
women who build and protect
Canada's greatest brand assets.

www.superbrands.com

CONTENTS

Aeroplan
Aeroplan
5100 de Maisonneuve West,
Bureau 1154
Montreal, QC H4A 3T2

AIM Trimark
Aim Trimark Investments
120 Bloor Street East, Suite 700
Toronto, ON M4W 1B7

Air Canada
Air Canada
Air Canada Centre, 6th Floor
7373 Cote Vertu West
Saint Laurent, QC H4Y 1H4

Benjamin Moore
Benjamin Moore & Co. Ltd.
130 Mulock Avenue
Toronto, ON M6N 1G9

Buckley's
Novartis
2233 Argentia Road
Suite 205, West Tower
Mississauga, ON L5N 2X7

Budget Rent a Car
Budget Rent a Car Canada Ltd.
21 Four Seasons Place, Suite 500
Toronto, ON M9B 6J8

Calgary Stampede
Calgary Exhibition and Stampede
1410 Olympic Way SE – 2nd Floor
Calgary, AB T2G 2W1

Canfor
Canfor Corporation
1700 West 75th Ave., Suite 100
Vancouver, BC V6P 6G2

Castrol
Castrol Canada Inc.
3660 Lakeshore Boulevard West
Toronto, ON M8W 1P2

Cirque du Soleil
Cirque du Soleil
8400 2nd Avenue
Montreal, QC H1Z 4M6

CN Tower
CN Tower
301 Front Street West
Toronto, ON M5V 2T6

Coca-Cola
Coca-Cola Ltd.
3389 Steeles Avenue East, Suite 500
Toronto, ON M2H 3S8

Crown Royal
Diageo Canada Inc.
401 West Mall, Suite 800
Etobicoke, ON M9C 5P8

Energizer
Energizer Canada
6733 Mississauga Road, Suite 700
Mississauga, ON L5N 6J5

Esso
Imperial Oil Ltd.
111 St. Clair Avenue West
Toronto, ON M5W 1K3

Fido
Fido
800 rue de la Gauchetiere Quest
Bureau 4000
Montreal, QC H5A 1K3

Fisherman's Friend
TFB & Associates
600 Alden Road, Suite 102
Markham, ON L3R 0E7

Ford
Ford Motor Company of Canada
Limited
The Canadian Road
Oakville, ON L6J 5E4

Hbc
Hudson's Bay Company
401 Bay Street, Suite 700
Toronto, ON M5H 2Y4

Heart & Stroke Foundation
Heart & Stroke Foundation
2300 Yonge Street, Suite 1300
Toronto, ON M4P 1E4

Hitachi
Hitachi Canada Ltd.
2495 Meadowpine Boulevard
Mississauga, ON L5N 6C3

Honda
Honda Canada Inc.
715 Milner Avenue
Toronto, ON M1B 2K8

Hunter Douglas
Hunter Douglas Canada Ltd.
132 First Gulf Boulevard
Brampton, ON L6W 4T7

Hush Puppies
Hush Puppies Canada Ltd.
4600 Hickmore Street
Montreal, QC H4T 1K2

Intel
Intel Corporation
2200 Mission College Boulevard
Santa Clara, CA 95052
USA

Jaguar
Jaguar Canada
8 Indell Lane
Brampton, ON L6T 4H3

Land Rover
Land Rover Canada
8 Indell Lane
Brampton, ON L6T 4H3

Lay's
Frito-Lay Canada
55 Standish Court, Suite 700
Mississauga, ON L5R 4B2

M&M's
Effem Inc.
37 Holland Drive
Bolton, ON L7E 5S4

MasterCard
MasterCard Canada Inc.
2 Bloor Street West, Suite 1400
Toronto, ON M4W 3E2

Michelin
Michelin North America Inc.
3020 Jacques-Bureau
Laval, QC H7P 6G2

Moen
Moen Inc.
2816 Bristol Circle
Oakville, ON L6H 5S7

Monster
Monster.ca
276 rue St. Jacques Quest, 10th Floor
Montreal, QC H2Y 1N3

Purina
Nestlé Purina
2500 Royal Windsor Drive
Mississauga, ON L5J 1K8

RBC
RBC Financial Group
Royal Bank Plaza
200 Bay Street
7th Floor, North Tower
Toronto, ON M5J 2J5

RE/MAX
RE/MAX Promotions Inc.
7101 Syntex Drive
Mississauga, ON L5N 6H5

Rogers
Rogers Communications Inc.
333 Bloor Street East
Toronto, ON M4W 1G9

RONA
RONA Inc.
220 Chemin du Tremblay
Bouchardville, QC J4B 8H7

Royal Doulton
Royal Doulton Canada
305 Milner Avenue, Suite 700
Toronto, ON M1B 3V4

**STAPLES Business Depot/
Bureau en Gros**
Staples
6 Staples Avenue
Richmond Hill, ON L4B 4W3

Symantec
Symantec
3381 Steeles Avenue East, 4th Floor
Toronto, ON M2H 3S7

Texas Instruments
Texas Instruments
12500 TI Boulevard
Dallas, TX 75243
USA

Tim Hortons
Tim Hortons
874 Sinclair Road
Oakville, ON L6K 2Y1

TSX
TSX Group
The Exchange Tower
130 King Street West
Toronto, ON M5X 1J2

United Way
United Way of Canada
56 Sparks Street, Suite 404
Ottawa, ON K1P 5K9

**The Weather Network
and MétéoMédia**
The Weather Network
2655 Bristol Circle
Oakville, ON L6H 7W1

Yellow Pages Group
Yellow Pages Group
16 Place du Commerce, 10th Floor
Isle des Soeurs
Montreal, QC H3A 2A5

FOREWORD

This is our first volume of *Superbrands Canada*. It represents the culmination of the vision and efforts of a lot of people, both at Superbrands and at the many companies that are represented in this first issue. I thank you all for your ability to recognize a great product and understand its importance to the ongoing task of branding.

Superbrands Canada provides readers with a benchmark of some of the truly great brands that have flourished in this country. Some are home grown; some have come from other countries and established themselves here, evolving into household names.

What makes a Superbrand and how does one make the cut? The Superbrands Council of Canada creates the list of Canadian Superbrands. The Council Members, who are some of the most distinguished figures in branding, marketing, advertising and public relations in this country, have used their expertise, gained through years of branding experience with many different products and services, to choose which Canadian companies qualify as Superbrands. Most of these companies and organizations are instantly recognizable to the general public because they have built their identity on high-quality products and excellent service. These companies compete in markets driven by price, quality, service and reputation. To be declared a Superbrand demands that a company withstand the pressures from the market and continually deliver on all their promises.

The profiles on the pages that follow illustrate how these brands have evolved and continually adapt to meet new challenges from the marketplace. Whether the market demands better fuel efficiency, lower trans fats, increased ergonomics or a cool factor that makes consumers want to own it, the companies featured here have met and exceeded those demands year after year.

We also asked the Brand Council and the featured brands in this volume to select two charitable organizations which they feel qualify as Canadian Superbrands. We are proud to feature The United Way of Canada and the Heart & Stroke Foundation in this first edition of Superbrands Canada. These nonprofit institutions raise money and awareness in the pursuit of the betterment of the health and welfare of humanity and are thus truly deserving of Superbrand status.

Richard E. Brown
Superbrands Canada

"Whether the market demands better fuel efficiency, lower trans fats, increased ergonomics or a cool factor that makes consumers want to own it, the companies featured here have met and exceeded those demands year after year."

THE SUPERBRANDS COUNCIL

**DR. ALAN MIDDLETON
Director
Executive Programs,
Marketing Specialization,
Schulich School of Business
York University**

We know the fundamentals of strong brands: they have clearly defined target groups, whose functional and symbolic needs they meet, at a price that is judged good value and with marketing communications that communicates both the performance benefits but also the personality or personae of the brand and with service levels that beat expectations. Marketers achieve this powerful brand positioning by consistent, sufficient and appropriate investment in product, distribution and communications research and development. Also, they learn to integrate and align all customer touch-points with the brand positioning, including the training and motivation of staff.

If we know this, why does there appear to have been a weakening of brand attractions?

My answer is impatience. The short termism of most businesses does not allow the time or consistency of investment to achieve the strength so admired in strong brands. So, what makes a great brand? The two Ps: professionalism and patience.

**ANDREA SOUTHCOTT
President,
TBWA Vancouver**

Today, it seems, branding is on everyone's mind; law firms are branded, realtors are branded, politicians are branded. So, what then does it take to go from brand to Superbrand? At minimum, the branding process needs to deliver on the essence of what you're selling. A strong brand also delivers on a character unique to that brand, with tone, look and message all helping reinforce the values inherent in what the brand delivers.

But a Superbrand goes beyond that. Superbrands connect in a fully dimensionalized way. They become a market force that others follow. They grow and build on the values that make them distinctive. A Superbrand's consumer feels so connected and understands the brand so well, that they begin to contribute ideas, insights and communications that demonstrate their co-ownership. Superbrands are alive, they grow and change.

**GARRY LEE
President,
Cundari Integrated Advertising**

I'm staying away from terms like differentiation, relevancy, equity, etc. To be honest, I'm tired of them and I think there is a bigger explanation for what constitutes a Superbrand.

Exceptional brands have two main functions in life: to make consumers decisions simpler and more gratifying. In exchange for this welcomed act, consumers reward them first through purchase, then through loyalty and lastly through their willingness to pay a premium. This consumer attitude doesn t just happen however. Great brands must stay true to themselves and never lose sight of what they stand for in their category. And if they hope to endure, great brands must never be satisfied with the state of their customer relationships.

In the end, Superbrands are like human beings. They learn, grow, make mistakes, and rebound. Naturally, one thing is a given. They always take the lead.

**NOEL O'DEA
President,
Target Marketing & Communications Inc.**

John Smale, Chairman of Procter & Gamble, reported in 1995 that while Procter & Gamble was valued at $48 billion, its assets totalled only $6 billion. The $42 billion difference, he said, represented the brand equity the company had built into its products through advertising .

As brand architects, we see brands as complex bundles of meanings, emotions, symbols, and associations created and shaped by advertising and other brand cues and adopted by people to fit their aspirations, dreams, and self-concept or as a tribal badge.

Advertising is one of our most powerful tools for building strong, profitable brands. Advertising gives the brand its voice. It communicates what the brand stands for. It delivers a powerful articulation of the brand's benefits. And, at its most powerful, advertising sneaks into our hearts and minds and creates an enduring emotional bond.

That's the point when a brand becomes a Superbrand.

**RICHARD PADULO
Chairman & CEO,
Padulo Integrated Inc.**

What makes a great brand? Pervasive awareness, an image of quality, the ability to drive share of market . . . True. But too obvious. Let's go deeper . . .

There's a flurry of Remember when? e-mails circulating the Internet, exchanged by Baby Boomers shocked to realize they're old enough to be reminiscing. Remember when Coke cost a quarter? Remember when Double Bubble was where you found baseball cards? Remember Tony the Tiger? To me, that's what makes a great brand: it's a brand you'll mention when it's your turn to write a Remember when e-mail.

Such a brand is no longer external — it's family. It's literally a part of how you re going to remember your life. A point on your compass. Even if the product itself isn't perfect, something would be missing if the brand went away.

That's the essence of a Superbrand.

BOB KINCAIDE Managing Director, Hazelton Group

A brand is a promise to consumers of a meaningful, unique experience. Easy to say, tough to do.

Superbrands go beyond the immediate tangible experience (e.g. comfortable run with Nike shoes) and deliver a bigger experience (e.g. feeling of accomplishment with a successful run). The benefits of a Superbrand are both rational and emotional — they touch the heart as well as the mind in an integrated way.

Superbrands walk the talk — and for them, advertising only adds value to a benefit that people already want to include in their lives. A Superbrand has a life of its own. Consumers recognize it immediately as a meaningful, differentiated and compelling answer to their needs. The Superbrand is a simple but demanding concept as witnessed by how few Superbrands exist today. However, creating a Superbrand is a worthy goal as it delivers sustainable competitive advantage with superior financial rewards.

PROFESSOR DAVID DUNNE Marketing, Joseph Rotman School of Management University of Toronto

What makes a great brand? Consumers make a brand great. A great brand is like a great opera, where the orchestra, soprano and chorus merge to bring the audience to a crescendo of emotion. Similarly, for a brand to be great, everything has to work: the product, the advertising, the trade deals, the service.

But the key to greatness is what the brand's opera produces in consumers' hearts. That's why Apple is a great brand: it connects with its audience. Who cares if it isn't market leader? Its users love it and will pay for it. IKEA furniture looks great and saves its customers money, and they travel far and wide to find an IKEA store. To marketers of great brands, customers aren't just market segments: they are real, living, feeling human beings. Knowing your customers like you know your own family: that's the stuff of greatness.

EDWARD GOULD Senior Vice-President, National Public Relations

Great brands connect with people. They exude personality and know how to communicate to the head and the heart. They have the ability to anticipate where the customer relationship is going. Yet, these are challenging times for even the best of brands. Competitive advantage is ephemeral. New players with new technologies are delivering more functionality at a lower price. But perhaps the greatest risk to the future of brands may be society's perception of the conduct of corporations. Misconduct and scandal have eroded confidence in the sacred trust between consumer, product and producer.

Character counts. When consumers are reaching for brands, they are passing judgment on the reputation of the corporation. Trust is part of the transaction.

Here's to the Superbrands that have the imagination to anticipate needs, the commitment to deliver quality and above all, the integrity that earns the trust of those who define their success.

ROB GUENETTE President, Taxi Toronto

What makes a great brand? A great brand has soul. It evokes a feeling and creates value.

To evoke feelings, great brands must stand for something, be salient and be reasonably consistent over a long period of time. Durability will be the outcome of a personality that invites trust, respect and loyalty.

Brands that achieve greatness build on a powerful emotional connection while delivering value for both their consumers and their stakeholders. Everyone's happy when brand equity is high. The notion of equity has come to connote money value, but its roots are in the meaning of just or fair. Herein lies the most powerful interpretation of brand equity; this notion of perceived value.

The greatest brands have been tested and retested proving their resilience. They have become part of our culture in a very special way, woven into the fabric of everyday life.

MONICA RUFFO President, Nucleus Cossette Montreal

Superbrands break at least one law of marketing. They do things their own way. They surprise and they pioneer. They are "the first." They are studied and benchmarked. Coca-Cola's use of Norman Rockwell in the 40's was gutsy and fresh. A Superbrand if ever there was one. In some cases, as is the case with McDonald's, their positioning is broad enough that (gasp) it has different meaning to different targets and it is hard to put into a nice neat box. Ubiquitous superbrands are scary since no brand can "be all things to all people," . . . right?

In other cases, Superbrands have gone beyond "dialogue" and interactivity with consumers to true co-creation. Internet brands such as MySpace have led the way, but many brands in traditional categories are now following suit. Where Superbrands go, others inevitably follow. Of course there are many measurable variables that make a brand a Superbrand, including awareness and so forth. But Superbrands also possess an elusive quality: a uniqueness not only of positioning but also of marketing practice. They dare to be first and alone. And for this they are admired.

DAVID LEONARD President, DDB Canada

Marketing communications professionals get so caught up in the world of eloquent lingo and sophisticated banter about brands that I sometimes wonder if we've lost sight of our role in this business. Are we not about making things simple for people — helping to connect a promise with a need or desire? Is it not that simple?

My take on this topic is that it all comes down to the most precious of relationships, between family, friends, and pets. Yes, it's the L word. Love. Irrational, unexplainable, overwhelming — so powerful that it drives us to do the craziest things.

A special relationship endures, evolves and becomes more precious with every passing day. Like special people in our lives, a Superbrand takes on a powerful, emotional, often irrational role in our world.

The degree of commitment, involvement, passion and respect that is built is beyond explanation. It's the magical love affair going on between people and the things they love. They can't imagine their lives without their favorite brand of java, jeans, beer, airline even shampoo and deodorant!

aeroplan

Miles. Possibilities.

THE MARKET

The Canadian loyalty marketing industry provides loyal customers with collectible incentives that, when converted into rewards, form part of a compelling value proposition that encourages the purchase of products or services. Loyalty programs have consequently become prevalent in many sectors, including mass merchandising, retail, financial services and travel. Accordingly, loyalty marketing has become a key element in the marketing mix of many companies. Today, 80 percent of Canadian households — with incomes of over $100,000 — have one or more Aeroplan Members, making Aeroplan one of Canada's loyalty market leaders.

ACHIEVEMENTS

In 2004, Aeroplan celebrated its 20th anniversary, a milestone that few other loyalty marketing companies can claim in Canada. Today, Aeroplan's leading market position and strong brand make it highly attractive to existing and potential commercial partners. According to a 2005 in-house survey, Aeroplan is also most often identified by its members as their "preferred loyalty program."

In early 2004, Aeroplan received an Industry Impact Award from *InsideFlyer* magazine to honour its introduction of personalized and expanded benefits to Air Canada's top-tier members. Moreover, the prestigious U.S.-based *Communication Arts* magazine also recognized the design quality of Aeroplan's new tangerine-coloured brand logo, which was in its 2004 Design Annual edition.

Since its inception, Aeroplan has joined forces with more than 60 commercial partners, representing over 100 leading brands, who have actively participated in the program — due mostly to the sustained purchasing behaviour of Aeroplan Members. Over time, Aeroplan's brand has also become associated with a very appealing base of Canadian consumers — in terms of household income and spending habits. With a growing number of partners and, in turn, ever more opportunities to collect and redeem Aeroplan Miles (Aeroplan's highly valued currency), high value members have chosen to remain loyal to the program.

HISTORY

Aeroplan was founded by Air Canada in July 1984 as an incentive program for its frequent-flyer customers. By the end of its second year, over 100,000 frequent flyers had enrolled in Aeroplan.

By 1990, Aeroplan had grown to over 700,000 members. That year, Aeroplan began rewarding its top-tier members with Air Canada Elite® and Air Canada Prestige® status — along with the accompanying premium benefits and privileges. Given the popularity of this initiative, Aeroplan introduced a third status level in 1999 — Air Canada Super Elite® — to reward members who earned over 100,000 Aeroplan Miles per year.

When Aeroplan first formed a co-branded financial card partnership with Canadian Imperial Bank of Commerce in 1991, its membership took off. That year, the CIBC Aerogold VISA card was launched, allowing cardholders to earn miles on every card purchase. Today, according to the Canadian Banking Association, it's Canada's most widely used premium credit card.

The period of Aeroplan's most profound transformation is recent. In January 2002, Air Canada spun off Aeroplan as a wholly owned subsidiary (now the world's first publicly traded loyalty program following a recent IPO). By the time Aeroplan marked its 20th anniversary in 2004, it had evolved into Canada's premier loyalty marketing company — and one of Canada's longest-standing loyalty programs. Aeroplan offers airline seats on the Star Alliance network and an ever wider selection of upscale lifestyle rewards. Its relationship with financial partners also expanded in early 2004 — when Amex Bank of Canada introduced American Express AeroplanPlus cards, a family of co-branded charge cards for swift mileage accumulation. Aeroplan also signed multi-year partnership contracts with some of Canada's leading retailers, including Bell, Esso and Future Shop.

THE PRODUCT

Through its partnerships with Air Canada, Amex Bank of Canada, Bell Canada, Canadian Imperial Bank of Commerce, Future Shop, Esso, Star Alliance member airlines and numerous hotel chains and car rental companies, Aeroplan offers over 5 million active members the ability to accumulate Aeroplan Miles through the purchase of products and services. In 2004, members accumulated over 58 billion Aeroplan Miles, representing an equivalent of approximately $40 billion in consumer spending.

Once members accumulate enough Aeroplan Miles for an Aeroplan Reward, they can redeem them by selecting from approximately 15,000 daily

flights to 795 destinations in 139 countries, stays at over 2,000 hotels across Canada, the U.S. and the Caribbean, car rentals worldwide, plus a wide choice of electronics and lifestyle rewards.

One of Canada's longest-standing rewards programs, Aeroplan is Canada's premier loyalty marketing company. Long recognized for its innovative programs to encourage mileage accumulation and redemption, Aeroplan provides its commercial partners with loyalty marketing services to attract and retain customers and stimulate demand for their products and services — through access to its members and marketing programs aimed at increasing revenue, market share and customer loyalty.

Aeroplan has also expanded its strategy beyond the consumer realm to encompass solutions designed specifically for the needs of Canadian businesses. Aeroplan's B2x strategy has been developed to leverage the appeal of Aeroplan Miles in non-traditional markets and applications. Together with its business partner, Elevate Incentives, Aeroplan offers Business-to-Employee and Business-to-Channel solutions to Canadian businesses, offering the ability to award Aeroplan Miles to their employees and distribution channels that meet or exceed performance goals. With the Aeronote™ program, Aeroplan has developed a Business-to-Customer solution that leverages the power of the Aeroplan Mile, offering businesses turnkey, certificate-based marketing tools (available in various denominations of Aeroplan Miles) to attract new customers or increase customer loyalty.

RECENT DEVELOPMENTS

In recent years, Aeroplan has initiated a number of significant changes aimed at improving customer service. Between 2001 and 2005, Aeroplan's customer satisfaction levels have climbed steadily. This is due to the ongoing development of its call centres. It can also be attributed to the dramatic growth of Aeroplan's Web

presence — via aeroplan.com. This has increased online bookings over time, which now approximately represent over 40 percent of air reward travel. In addition, Aeroplan recently introduced an interactive voice recognition system to facilitate member access to customer services, further improving its self-service aspect.

In 2003, Aeroplan made a strategic shift to expand its reward portfolio beyond airline seats,

introducing a flexible suite of experiential and merchandise rewards. It is now amongst the largest of its kind in Canada.

In 2004, Aeroplan marked another important change in direction: a new brand strategy and the

creation of a new brand identity. At the same time, Aeroplan introduced its new and distinctive, tangerine-coloured, "swipable" membership card, which has the potential for limitless mileage accumulation and redemption.

PROMOTION

Aeroplan maintains a broad range of mass advertising, promotional, direct mail, sponsorship and e-marketing activities.

Traditionally, Aeroplan's marketing activities have been focused on dedicated and coalition marketing promotions for commercial partners, which often take the form of multi-channel national campaigns, including point-of-sale promotions, national advertising, Web banner advertising and direct marketing.

Regular communication with members through newsletters, statements and periodic special mailings is a cornerstone of Aeroplan's marketing approach. Its communications were recently revised to offer members more choice in channels, more flexible tools and increased potential for highly targeted and relevant messages.

Nearly 2 million members receive statements and other targeted information from Aeroplan via e-mail. Now half of its content is targeted, member-centric content, and up to 100 percent more media space is available for partner offers.

Aeroplan's new newsletter, *Tangerine*, is another innovative tool that offers high quality, highly anticipated, targeted content. In the spirit of providing members with a value-added experience, Aeroplan recently launched its first rewards catalogue — also available in an electronic version.

BRAND VALUES

Aeroplan enjoys a solid relationship with its 5 million active members, who may very well consider Aeroplan Miles a precious commodity — currency for not only the cost of a reward, but also enriching the discretionary side of their lives, a way of making special experiences happen.

According to in-house research in 2003, "enriching life" and "personal fulfilment" were two phrases that were repeatedly mentioned by members. For them, Aeroplan is about unique, memorable experiences that represent a very emotional and precious dimension in their lives. As it enters the next phase of its evolution, Aeroplan intends to make the benefits of its program even more member-centric — and strengthen the familial bond with its membership.

THINGS YOU DIDN'T KNOW ABOUT AEROPLAN

○ Aeroplan is Canada's premier loyalty marketing company — and among the top rewards programs in North America.

○ Aeroplan has more than 5 million active members worldwide, almost 500,000 of whom reside outside Canada.

○ Twenty-seven percent of Canadian households include an Aeroplan Member — and more than 80 percent of those households have incomes of over $100,000.

○ According to the Ipsos-Reid 2004 *Canadian Business Travel Study*, 92 percent of frequent Canadian business travellers are Aeroplan Members.

○ In 2004, over 58 billion Aeroplan Miles were accumulated by members, representing an equivalent of approximately $40 billion in consumer spending.

○ Aeroplan issued 1.35 million reward tickets in 2005.

○ Aeroplan is the world's largest issuer of Air Canada tickets.

○ The prestigious U.S.-based *Communication Arts* magazine has recognized the design quality of Aeroplan's new brand logo, including it in its 2004 Design Annual.

Knowing Pays.

AIM TRIMARK

LOOK HARDER. YOU'LL SEE 140 YEARS
OF PENSION INVESTMENT EXPERIENCE.

The investment team at AIM Trimark has an extensive and successful background in providing disciplined and proven solutions for pension plans in Canada. In fact, we have more than 140 combined years of pension investment experience – experience that is skillfully applied to five defined benefit pools: Canadian balanced, Canadian equities, global equities, international equities and U.S. equities.
Learn more by calling 1.800.874.6275

Knowing Pays: **AIM TRIMARK™**

INSTITUTIONAL INVESTMENTS

¹AIM, the chevron logo and all associated trademarks are trademarks of A I M Management Group Inc., used under licence. ²Knowing Pays, TRIMARK and all associated trademarks are trademarks of AIM Funds Management Inc.

THE MARKET

Mutual funds originated in Europe in the 1820s, but it took a hundred years before they appeared in Canada. Mutual fund growth was slow from the 1920s until the mid- to late 1980s. That's when they caught the eyes of investors and advisors who recognized the return potential mutual funds offered. They made sense in a lot of other ways. How else, for instance, could the average investor gain access to the professional expertise of the best investment managers for as little as a $100 investment? Inexpensive, accessible and easy to buy and sell, mutual funds suddenly — and smartly — became the investment of choice for millions of people.

Today, there are over 2,300 mutual funds available in Canada with over $540 billion invested. Equally impressive is the one-third of Canadian households that rely on mutual funds to support them in retirement, put their kids through school or meet any number of other financial goals.

ACHIEVEMENTS

AIM Trimark is one of Canada's largest investment management companies, with over $43 billion in assets under management and more than 2 million investors in Canada and around the world.

One of the company's co-founders and chief investment officer, Robert Krembil received a career achievement award in 1999 upon his retirement. But winning awards is par for the course at AIM Trimark. The company's impressive track record and excellent investor relations have been acknowledged dozens of times over the years with a growing list of awards and accolades.

AIM Trimark has won nineteen awards for excellence in investment management and was named Advisors' Choice Fund Company of the Year eight times in 10 years starting in 1996.

Voted tops in the industry in 2005 for service among high volume contact centres for the fourth year in a row, AIM Trimark also won an award for having North America's best advisor Web site in 2005 among the continent's 24 largest fund companies, including Fidelity Investments, Franklin Templeton, Oppenheimer and American Funds. And it was ranked fourth-highest in terms of percentage growth in pension assets by *Benefits Canada* magazine.

HISTORY

The history of AIM Trimark Investments starts in two very different places.

In Canada, Trimark Investment Management Inc. was created by Robert Krembil, Arthur Labatt and Michael Axford in July 1981. The three men created two mutual funds — Trimark Fund and Trimark Canadian Fund — with seed capital of $800,000 that came from friends and associates. Over the course of the next 12 years, 29 funds were added to the Trimark mutual fund lineup, leaving the firm with $25.5 billion in assets under management at December 31, 1999.

Meanwhile, south of the border, another trio of men consisting of Ted Bauer, Bob Graham and Gary Crum were busy founding their own company called A I M Management Group Inc. in 1976. With nothing more than a card table, two chairs, a coffee pot and telephone, the three opened what was then essentially a fixed-income or bond shop. Over the next 25 years, AIM would purchase or launch more than 100 mutual funds

and reach the US$183 billion mark in assets, serving more than 7 million U.S. shareholders.

The two firms became one in 2000, creating AIM Trimark Investments. Now, Canadian investors had the best of both worlds — two complementary but distinct fund families to choose from, both with proven track records of success.

THE PRODUCT

Success in the mutual fund industry isn't accidental, so AIM Trimark Investments adheres to proven investment disciplines that have built and protected investors' wealth for more than two decades.

When it comes to investing in companies, Trimark investment managers go about it as if they were buying the company for themselves with their own money. This approach is encapsulated in the phrase "Business people buying businesses." As prospective business owners, Trimark managers form a proprietary view of a company using independent thought and judgement. This proprietary view is arrived at by adhering to three fundamental principles:

Know the business inside out. Trimark managers apply rigorous financial, competitor and supplier analysis to companies under consideration.

Focus on management. Determine the overall calibre and credibility of the people running the company through one-on-one interviews.

Identify attractively priced businesses. Even with a great business in sight, Trimark managers will only invest in it if it's selling at the right price.

AIM investment managers apply one of four investment disciplines to identify investment opportunities with superior growth potential.

The earnings-driven discipline is based on the belief that earnings drive stock prices over time, so AIM investment managers seek high-quality companies with encouraging future earnings events.

The quantitative discipline relies on statistical analysis to find the best stocks worldwide with the greatest opportunities to outperform.

The **catalyst-driven discipline** seeks companies with an emerging variable or cause for change that will unlock the company's true value.

The **growth discipline** applies deep, rigorous fundamental analysis to uncover companies with above-average growth potential over the long term. AIM and Trimark: Taken together, the two fund families offer investors the promise of building and protecting wealth through a wide variety of investment options.

A full range of mutual funds spanning the risk-return spectrum offers investors the ease, convenience and peace of mind that comes from knowing that one company has two complementary, proven fund families that provide investors specialized services for their individual needs.

Dialogue Wealth Management is AIM Trimark's comprehensive wealth management solution that offers a range of fully personalized or fund-of-funds portfolios with both options providing asset rebalancing and features enhanced client reporting.

AIM Trimark Core Bundles incorporate the company's complementary investment disciplines into one investment.

AIM Trimark Private Pools are designed for investors with more than $100,000 to invest and deliver the benefits of reduced management fees, tax-deferred switching between pools and enhanced portfolio manager commentaries.

RECENT DEVELOPMENTS

As smart and as beneficial as the AIM and Trimark union was for investors, it did not come without challenges from a brand perspective. As recently as 2002, the two companies had very different cultures, were in different phases of development, and the post-merger logo looked like a co-sponsorship initiative because it contained both corporate logos. More important, few employees could articulate what it was that made the newly merged company unique. Further, the newly created AIM Trimark Investments lacked a unified vision and brand essence.

WE LIKED WHAT WE SAW IN THE BEDROOMS OF EUROPE. AND SO DID OUR INVESTORS.

It was the positive earnings reports we'd seen from a European bedroom furniture store that made us look into the bedrooms of Europe. What we discovered there was an obsession with getting a deal. And a retailer totally focused on undercutting its competitors and increasing its market share. We thought this discount retailer had great growth potential, so we invested in it. Less than three years later, our investment had quadrupled in value. Ask your advisor about AIM Trimark or visit www.aimtrimark.com.

Knowing Pays: AIM TRIMARK

Commissions, trailing commissions, management fees and expenses may all be associated with mutual fund investments. Mutual funds are not guaranteed, their values change frequently and past performance may not be repeated. Please read the prospectus before investing. Copies are available from your advisor or from AIM Trimark Investments. †AIM, the chevron logo and all associated trademarks are trademarks of A.I.M Management Group Inc., used under licence. *Knowing Pays, TRIMARK and all associated trademarks are trademarks of AIM Funds Management Inc.

The first step to meeting these challenges was the development of a mission statement. Second, an all-employee Town Hall meeting was held to help fine-tune the statement and develop core values, or principles. All employees were invited to attend focus groups where they were asked what AIM Trimark meant to them. This was an ambitious undertaking, but it was important to build the brand from the inside out as opposed to the top down. The company's six core principles were created from these sessions, and they now act as signposts to guide employee behaviour, aid decision making and solidify a common brand experience for the company's staff and clients.

PROMOTION

After comprehensive brand equity research and careful analysis of investor/advisor perceptions and their needs, the decision was made to signify the depth and value of AIM Trimark's investment expertise in the statement: Knowing Pays.

These words now appear as the AIM Trimark tagline and have become synonymous for the way the company rigorously analyzes companies, thoughtfully invests its clients' money and gives its investors confidence regarding their investments. The tagline and logo now form the focal point of print, broadcast and out-of-home advertising, with each having to satisfy the Knowing Pays thought. This unified approach was introduced to investors/advisors in early 2004 with the following results:

• Twenty-one percent year-over-year rise in investors' claimed awareness of our TV advertising, according to Ipsos-ASI Brand/Ad Tracking Report
• Viewed as Canada's Best Mutual Fund

Company Overall by 47 percent of advisors, with the next closest competitor at 16 percent, according to Ipsos-Reid Advisor Tracking Study
• Scored highest in terms of brand awareness among competitive set and ranked number one for aided awareness of the AIM Trimark name by investors in 2005, according to Ipsos-ASI Brand/Ad Tracking Report

BRAND VALUES

AIM Trimark's six core principles were created by its 900-plus employees to meet president and CEO Phil Taylor's desire to build a company "not for which employees work, but to which they belong."

Inspired by the its misson statement, "AIM Trimark is the premier provider of enduring solutions for investors and their advisors," the company was built on a bedrock of the values and principles that continue to drive AIM Trimark's exceptional success in the mutual fund industry.

1. Exceeding expectations sets us apart.
2. People are the foundation of our success.
3. Leadership is within all of us.
4. Working together, we achieve more.
5. Communication builds trust among us.
6. Helping others is part of who we are.

So entrenched are these principles that 92 percent of all employees surveyed in 2004 understand them, and 91 percent believe they live the principles every day, according to AIM Trimark Employee Opinion Survey.

THINGS YOU DIDN'T KNOW ABOUT AIM TRIMARK INVESTMENTS

○ The company is a National Partner, Bowl for Kids Sake, Big Brothers and Big Sisters.

○ Ninety three employees have assisted in the building of four homes for Habitat for Humanity.

○ From April 2000 to October 2005, employees have submitted over $820,000 in donations to 350 charities.

○ Every dollar contributed by employees to a registered charity is matched by AIM Trimark up to $3,000 a year per employee.

I am the brand

AIR CANADA

THE MARKET

At a time of turmoil in the North American airline industry, Air Canada is flying high with a successful business plan and accumulating awards as the best airline in North America.

Launched on September 1, 1937, Air Canada has survived the many challenges of the airline industry and has become one of the biggest Canadian success stories of all time.

Today, Air Canada, a business unit of the parent company ACE Aviation Holdings Inc., provides scheduled and chartered transportation to over 150 destinations. These destinations include **60** Canadian cities, **51** U.S. locations and **59** European, Middle Eastern, Asian, Australian, Caribbean, Mexican and South American travel spots. Air Canada mainline operates on average **635** scheduled flights a day, proudly serving more than 30 million scheduled and chartered customers annually. Air Canada's extensive global network, convenient schedules and customer services are enhanced through its membership in the Star Alliance™ network. Above all, Air Canada is dedicated to value-added customer service, technical excellence and passenger safety.

ACHIEVEMENTS

Brand image and superior customer service are key factors in the competitive airline industry, and both must be strategically maintained in order to maintain customer loyalty. New terminals in Toronto and Montreal gave Air Canada the opportunity to improve passenger processing, refurbish its Maple Leaf Lounges and add "self check-in" kiosks. And when customer research revealed that travellers thought the airline's interiors were uninspired, Air Canada moved to develop a new and refreshed brand identity. The restyling included the creation of new uniforms for flight attendants and

Best Airline—North America

a complete makeover of the aircraft's interiors. The new creative platform was inspired by Air Canada's emblematic red maple leaf.

These changes were made simultaneously with several other initiatives: a simplified fare structure, an overall fleet modernization with the acquisition of Embraer aircrafts and a new advertising campaign.

As one of the most innovative companies in North America's airline industry, Air Canada's rebranding was a natural evolution of a company that has always been the leader of the pack. The company made headlines in 1999 when it became the first airline in the country to introduce convenient self-serve check-in kiosks at all major airports across Canada. Air Canada now offers web-based electronic ticketing and Web check-in on most North American and international routes.

In 2005, the company was voted Best Airline in North America at the Skytrax World Airline

Awards. That same year, the now famous "You and I Were Meant to Fly" ad campaign garnered multiple honours, winning awards for Best Airline Integrated Advertising Campaign and Best Travel Integrated Advertising Campaign.

Today, Air Canada continues to dominate the field with creative ideas for both business and economy class customers. The latest generation of "lie-flat bed," which use the most advanced technology in seat design, have made Air Canada's Business Class a haven of comfort for long-haul flights. And new, more comfortable seats have been installed in Economy Class as well.

In addition to the new look and feel of the cabins, Air Canada has also upgraded its on-board entertainment systems. Travellers now enjoy Video-on-Demand across the fleet, which delivers video and entertainment choices via personal touch-screen television monitors, digital imaging and "Surround Sound."

In addition, the launch of the prepaid multi-trip Flight Pass has given passengers the opportunity to have tailor-made, customized passes created just for them based on their travel needs and dreams.

HISTORY

On September 1, 1937, Air Canada's predecessor, Trans-Canada Air Lines, took flight from Vancouver to Seattle with two passengers and a bundle of mail aboard the Lockheed 10A. The 50-minute flight launched one of the biggest and most recognized brands in the world. By 1964,

TCA had grown to become Canada's national airline, and in 1965, Air Canada was born. A new, brighter look and the famous red maple leaf dominated the skies. The airline became fully privatized in 1989. Today, Air Canada is the 14th-largest commercial airline in the world.

THE PRODUCT

Air Canada is the airline proud to offer more non-stop flights within Canada and between Canada and the U.S. than any other carrier. Its unique North American one-way fare structure allows fliers to customize their experience depending on their travel needs and desires.

Executive First®, Air Canada's award-winning international premium service, offers first-class comfort and sophistication at a business class fare. And Air Canada's 19 luxurious Maple Leaf™ Lounges welcome Executive First and Executive Class® ticket holders (as well as Aeroplan top-tier members and Diners/enRoute Maple Leaf Club cardholders) to kick back and relax before, between and after their flights. Each lounge comes complete with a state-of-the-art business centre and is ideal for travellers who wish to work en route.

Air Canada also offers personalized Concierge® Service for Executive First and Super Elite® passengers at all major Canadian, U.S. and international airports. When it comes to customer service, customer safety and customer value, Air Canada is flying high.

RECENT DEVELOPMENTS

The airline industry has been battered by many unforeseen external factors, including escalating

oil prices that have left the bottom line of many airlines awash with red ink.

Air Canada has faced these challenges with a renewed commitment to customer service, a very competitive business model and an uncompromising attitude towards safety as its number one priority. Today, passenger numbers are on the increase, as is operating income. And with innovative hedging practices moderating fuel prices, Air Canada has created a business model that is capable of competing in domestic and international markets.

In addition, Air Canada's commitment to enhancing the Canadian travel experience and its dominance in the field have made it the airline that most Canadians automatically choose when travelling on business or for pleasure.

Some of the company's most recent developments include convenient Web check-in and electronic ticketing on most North American and international routes. Most recently, user-friendly international Web sites have been added to Air Canada's digital realm. And state-of-the-art Executive First seating on all long-haul aircraft are a welcome addition to Air Canada's fleets.

Even more luxurious, the Executive First® Suite made its first appearance in the summer of 2006 on select aircraft.

It caters to every aspect of the travel experience with your time, your space and your choice in mind. Each suite features a truly horizontal lie-flat bed. Equipped with a wide selection of on-demand entertainment features, the Executive First Suite also provides the business traveller with convenient work surfaces and an individual power supply. And the Executive First Suite comes with its own reward: 150 percent Air Canada Status mile earnings with each booking.

The launch of prepaid multi-trip passes will also streamline the lives of many frequent fliers. These passes allow travellers to book multiple flights at a time in one single transaction. Passes save money, time and offer a tailor-made, customized travel experience.

PROMOTION

Air Canada is no stranger to the public eye. Over the years, ad campaigns, PR events and sponsorship efforts have attracted the press and the imagination of travellers worldwide. In 2004, a unique idea, one big enough to generate its own news, blitzed the media. It started with a theme, "You and I were meant to fly," and was embraced by Canadian superstar Céline Dion. The song about the joy of flying quickly became a hit around the world and when linked closely with the Air Canada brand via TV, radio and print ads, the campaign hit a high note with consumers.

But spectacular ad campaigns are only one part of Air Canada's promotional strategy. Innovative ways of communicating with the public have also created a buzz and raised the airline's profile. In 2005, Air Canada promoted the new North America Unlimited Pass by creating the first-ever sky parade. Live news coverage of the event coupled with parade "sightings" by thousands of Canadians at prime times during the day made for a huge promotional success.

Air Canada also connects with the public with the future in mind, through its Kids' Horizons programs which help improve the lives of children across the country through several community-building initiatives.

BRAND VALUES

Air Canada focuses on building lasting customer relationships by delivering the most rewarding attributes of choice, ease and value to travellers worldwide. Choice gives customers greater control over how they travel — selecting and paying

only for those products and services they want or need. Ease of booking and boarding help simplify the travel experience. And value to customers is offered through a combination of innovative pricing, superb product and service offerings, modern aircraft and the convenience of a vast domestic and global network.

THINGS YOU DIDN'T KNOW ABOUT AIR CANADA

- In one year, Air Canada transports over 30 million passengers.
- An Air Canada flight takes off or lands every minute of the day or night world-wide.
- To date, Air Canada has given over 2,300 seats to 14 Canadian children's hospitals to transport kids in need of treatment to specialized facilities.
- Two and a half million people visit aircanada.com every month.

THE MARKET

Colour is an essential element in our lives. Colour expresses and stimulates feelings. In fashion colour flatters, conceals, attracts and provokes. In living and working environments colour soothes, inspires, relaxes and astonishes.

Ideas of how colour should be used change, but the need for colour is constant. People who understand colour and its importance — architects, designers and design-conscious homeowners — are always looking for new colours and new combinations.

One hundred years ago, Benjamin Moore was simply a manufacturer of quality paints and finishes. Today the Benjamin Moore brand has a powerful retailing presence, is highly visible in the media, has a reputation as a leader in all aspects of interior design and has pioneered services that put beautiful colour and great design within the reach of all consumers.

ACHIEVEMENTS

From the start, Benjamin Moore was determined to give the best quality and the best value. Discerning customers have responded by making Benjamin Moore the most popular (*PMB annual surveys, since 1997*) and most trusted (*Reader's Digest Ipsos/Reid survey, 2003–04*) brand in its category in Canada.

Benjamin Moore has always sold its products through independent Retailers. A program for extending the brand to these Retailers while enhancing the visibility of their locations, the Signature Store Program, has been a continuing success. It was recognized by the Retail Council of Canada with the Excellence in Retailing 2000 — New Retail Concept award.

The company is a leader in using technology both to widen choice and to assist customers at the point of sale. Benjamin Moore was first with a customized colour mixing system and with computer colour matching. Benjamin Moore customers were the first to receive forecasts of colour trends for use in the home. Benjamin Moore was an early supporter of the Canadian Environmental Choice initiative.

One result of this continuous attention to users' needs is that in 2004 loyalty of regular users of Benjamin Moore paints stood at 80 percent — the highest of any single brand in the category.

HISTORY

In 1883, in New York, Benjamin Moore established the company that bears his name, with his brother Robert. They were immigrants from Ireland. Their first product, a calsomine coating for walls and ceilings, was the foundation for a growing product line. In 1906 a Canadian company was established, in Toronto, with Benjamin as its first president. In 1911 Fred Moore was appointed managing director.

Benjamin Moore is now owned by Berkshire Hathaway, the holding company controlled by Warren Buffet. The change of ownership provides financial and management resources that allow Benjamin Moore to remain independent and to strengthen its manufacturing and marketing programs. Benjamin Moore manufactures at two locations in Canada: Burlington, Ontario and Montreal, Quebec.

THE PRODUCT

Benjamin Moore, the man, set "Integrity, Intelligence and Industry" as the guiding principles of his company. Today, the quality of Benjamin Moore products is never in doubt. With a history of innovation and a full range of interior and exterior paint and stain coatings, all available from trusted Retailers, users can be confident of finding the perfect product for any project.

Consumers can be equally confident of finding the right colours. Retailers offer over 1,800 colours, arranged in four collections, each with a distinct character. The colours in **Colour Preview** are clean and luminous, thoroughly modern in spirit. **Historical Colours** have the timeless quality of 18th and 19th century interiors. **Designer Classics** have proven popular in Canadian households over the last 30 years. The **White and Off-White Collection** simplifies the search for the exact shade of white, and for pale neutrals.

Inside a home the sheen of the paint surface is important, since it influences the way colour is perceived. Latex paints for interior use are available in seven sheen levels, from High Gloss to Ulti-Matte, a super-flat, washable finish that maximizes the impact of colour by reducing reflection.

Benjamin Moore Collection Ulti-Matte received a Gold Medal for quality from the Brussels-based assessment organization, Monde Selection.

Benjamin Moore colours are constantly fine-tuned to offer long term appeal while anticipating changes in taste and style. Through its designers, the company takes a leading role in explaining and introducing new colours and styles to the general public. One example: every year the Benjamin Moore Design Team creates an introduction to the newest colours in home décor. They are presented as a series of palettes suitable for a number of popular styles. This colour card, backed by one-on-one advice from a Benjamin Moore Retailer, becomes the starting point for many home decorating projects.

RECENT DEVELOPMENTS

Over the years, Benjamin Moore has made many improvements in products and services to ensure continuing satisfaction among its customers. A major change took place in the late '90s, when the arrival of Big Box stores challenged the way home improvement products were delivered to consumers.

The Benjamin Moore defence strategy was to build on the established reputation of the brand. Retailers who were prepared to focus on the needs of house-proud homeowners received a dramatic makeover for their stores. The most noticeable difference was a large red sign which enabled the name "Benjamin Moore" to dominate the streetscape.

"The powerful association between the brand and the Benjamin Moore Stores creates important new synergies," said Thomas Stack, vice-president of sales and marketing, at the time. "For one thing, it is now possible to link our consumer advertising and publicity directly with the stores, by using common logos. Brand development now drives customers directly to our Retailers."

By 2005, there were over 400 Benjamin Moore Signature Stores across the country, providing local centres of inspiration for homeowners. The company had transformed itself from a successful, but slightly old fashioned manufacturer into a dynamic and highly visible retailing presence.

Knowledge, expertise and innovation are the hallmarks of a Benjamin Moore Retailer. By understanding the specific needs of their customers, they play an important role in bringing a decorating enthusiast's dreams to life.

Not all consumers have the time or inclination to Do-It-Yourself. In 2004 Benjamin Moore reached out to idea-rich but time-poor homeowners with the Painting & Decorating Services (PDS) program. Customers can call on a Colour Consultant to assist in colour selection and a professional painter to do the work. PDS partners are independent business people, with user satisfaction guaranteed by Benjamin Moore.

PROMOTION

Benjamin Moore prefers a "grassroots" approach to marketing communications. The selected channels are strategically directed to reach upscale homeowners with an appreciation of and passion for colour and design. This focus on the emotional value of colour is not new. In the 1930s "Betty Moore" became the brand's fictitious spokesperson, and talked about colour in the home until the mid-1960s.

In Canada Benjamin Moore is a leader in the lifestyle revolution. Pioneering initiatives included the publication of design project books that sold in the hundreds of thousands, and appearances by members of the Benjamin Moore Design Team at Retailer seminars, Home Shows, on network lifestyle programs and on specialty TV channels.

Benjamin Moore has become an important colour resource for the professional market. Support ranges from technical consultation to regular get-togethers to exchange views on trends in colours and design.

Benjamin Moore, seeking new ways of reaching its consumer audience, created a Canadian Web site that can be browsed like a magazine. Shortly after its launch the site was recognized by the Canadian Marketing Association for its innovative use of interactive communication techniques.

BRAND VALUES

Although the brand character has been consistent from the earliest days, it was not expressed in words until the late '90s. Here is an excerpt from the company's Brand Charter.

- **Vision:** Together, we will create a uniquely colourful decorating experience, with the highest level of products and expertise, to inspire customers to achieve the ultimate expression of their personal style.
- **Position/Image:** Benjamin Moore is in the business of helping discerning customers create an atmosphere, express their style and personality and add value to their home, through colour.
- **Attributes:** Knowledgeable, trusted, warm, timeless, imaginative.
- **Personality:** Benjamin Moore is a wise family friend, rich in experience and personality. Someone we look up to for a sense of quality and style, a good listener and a trusted advisor who makes decisions easier.

THINGS YOU DIDN'T KNOW ABOUT BENJAMIN MOORE

- ❍ The triangle which is part of the Benjamin Moore logo is derived from the founder's motto of "Intelligence, Industry, Integrity."

- ❍ Since 2002, throughout October, Benjamin Moore Retailers and the company have raised an ever-increasing total for the Canadian Cancer Society through their national Decorate for a Cure campaign.

- ❍ Benjamin Moore is the most-specified paint brand with designers and architects in Canada.

MARCHÉ

La couleur est essentielle à la vie : elle exprime et stimule nos sentiments. Dans le milieu de la mode, la couleur flatte, dissimule, attire et provoque. À la maison et au bureau, la couleur apaise, inspire et surprend.

Notre façon d'utiliser la couleur a changé, mais nos besoins en couleur persistent. Les personnes qui comprennent l'importance de la couleur — les architectes, les designers et les consommateurs soucieux du design — sont toujours à l'affût des nouvelles couleurs et de leur agencement.

Il y a cent ans, Benjamin Moore n'était qu'un fabricant de peintures et de finis de qualité. Aujourd'hui, elle a une forte présence dans le commerce de détail et dans les médias, elle est la référence dans le design d'intérieur et offre des services d'avant-garde mettant à portée de la main de tous les consommateurs de superbes couleurs.

RÉALISATIONS

Dès le début, Benjamin Moore décide d'offrir la meilleure qualité. Ce n'est pas étonnant qu'aujourd'hui elle soit la marque la plus populaire (*d'après le sondage annuel de PMB, depuis 1997*) et la plus fiable (*d'après le sondage du Sélection du Reader's Digest Ipsos/ Reid, en 2003-2004*) de sa catégorie, au Canada.

Ayant toujours vendu ses produits par l'entremise de détaillants indépendants, l'entreprise crée le programme des boutiques Signature dans le but de leur faire bénéficier de sa marque tout en assurant leur visibilité. En 2000, le Conseil canadien du commerce de détail lui décerne le prix d'excellence dans le commerce de détail — nouveau concept de détail.

L'entreprise est un chef de file dans l'utilisation de la technologie, ce qui lui permet d'offrir une vaste sélection de couleurs et de répondre aux besoins des clients en magasin. Elle est la première à avoir développé un système de colorant personnalisé et un système d'appariement des couleurs aux points de vente. De plus, elle adhère très rapidement au programme canadien Choix environnemental.

Cette attention constante portée sur les besoins des consommateurs a permis à Benjamin Moore d'obtenir, en 2004, le pourcentage de loyaux utilisateurs le plus élevé dans sa catégorie (80 %).

HISTOIRE

L'entreprise est établie en 1883, à New York, par deux immigrés irlandais, Benjamin Moore et son frère Robert. Leur premier produit, un revêtement à base de calsomine pour les murs et les plafonds, ouvre la voie à toute une gamme de produits. En 1906, l'entreprise canadienne voit le jour à Toronto; Benjamin est son premier président, et Fred Moore devient son directeur général en 1911.

Benjamin Moore appartient maintenant à Berkshire Hathaway, la société de portefeuille dirigée par Warren Buffet. Cette nouvelle structure fournit à Benjamin Moore les ressources financières et managériales lui permettant de rester indépendante et de consolider ses programmes de fabrication et de marketing. L'entreprise possède deux usines de fabrication au Canada : une à Burlington, en Ontario, et une autre à Montréal, au Québec.

PRODUIT

Dès les premières années, Benjamin Moore adopte trois valeurs fondamentales pour définir les principes de la société : l'intégrité, l'intelligence et l'industrie. Aujourd'hui, la qualité des produits Benjamin Moore est indéniable. L'histoire de l'entreprise, marquée par l'innovation et par une gamme complète de peintures et de teintures pour l'intérieur et l'extérieur offertes par un réseau de détaillants fiables, fait en sorte que les consommateurs peuvent en toute confiance trouver les produits et les couleurs qui conviennent à n'importe quel projet.

Les quelque 1 800 couleurs Benjamin Moore sont réparties en quatre palettes au caractère distinct. Les couleurs du système **Inspiration Couleur** sont pures et lumineuses, et résolument tournées vers l'avenir. Les **Couleurs historiques** reproduisent à merveille les qualités intemporelles des décors des 18e et 19e siècles. Les **Classiques des designers** sont les couleurs les plus populaires auprès des consommateurs canadiens depuis les 30 dernières années. La **Collection des blancs** simplifie la recherche du blanc parfait et des divers tons de neutre.

Le lustre est une caractéristique importante d'une peinture

d'intérieur puisqu'il influe sur la façon dont nous percevons la couleur. Les peintures d'intérieur latex comportent sept niveaux de lustre : du très lustré à l'Ulti-Mat. Ce dernier, un produit au fini parfaitement mat et lavable qui rehausse l'impact de la couleur en réduisant les reflets, a reçu en 2004 et en 2005 la médaille d'or de Monde Sélection, l'institut d'évaluation de la qualité basé à Bruxelles.

Les couleurs Benjamin Moore font continuellement l'objet de mises au point afin d'entretenir leur beauté et de répondre au goût et au style du jour. Par l'entremise de ses designers, l'entreprise joue un rôle dominant dans la présentation des nouveaux styles et couleurs au public. Ainsi, chaque année, l'équipe du design de Benjamin Moore crée un événement pour présenter les nouvelles couleurs en décoration intérieure. Grâce à la carte de couleurs et aux conseils individualisés d'un détaillant Benjamin Moore, il est facile de les utiliser pour réaliser des projets de décoration.

ÉVOLUTION RÉCENTE

Au cours des dernières années, Benjamin Moore a amélioré et créé bon nombre de produits et de services dans le but de continuer à satisfaire les exigences de sa clientèle et de contrer l'influence des grandes surfaces qui, à la fin des années 90, ont révolutionné la façon dont les produits de rénovation étaient offerts aux consommateurs.

La stratégie de Benjamin Moore a consisté à tirer profit de la réputation de sa marque. Les détaillants prêts à répondre aux besoins des clients avisés ont transformé leur magasin de fond en comble en adoptant, notamment, la nouvelle enseigne rouge où figure en proéminence le nom « Benjamin Moore ».

« L'association puissante de la marque aux boutiques Benjamin Moore crée d'importantes nouvelles synergies, explique Thomas Stack, alors vice-président des ventes et du marketing. Il est maintenant possible de faire le lien entre nos publicités et nos magasins au moyen de nos logos. L'expansion de notre marque incite les clients à venir directement chez nos détaillants. »

En 2005, on dénombrait plus de 400 boutiques Signature Benjamin Moore au Canada. Aujourd'hui, l'entreprise a transformé son rôle de fabricant primé, mais traditionnel en devenant une organisation dynamique et bien en vue dans le commerce de détail.

Un détaillant Benjamin Moore se distingue par ses connaissances, son expertise et son innovation. En comprenant les besoins propres à chacun de ses clients, il joue un rôle essentiel dans la réalisation de leurs rêves.

Puisque ce n'est pas tous les consommateurs qui ont le temps ou l'envie d'effectuer leurs projets eux-mêmes, Benjamin Moore lance en 2004 son programme des Services de décoration et de peintres (SDP). Les conseillers en couleur contribuent au choix des couleurs et les peintres professionnels effectuent le travail! Les membres du programme SDP sont des entrepreneurs indépendants, et la satisfaction du client est garantie par Benjamin Moore.

PROMOTION

Pour ses communications de marketing, Benjamin Moore préfère une approche locale. Les médias choisis s'adressent aux consommateurs sophistiqués qui aiment la couleur et le design. L'importance de la valeur sentimentale de la couleur ne date pas d'hier. Déjà dans les années 30 jusqu'au milieu des années 60, « Betty Moore » était devenue la porte-parole fictive de la marque, insistant sur la place d'honneur de la couleur à la maison.

Au Canada, Benjamin Moore est à la tête de la révolution du mode de vie. Au nombre de ses initiatives, on retrouve des livres sur des projets de design, qui se sont vendus par centaines de milliers, et la participation des membres de l'équipe du design de Benjamin Moore aux ateliers offerts aux détaillants, aux salons de l'habitation et à des émissions spécialisées sur la décoration.

Benjamin Moore est devenue une ressource incontournable pour les professionnels, en offrant des conseils techniques et des rencontres d'échanges de points de vue sur les tendances en matière de couleur et de design.

En outre, dans le but de diversifier ses façons de toucher ses consommateurs, elle a créé un site Web canadien qui a été primé par l'Association canadienne du marketing pour son usage novateur de techniques de communication interactives.

VALEURS DE LA MARQUE

Bien que les attributs de la marque aient été définis dès la fondation de l'entreprise, ils n'ont été exprimés que vers la fin des années 90. Voici un extrait de la *Charte de la marque* :

- **Vision** : Ensemble, grâce à la qualité de nos produits et à notre expertise, nous ferons vivre à nos clients une expérience unique en décoration et riche en couleurs, laissant libre cours à l'expression de leur propre style.
- **Positionnement** : Benjamin Moore est en affaires pour aider les clients avisés à créer une ambiance, à exprimer leur propre style et à accroître la valeur de leur maison, et ce, grâce à la couleur!
- **Caractéristiques** : Experte, fiable, chaleureuse, intemporelle, imaginative.
- **Personnalité** : Benjamin Moore est un ami avisé de la famille ayant une expérience et une personnalité riches. Quelqu'un qui est respecté pour son sens de la qualité et du style. Un conseiller digne de confiance qui sait écouter et qui facilite la prise de décision.

QUELQUES PARTICULARITÉS MOINS CONNUES DE BENJAMIN MOORE

○ Le triangle qui fait partie du logo Benjamin Moore a été créé à partir des trois « i » de la devise du fondateur : intelligence, industrie et intégrité.

○ Depuis 2002, pendant tout le mois d'octobre, Benjamin Moore et ses détaillants collectent des fonds pour la Société canadienne du cancer dans le cadre de leur campagne nationale *Décorez, pour l'espoir*.

○ Benjamin Moore est la marque de peinture la plus recommandée par les designers et les architectes au Canada.

Services de décoration et de peintres

Buckley's

It Tastes Awful. And It Works.

THE MARKET

The Canadian cough/cold market is a dynamic and competitive category driven by consumers battling the symptoms of coughs, colds and flu. In 2005 consumers purchased nearly $300 million worth of these products, posting a growth of 9 percent.

The market meets the needs of both adults and children, with relief available in a number of different formats including liquid, tablets/caplets, powders and thin strips. These products are available through a variety of outlets such as grocery stores, drugstores, mass merchandisers, corner stores and gas stations. Their availability is regulated by provincial guidelines depending on the active ingredients and the type of retail outlet.

ACHIEVEMENTS

Buckley's has been a leader in the cough/cold market since its introduction in 1919. The well-known Buckley's Mixture (200ml) has been the top-selling cough syrup product in Canada since 1992 and is the number 3 product in the whole category — a huge achievement for a "little" Canadian brand, competing with larger brands with deeper pockets.

Buckley's has always been focused on making products that work — a fact that has created a loyal following since the first batch of Buckley's went on the market. Even though the adult products all taste awful, Buckley's users LOVE the brand that has been a mainstay of the family medicine chest for generations. Buckley's fans write glowing testimonials about a cough syrup that doesn't even try to be tasty — and many of them choose to carry a bottle of Buckley's even when they are not sick!

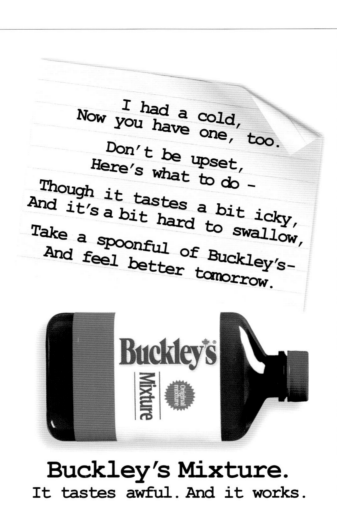

I had a cold,
Now you have one, too.
Don't be upset,
Here's what to do –
Though it tastes a bit icky,
And it's a bit hard to swallow,
Take a spoonful of Buckley's–
And feel better tomorrow.

Buckley's Mixture.
It tastes awful. And it works.

HISTORY

The creation of Buckley's Mixture was a classic case of recognizing a good thing when it appears. When pharmacist William Knapp Buckley took over a Toronto drugstore in 1919, he discovered the merits of several natural ingredients used in the treatment of coughs and colds. He combined them to create a unique and effective remedy which he called Buckley's Mixture. Never one to hesitate in the face of opportunity, he formed W. K. Buckley Limited on March 20, 1920, and began marketing his product.

Realizing the power of catchy copy and smart media buying, W.K. concentrated his efforts on print and radio advertising to sell his product. In an era when advertising was a relatively new and poorly understood phenomena, W.K. was ahead of his time. His son, Frank Buckley, says, "My father was first and foremost a born salesman." He believes that advertising on radio in the early days

of broadcasting built the business and was a key factor in establishing Buckley's as a household name.

The '20s was a period of rapid growth at W. K. Buckley Limited with new products being introduced and distributed throughout Canada. Despite this growth, W.K.'s Drug Store in Toronto remained the headquarters for development of new products, including products outside the cough and cold category.

When the Great Depression hit, many of the secondary Buckley products were discontinued, and W. K. Buckley Limited went back to what it did best: cough and cold preparations. The company introduced a smaller size of Buckley's Mixture priced at a more manageable 40 cents to help consumers through the lean years. It was during this period that W.K. introduced his "medicine chest in a jar," Buckley's White Rub.

Buoyed by ongoing success in Canada, W.K. decided to expand his horizons. By the late thirties, W. K. Buckley Limited took its Mixture to the United States and Caribbean, and ten years later, the company expanded its reach even further to include New Zealand, Australia and Holland.

After WWII, W.K.'s son, Frank Buckley, joined the family business as a salesman. With a bachelor of commerce degree and a fascination with anything mathematical, Frank began to apply modern financial concepts and practices

to the running of the business. With W.K.'s entrepreneurial energy and Frank's financial skills, father and son made a formidable team.

By the 1960s, it was clear that pharmacies were changing rapidly. Small, individually owned drugstores gave way to drug supermarkets, and every pharmaceutical chain began advertising.

The creative marketing strategies that had made Buckley's so successful and unique were now being used by everyone. Buckley's no longer held a creative competitive edge, and sales began to slide.

In 1978, W. K. Buckley passed away, and his son Frank took the helm of a struggling family enterprise. In the early '80s, the company decided on what Frank Buckley calls, "the back to basics"

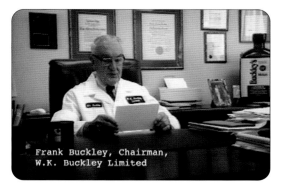

Frank Buckley, Chairman,
W.K. Buckley Limited

strategy. Since radio and print media had built the business, Buckley's rolled the dice with a creative ad campaign that would make Buckley's Mixture into a consumer favourite once again.

THE PRODUCT
In our complex and constantly changing world, consumers are looking for products that are simple to use and deliver results each and every time. The Buckley's product line offers nothing less. In a market where people are concerned about potential dangers and contraindications, Buckley's

No one said it would be easy.

It tastes awful. And it works.

Mixture stands out as the tried and true: a non-drowsy alcohol-free, sugar-free, highly effective formula that also offers the comforts of the familiar.

Over time the Buckley's brand has grown to include a number of products designed to meet the various consumer needs of both adults and children. Today, the six-product adult line-up includes:
- Buckley's Mixture for Coughs & Congestion
- Buckley's DM for Coughs
- Buckley's DM-D for Coughs & Colds
- Buckley's Bedtime for Coughs & Colds
- Buckley's Day/Night Caplets for Cough, Cold, and Flu Relief
- Buckley's White Rub, a vapourizing decongestant

And the flavoured Jack and Jill line of products makes Buckley's palatable for children.
- Buckley's Jack & Jill DM Cough Suppressant (Cherry)
- Buckley's Jack & Jill DM-D for Coughs & Colds (Cherry)
- Buckley's Jack & Jill Expectorant (Raspberry)
- Buckley's Jack & Jill Bedtime Cough Suppressant (Grape)
- Buckley's Jack & Jill Chewable Tablets for Cough, Cold, and Flu Relief (Grape)
- Buckley's Jack & Jill Thin Strips for Long Lasting Cough Relief (Cherry)
- Buckley's Jack & Jill Thin Strips for Bedtime Cough & Cold Relief (Grape)

RECENT DEVELOPMENTS
Buckley's works hard to develop products that help consumers deal with cough, cold and flu symptoms in the most efficient manner. In August 2005 Buckley's launched two different thin strips into its Jack & Jill line of children's products. This new product format makes it easier than ever for parents to give their children the right dosage of medication at any time. The thin strips come in individually sealed packets, and dissolve when placed on the tongue.

PROMOTION
Buckley's is best known for its famous Bad Taste campaign, which launched the company's famous tag line: "It Tastes Awful. And It Works."

The advertisements highlight the two main characteristics of Buckley's Mixture — terrible taste and proven efficacy. Building on those facts, Buckley's produced an award-winning advertising campaign that made Buckley's Mixture and Frank Buckley into household names in Canada.

In 1986, the first transit ads featured Frank Buckley quipping, "I came by my bad taste honestly — I inherited it from my father" and "I wake up with nightmares that someone gives me a taste of my own medicine." The campaign ran nationally, and the company's simple, honest and humourous approach to advertising attracted a lot of attention and, more importantly, new users.

The Bad Taste campaign significantly increased Buckley's market share in the Canadian cough and cold category and won numerous advertising awards. And it appears that Bad Taste traveled well,

Q. Do I have to?

A. Do you want relief so you can feel better?

It tastes awful. And it works.

www.buckleys.com

as these humourous advertisements were also very successful in the Caribbean, Australia, New Zealand and the United States.

BRAND VALUES
When it comes to being sick, there are two kinds of people in this world. Those who want to be coddled and those who want to get better.

Buckley's makes medicine for the second kind of person — someone who knows life is too good to miss hiding under the covers. When they're sick, they are for some stern medicine in order to get better fast. Buckley's makes medicine for people who know what they want, know nothing comes easy and aren't afraid of a little bad taste and tough love on the road to better health.

That's the way it's always been when it comes to Buckley's Mixture. Which is why the company is proud to say, "Let the people who love you give you comfort. We're here to make you better."

THINGS YOU DIDN'T KNOW ABOUT BUCKLEY'S

- Frank Buckley, born in Toronto on April 8, 1921, likes to believe he was conceived around the same time his father, William Knapp Buckley, founded W. K. Buckley Limited (1920).

- Now in his 80s, Frank Buckley is still the spokesperson for the Buckley's brand.

- In 2003, Frank was deeply honoured to be appointed a member of the Order of Canada.

- The Buckley's "It Tastes Awful. And It Works." campaign has been spoofed by Canadian sketch comedy shows *Air Farce* and *This Hour Has 22 Minutes.*

- Rush Limbaugh and Howard Stern have both tried Buckley's Mixture and touted the brand on their radio programs.

Budget.

Escape the everyday.®

Today, Budget is the leading car rental company in Canada with more points of distribution and airport locations than any of its competitors. Budget continues to focus on appealing to value-minded renters by offering quality vehicles and a rewarding rental experience.

THE PRODUCT

Budget Rent a Car is in more places in Canada than any other car rental company. With over 350 points of distribution including service to 90 percent of airports in Canada and nearly 300 off-airport locations, Budget is part of Canadian neighbourhoods and airports from Tofino to Gander, Gaspé to Sandspit and Whitehorse to Windsor.

With the largest fleet in Canada, Budget is perfectly positioned to service all car rental needs. Fleet buying is customized to time of year, local demand and climatic conditions. Most vehicles are rotated out of fleet every six months, ensuring that customers have access to reliable new vehicles with the most size and style options. Budget can deliver specialty car categories such as Luxury, Sport Utility, Minivan and even Convertible. Accessories are tailored to seasonality and location — ski racks, moving supplies and child booster seats are popular choices for customers.

Budget's fleet of Light Duty Trucks is the largest of any rental company in Canada. The 4,500 trucks in Budget's fleet include pick-ups, cube vans, cargo vans and five-ton trucks. Extensively used for personal moving as well as commercial purposes, Budget's truck fleet is inventoried specifically for the local markets.

Budget's local know-how doesn't stop with the attention to fleet. Local Budget operations pay

THE MARKET

It has taken the Canadian travel industry a long time to recover from the serious economic blows of events such as 9/11, the Iraq War and the SARS outbreak. Recovery has been slow but steady, and in Canada, the rental car industry has been on an upward track since 2001. According to Statistics Canada, total vehicle rental demand was in excess of $1.5 billion in 2004, with over $1 billion from domestic demand.

Due to consolidation, expansion and attrition, the business of renting cars has changed considerably in the past few years. Vehicle rental occasions in Canada are now split between eight major car rental brands, as well as a number of smaller regional suppliers. Competition between brands has always been fierce, with heavy emphasis on price-based promotions and value-adds to increase customer demand for a particular brand. Through it all, Budget has remained a dynamic, entrepreneurial brand and has emerged as the car rental company with the largest share of all rentals in Canada for both business and personal occasions.

ACHIEVEMENTS

Setting Budget apart from the competition is the positive recognition received from the travel industry and customers. For the past four years,

Budget has won the prestigious Agent's Choice Award as the top rental car company, as travel agents from across Canada vote to select their favourite travel suppliers. The competition is sponsored by Baxter Group, a travel industry publisher.

In addition to the positive industry feedback, the Canadian Professional Sales Association (CPSA) also voted Budget as Canada's best car rental company in 2004. The recognition of a seasoned group of "road warriors" such as the CPSA members is much appreciated by Budget and celebrates the company's commitment to be the number-one choice for Canadians looking for rental vehicles.

HISTORY

Budget Rent a Car was founded in the United States in 1958 as a car rental company for the "budget-minded" renter. In 1962, the first two Budget locations were opened in Canada. By 1966, Budget was officially operating in all airports in Canada. From there, the Budget brand flourished, spreading from coast to coast under the guidance of a team of savvy entrepreneurs. These leaders focused on providing rentals suited to the different climatic and economic conditions in Canada, while diversifying their business interests into self-storage and parking.

careful attention to local markets to develop promotions and relationships that work. Neighbourhood businesses, on-site film crews and local insurance providers take advantage of Budget's extensive fleet for specialty vehicle or long-term rentals.

Relationships — local, national and international — are an important part of Budget Canada's business. Budget's Fastbreak program is a relationship-based program that helps frequent renters "Get In, Get Out, Get Going"[SM] with expedited reservation, pick-up and drop-off service. Perfect for the busy road warrior or a frequent city renter, Fastbreak gets Budget customers on the road fast.

Budget also maintains a national portfolio of corporate-contracted business, travel agent and association relationships. Budget Rent a Car Canada's corporate headquarters is located in Toronto and manages national sales, partnerships and advertising. With over 30 executives dedicated to maintaining brand integrity, Budget has

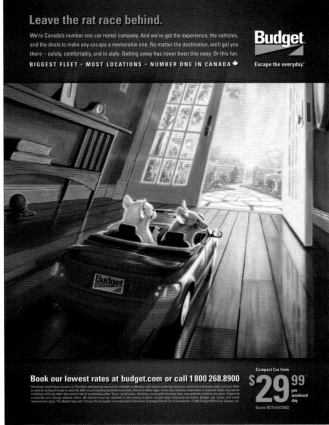

the largest franchise and brand management rental car infrastructure in Canada. Budget employs over 3,000 people dedicated to provincial, regional and local promotions and customer satisfaction.

Budget has become the leader in the industry because Budget knows how to deliver: get customers where they need to go — reliably, comfortably and in style.

RECENT DEVELOPMENTS

In November 2002, the Budget brand was purchased by Cendant Corporation (NYSE:CD), a diversified global provider of business and consumer services within the travel and real estate sectors. Budget Rent a Car Systems Inc. became the owner and franchisor of Budget, which is now one of the world's best known car rental brands with nearly 2,000 rental locations in the United States, Canada, Europe, Latin America, the Caribbean, Australia and New Zealand.

PROMOTION

Budget's promotional efforts are multi-faceted. The car rental industry is a mature market where retail consumers do not easily differentiate between the major brands — except when it comes to price.

Differentiating the brand at the point of purchase, capitalizing on Budget's high brand recognition and positive consumer opinion are important parts of Budget's advertising and promotional activities.

Travel and industry partnerships help Budget to deliver value-adds at point of purchase:
- Online merchants give consumers the opportunity to shop for the best rates or take advantage of specific sale opportunities.
- Strategic partnerships with Canadian brands like WestJet Airlines Ltd., Canadian Tire Corporation and KidsFutures, Inc., help Budget to bring value-added savings to transactions.
- Strategic relationships with travel professionals and credit card companies allow Budget to deliver promotional offers and savings directly to customers.

Budget looks for opportunities to help customers get more out of renting a car, to escape the everyday routine and to have a great car rental experience for business or leisure travel.

BRAND VALUES

Budget wants to help customers escape the everyday. Whether the escape is literal or figurative, Budget's goal is to help customers have a great vacation, shorter pick-up times before a business meeting or just a little behind-the-scenes help with a car that works great in the snow. Budget tries to make each rental experience a positive experience that enhances every trip.

"Escape the everyday."® and Budget's creative graphics break through the

clutter of traditional, tired car rental advertising. Appealing characters and whimsical headlines combine to stand out from the crowd and develop empathy between the brand, customers and characters. "Escape" is presented as a very real possibility — even for something as mundane as a mouse.

Budget's brand position in Canada is one of value pricing and high value. Available fleet is of the newest and highest quality in the industry and is offered at lower prices than comparable competition. Supporting this is Budget's comfortably Canadian appeal. Budget's long history in Canada and its inclusion in so many Canadian communities promotes a familiarity and ease with the Budget brand and it gives Budget an in-depth and ongoing understanding of the communities it serves.

According to a recent study done by Chadwick Martin Bailey, at 98 percent, Budget has the highest brand awareness in the car rental industry. In Canada, Budget received the highest ranking on every one of the top-five most important attributes of a vehicle rental company as it relates to consumers: low cost, efficient, uncomplicated, honest, consistent and responsive.

Budget's commitment to consistently meet or exceed consumer expectations is underpinned by measuring performance against seven key attributes:
- Helpful, knowledgeable and courteous reservation services
- Environment and first impressions
- Making customers feel welcome and wanted
- Professional behaviour
- Value and appreciation
- Clean, safe and reliable vehicles
- Convenient return process

THINGS YOU DIDN'T KNOW ABOUT BUDGET

- ○ Budget's original rate for a mid-size vehicle in the early '60s was $5 per day and $0.05 per mile.
- ○ The Budget logo is made up of the Budget name with a stylized road curving underneath it.
- ○ Budget Canada's northernmost location is Yellowknife, NWT; the southernmost is Windsor, Ontario.
- ○ Budget now has locations in over 125 countries. It is also the leader in most of the Caribbean countries, Holland, South Africa and Australia.

CALGARY EXHIBITION & STAMPEDE

THE MARKET

One truth is central to the attraction, and therefore the market, of the Calgary Exhibition & Stampede: there are still real working cowboys.

That's what gives the brand relevance today and what makes it meaningful to anyone looking for genuine hospitality and an authentic western experience.

The appeal of the Stampede stems from romantic imagery — tales of adventure and heroism — in short, the mythology of cowboys and the settlement of the western half of North America.

But today's Stampede is built on much more than mythology. It's a festival of all things western. Its market is chiefly Calgarians, but visitors come from across North America and around the world. They come to get a taste of the old west and of the still-vibrant real west — a world that lives outside cities and highways where farming and ranching and rodeo are still practiced.

Of course, this world thrives 365 days a year, and so does the Calgary Stampede. The heels are kicked up highest during ten days in July, but the Stampede is a year-round enterprise.

The Stampede's market comprises those seeking to have fun, to learn and to re-connect with

western values — through family connections, cultural connections such as movies or books or personal recollections of childhood games, dressing up as cowboys and Indians.

Though expressed through contemporary culture and commerce, a visit to the Calgary Stampede still offers an authentic, western-based experience characterized by friendliness, western hospitality, hard work and handshake honesty.

ACHIEVEMENTS

Visitors to the Calgary Stampede come for a variety of reasons — and they come in droves!

2006 was another record-breaking year for attendance: over 1.2 million over the course of ten days, an average of over 120,000 a day. The attendance for the afternoon rodeo and sold-out evening grandstand shows continued to climb – both routinely averaged over 15,000.

And that's less than half the story. Over the entire year, attendance at more than 1,300 other events totalled an additional 1.4 million.

Not only are Stampede guests numerous, they're happy — over 90 percent rated their experience as "good" or "excellent."

The Stampede succeeded in upping the ante significantly for the rodeo and chuckwagon racing events in 2006. Combined, the purse for these competitions is over $2.5 million — enough to attract the top rodeo athletes and chuckwagon outfits in the world.

HISTORY

It was 1886 when the city of Calgary held its first agricultural fair. The population at the time was 2,000, and the fair attendance that year was 500.

In 1912 the first Calgary Stampede was held, largely due to the efforts of cowboy, promoter and celebrated trick roper Guy Weadick. His background was entertainment — the Wild West shows made famous by Buffalo Bill and the like. But Weadick combined his showman's flair with a true respect for agriculture, ranching and real cowboys. His vision was grand: "hundreds of cowboys and cowgirls, thousands of natives . . . Mexican ropers and riders . . . we'll make Buffalo Bill's Wild West Extravaganza look like a side show."

Weadick's inclusion of Treaty 7 First Nations people is significant. In 1912, the Stampede's influence helped natives receive the necessary approvals to attend the exhibition and ride in the parade. They've been involved ever since.

By 1923 this vision had expanded, and the festival included the Stampede Parade, chuckwagon racing, rodeo events and agricultural exhi-

bitions. What he pictured came to be known as "The Greatest Outdoor Show on Earth."

Over time the festival and the city's identity has become intertwined (since 1945 the Calgary CFL football team has been called the Stampeders). The two remain as paired strands of the same DNA. Who could imagine Calgary without the Stampede? Or the Stampede taking place anywhere else?

As Calgary has grown (the population is now 1 million), so has the Stampede. Especially in terms of brand and reputation, the city and the Stampede have become ever more interdependent: the city grows rapidly and the Stampede embarks on an ambitious expansion; the city becomes more

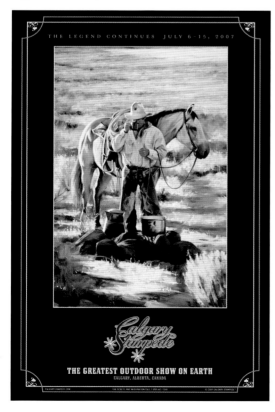

THE LEGEND CONTINUES JULY 6-15, 2007

THE GREATEST OUTDOOR SHOW ON EARTH
CALGARY, ALBERTA, CANADA

diverse and the Stampede plays a more significant role in unifying the community.

THE PRODUCT

The Calgary Exhibition & Stampede is a not-for-profit, volunteer-supported community organization dedicated to preserving and promoting western heritage and values. The importance of volunteers to the organization cannot be overstated — 2,200 Calgarians willingly give time, experience and energy to help organize and stage the many events.

As such, what the Stampede really offers is a celebration of community.

Of course, there are more concrete offerings as well: one of the world's premier rodeos, the world's top chuckwagon competition, as well as the evening grandstand show. Agricultural exhibitions and demonstrations, performances by top entertainers, western art displays and North America's largest mobile midway round out the product offering.

During the other 355 days of the year, Stampede Park hosts over 1,300 other exciting events of all kinds that take advantage of the excellent facilities and the Stampede spirit. The spirit burns brightest in July, but the warmth of its welcome lasts all year long.

RECENT DEVELOPMENTS

The year-round aspect of the Calgary Exhibition & Stampede continues to rise significantly in importance.

In June 2006, a groundbreaking ceremony marked the beginning of an ambitious $600 million expansion, including expanded trade and entertainment facilities, expanded green space, a youth campus, a new agriculture arena, hotel, retail marketplace, heritage museum and a riverfront park.

The drive behind expansion is to extend the Stampede brand and its strength in order to create a year-round international gathering place with a distinctly western flavour where citizens and their guests gather to learn, socialize, conduct

business, shop, be entertained, remember and, of course, celebrate.

The plan is to carefully manage the brand — to capture the intensity of experience offered during the Stampede's ten days in July and apply the western values of the brand to activities and events held throughout the year.

PROMOTION

The party atmosphere that comes along with the Stampede is pervasive across Calgary during the ten day festival.

It begins with the Stampede Parade through downtown Calgary. Parade Day is an unofficial holiday for most downtown businesses. With free Stampede breakfasts all over the city, boisterous airport greeters, downtown activities and entertainment, Stampede parties and excitement every night in bars and clubs, there is absolutely no way to be in Calgary at that time and not know that the Stampede is on!

The Stampede brand is carried far and wide through a variety of traditional and innovative efforts. Formal means of promotion including TV, newspaper, transit and outdoor advertising are used to promote the ten day festival and corporate messages. On-line sales and Internet advertising are also leveraged to promote the Stampede, provide information and facilitate sales efforts.

Relationships are a key promotional tool for the Stampede as well and include a sponsorship program with long-standing partners such as Bell Canada, Coca-Cola, GM, TransAlta, Enmax and Budweiser. Relationships are also cultivated with the media, community and political leaders and cultural groups across the region.

In true western style, chuckwagon tarps are auctioned to sponsors and an annual poster is commissioned from leading artists to create the poster that promotes the Stampede worldwide.

BRAND VALUES

The Calgary Stampede brand originated from an authentic brand used to "brand" livestock. The brand (called the C, lazy S) is still in use today and appears on livestock from the Stampede Ranch that competes in over 50 rodeos across North America.

The brand's power is recognized by all Albertans. A recent Ipsos-Reid survey showed that the Calgary Stampede is considered the number one reason to visit the province — more than Banff and the Rockies put together!

Although clearly powerful in a commercial sense, the brand is deeply vested in the community. The Stampede has been described as the soul of Calgary. During the ten day festival the entire city is stampeding, a general-purpose verb meaning partying, dressing western and decorating storefronts, office buildings and community centres in a western theme.

As well, the tone and tempo of business in Calgary changes come Stampede time. Jean-clad CEOs flip pancakes and relax with colleagues amid a celebratory atmosphere. But it's not all fun and games. It's also a time to do business — much of it on the basis of a handshake. All this is part of the Stampede brand.

The power of the Stampede brand arises from the organization's core purpose: preserving and promoting western heritage and values. Those values — neighbourliness, hospitality, handshake honesty, entrepreneurship, integrity, hard work — shaped the West and are still in play today as the values of the Stampede brand.

THINGS YOU DIDN'T KNOW ABOUT CALGARY STAMPEDE

○ The Calgary Exhibition & Stampede has its own ranch. Covering almost 22,000 acres, it is home to roughly 450 bucking horses, 90 bulls and 40 saddle horses.

○ Every year since 1912, the Stampede has produced a poster, and the collection is on display. But the 1922, 1926 and 1930 posters are missing. In true western style, there is a reward ($1,000) for their return.

○ The Stampede Parade routinely includes over 800 horses, not to mention politicians, royalty, sports heroes and entertainment figures. It attracts a crowd of close to 400,000 every year and is televised all over the world.

○ The Stampede supports many youth programs, including the Stampede Showband, the Young Canadians, Stampede School, 4-H and even a course at the University of Calgary called "The Culture of the Stampede."

IT'S TRUE

THE MARKET

Shelter is one thing that is often taken for granted, but the fact remains, everybody needs a home. Hundreds of millions of houses are built around the world every year, and in many regions, wood has always been the building material of choice. Whether it is used to form the structure of a home or to add beauty and warmth, wood is a natural option. It is renewable, easy to use, and when compared to other building materials such as metal or concrete it requires little energy to manufacture.

Canfor is Canada's largest lumber producer, primarily making the 2x4 lumber and structural panels required to form the framework of a house. Over 2 million homes are built every year in North America, 95 percent of which use the 2x4 wood frame construction method. In addition to the key structural materials, Canfor also manufactures decking, fascia, siding and other products used to complete a home or project.

The forest products market is global, with supply and demand spread out across the world. Canfor's reach extends beyond North America into Europe and Asia, where Canfor supplies the key segments which define the industry: the DIY/Home Renovation market, the professional builder/renovator, the building component manufacturers and the industrial or remanufacturing segments.

ACHIEVEMENTS

Canfor is Canada's largest integrated forest products company. Canfor has grown from a single mill operation to a company that produces over 5.1 billion board feet of lumber, 1.7 billion square feet of structural panels, 135,000 tonnes of Kraft paper and 1.6 million tonnes of pulp, operating 33

production facilities in North America. As the industry leader, Canfor has always taken a highly responsible approach to forest management. Sustainability and environmental responsibility are driving forces in the way in which Canfor operates. Canfor has invested millions of dollars in production facilities to not only comply with, but exceed provincial and national standards for environmental protection. As a result, Canfor has become an industry leader in reducing greenhouse gas emissions from fossil fuels.

Canfor is de-commoditizing lumber by providing more than just wood, and has become a truly dependable and reliable supply partner. By offering not just straighter and more consistent quality lumber, but also better service, distribution and transportation alternatives, unique supply arrangements, inventory management, Web site transactions and order tracking facilities, the Canfor brand now means a great deal more to the trade than just lumber.

Canfor's customers want flexibility and reliability in their inbound logistics. To deliver this, Canfor operates multiple reload centres in North America in order to efficiently service key markets. This distribution network enables product to be inventoried in close proximity to Canfor's customers, reducing reliance on railcar shipments coming from the mills or through third parties.

As the lumber supply chain consolidates, leading lumber retailers and builders are becoming more and more reliant on Canfor's product and service offerings.

In the DIY market, Canfor is the largest supplier of SPF lumber to the leading home centre chains. In 1989 Canfor helped develop the premium grade of lumber that has now become the standard home centre grade.

Canfor is the largest supplier of 2x4 lumber to the Japanese market.

Canfor is also the largest producer of Machine Stress Rated Lumber in the world.

Today over 85 percent of Canfor's annual harvest volume from Canfor forest tenures is certified to the Canadian Standards Association (CSA) Sustainable Forest Management Standard. By the end of 2008, Canfor will have reached the 100 percent level. Canfor's forest tenures have the environmental management system in place certified to the ISO 14001 standard.

HISTORY

In 1938, John Prentice and Poldi Bently formed Pacific Veneer, a furniture and paneling veneer company that soon produced plywood for aviation and marine applications. In 1944, Vancouver Island timber rights were purchased along with a company called Canadian Forest Products Ltd. In 1947, all operations were re-organized under that name, and the company began to show a steady growth curve. Canfor moved into the pulp business in 1951 and continued to purchase sawmills and timber rights in BC and Alberta. In 1983, Canfor became a public company, Canfor Corporation, and kept on growing. Between 1989 and 2006, Canfor made a number of strategic acquisitions, including Balfour Forest Products, Northwood Inc., Daaquam Lumber Inc., Slocan Forest Products Ltd. and New South Companies Inc. Through these acquisitions, Canfor developed a wide range of products,

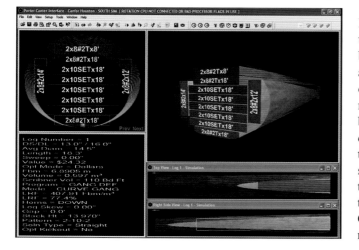

including Western SPF lumber, Eastern SPF lumber, SYP lumber, treated lumber, D Fir lumber, CSP plywood, hardwood plywood, OSB, NBSK pulp, thermo-mechanical pulp, paper, hardboard panels and other fibre products. As the company grew, so did its markets. Canfor now has sales offices in China, Japan, Europe, USA and Canada.

THE PRODUCT

Canfor manufactures a number of products. Some are sold under the house name, and others have individual brand names. JadeStar™ is Canfor's brand of premium J-Grade lumber that is sold in Japan. JadeStar is Japan's number-one lumber brand, tailored to the needs of the Japanese market.

SilvaStar® is a leading brand of specialty lumber products including fascia, decking and log cabin siding. Manufactured using premium lumber from Canfor's mills, SilvaStar adds beauty to a home at an affordable price. SilvaStar is manufactured to have zero defects and is 100 percent usable, a benefit that is not common in solid wood trim products.

Canfor framing lumber and Machine Stress Rated lumber are all sold under the Canfor name. These products are primarily Kiln Dried SPF lumber products, but also include Southern Yellow Pine. Canfor produces *a higher level of lumber*® that is reliably straight. Because lumber is manufactured from a natural raw material that is

slightly variable from log to log, Canfor's manufacturing facilities utilise laser scanning and laser grading technology. This advanced technology enables the machines to accommodate any variation in the wood, while still producing the best quality and lowest-cost lumber possible. As the

most important criteria in lumber is straightness, Canfor kiln dries all its lumber to ensure that the product is as straight and true as possible. Canfor values straightness above all else in terms of quality. The species mix, manufacturing expertise and advanced technology give Canfor a significant advantage over other companies. The "It's True" slogan is used by Canfor to reflect the straight and true nature of the product.

Canfor also manufactures structural panel products at four locations. Canfor OSB products are branded Polarboard™. In addition, Canfor manufactures plywood sheathing and added value plywood products.

RECENT DEVELOPMENTS

Canfor has two main priorities: to grow its global building products business, and to make higher-value structural and specialized lumber products for specific customer needs. To achieve these goals, Canfor has developed some of the largest, most advanced sawmills in the world. They are capable of meeting the growing global demand for consistent quality wood products as well as providing the low cost of manufacturing that is needed to survive.

In addition, Canfor's 2006 purchase of New South Companies Inc. has brought Southern Yellow Pine to the Canfor product mix and a significant import/export business. European wood is imported to supplement Canfor production and satisfy customers on the east coast of the U.S. And as the marketplace for lumber becomes truly global, Canfor continues to pursue strategic partnerships and joint ventures around the world.

China is an emerging marketplace for dimension lumber. To help build this market, Canfor has opened a school of construction in Shanghai. The Canfor Center of Wood Frame Construction teaches bricks and mortar builders the methods and advantages of wood frame construction, thus increasing the number of builders who are interested and capable of building the more environmentally friendly wood frame houses.

PROMOTION

The Canfor name is recognized by the trade as a leading supplier of consistent-quality lumber products. All lumber manufacturing facilities in Canada work to ensure that our product is of consistent quality, as straight and true as possible. Canfor's customers rely on this consistency. Direct advertising and promotion in North America, Asia and Europe promotes Canfor lumber as *a higher level of lumber*®, that is reliably straight and true.

The JadeStar™ brand and sales team are focused on Japan. Advertising explores the key initiatives within the company designed to improve the way in which Canfor does business

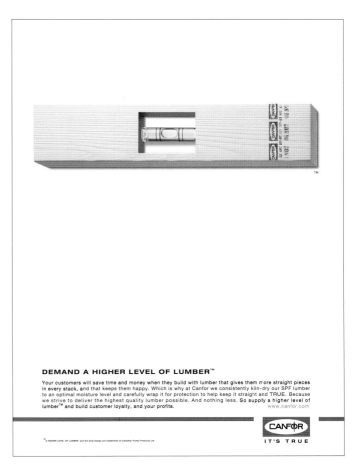

with Japan. JadeStar offers Japanese customers the supply security, customer service and product quality they need, and delivers it on their terms.

SilvaStar® is mainly promoted in the Western USA, as a cost effective way of adding real curb appeal to a home. The Silvastar brand is promoted directly to both builders and building material suppliers through trade press, trade shows and materials as an alternative to higher-priced cedar and composite products.

BRAND VALUES

"Canfor's reputation is built on the firm foundation of commitment to our customers, reliability of our supply and consistent quality of our product," says Jim Shepherd, chairman and CEO.

Canfor is respected in the industry for having the ability to manage our fibre supply and secure a stable supply of product for our customers. In a commodity marketplace, Canfor has earned its reputation as an established, branded manufacturer of the highest quality lumber that is always in demand around the world.

THINGS YOU DIDN'T KNOW ABOUT CANFOR

- ○ Canfor plants over 50 million trees every year, two to three times as many as are harvested.
- ○ Canfor uses lasers to scan the lumber it produces, producing a 3D image of each piece that can be interpreted by the master computer to help define the grade.
- ○ Canfor produces enough lumber to frame over 250,000 houses every year.
- ○ Canfor employs over 7,300 people and 2,200 contractors.
- ○ Canfor was voted Exporter of the Year for British Columbia in 2005.

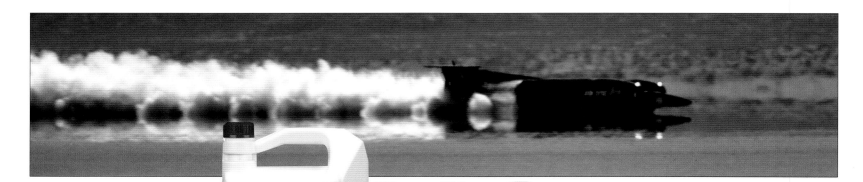

THE MARKET

With over 18 million light vehicles on the road, it is not surprising Canadians purchased more than 240 million litres of oil in 2005. The market has been relatively flat over the past several years, the consequence of extended vehicle servicing intervals and changing consumer behaviour. Counterbalancing these factors is an increasing population of vehicles and a propensity for consumers to drive farther and more often than ever before.

There are, however, segments within the market that show substantial growth. Sales of synthetics, spurred by manufacturers' recommendations and increased recognition of their benefits, have overcome a slow start and grabbed almost a 15 percent share of the market.

ACHIEVEMENTS

Castrol lubricants are tested and proven at the very limits of endurance. Many started as specialty formulations for competitive racing and endurance teams before becoming available to the everyday motorist. With a history of more than 100 years, this makes for a remarkable list of achievements. Castrol was first to:
• Add metallic soaps to oil, dramatically improving performance and life
• Produce a motor oil with additives, the breakthrough that every motor oil made today uses for better reliability and efficiency
• Market an affordable multi-grade motor oil for year-round use
• Patent anti-sludge technology to neutralize the components of sludge, thereby prolonging engine life
• Create fully synthetic lubricants for passenger jet engines
• Engineer an oil specifically designed to combat the stresses of hotter, higher-revving engines used in smaller cars

Castrol is used in more vehicles around the globe than any other brand of motor oil. In Canada, Castrol is the best-selling brand of passenger vehicle motor oil.

HISTORY

Castrol's roots lie with Charles Cheers Wakefield, who founded C. C. Wakefield & Company in the United Kingdom on March 19, 1899. The fledgling company focused on lubrication, an industry where Wakefield's legacy already included development of the Wakefield Box, a device to lubricate axles in steam engines that is still in use today.

Wakefield had the foresight to see the burgeoning potential of the gasoline engine.

His company concentrated on development of the lubricants that would become the lifeblood of automobiles, aircraft and other motorized vehicles throughout the 20th century.

Ten years after start-up, Wakefield introduced the brand that today is synonymous with premium quality, high performance and leading-edge technology: Castrol. By 1960, it was so highly regarded and well known it was adopted as the company name.

In 1966, Castrol merged with the British oil company Burmah to create Burmah-Castrol, which, in turn, was acquired by BP in 2000. Today, Castrol operates in over 60 countries.

THE PRODUCT

Castrol creates products that deliver superior performance and greater reliability with the goal of reducing customer operating costs. The most well-known Castrol product is GTX. Formulated with superior base oils, the GTX technology provides maximum protection against viscosity and thermal

breakdown. No wonder it's the first choice of North American motorists.

As a vehicle ages, engine performance decreases and oil breaks down faster. Over time, seals deteriorate, gaskets become brittle and oil consumption increases. Castrol GTX HIGH MILEAGE was developed specifically for older vehicles, to combat this aging process. It provides superior protection against oil burn-off, containing seal conditioners that help reduce leakage and proprietary additives that provide superior protection from wear and harmful deposits.

The fastest growing motor oil in the Castrol lineup is SYNTEC. In independent tests, it has been proven to provide engine protection and performance superior to all leading conventional oils. SYNTEC excels in protecting against corrosive particles such as rust, acid, soot and oxidized fuel

fragments that can cause costly damage to critical engine parts. SYNTEC neutralizes these particles, suspending them away from engine surfaces and preventing them from grouping and forming sludge.

While most frequently associated with automotive oils, Castrol offers lubricants for virtually all kinds of vehicles from motorcycles to heavy industrial trucks, off-road equipment, aircraft and marine. Each excels in its specific application.

RECENT DEVELOPMENTS

The company's focus on technology continues to deliver industry-leading products such as Castrol SYNTEC. Partnerships with technology-leading manufacturers such as BMW and Volkswagen have led to co-engineered development of Castrol products specifically designed to maximize the performance of their marques.

Castrol's commitment to technology is being leveraged in worldwide brand communications using the theme: "IT'S MORE THAN JUST OIL. IT'S LIQUID ENGINEERING."

PROMOTION

"Win on Sunday . . . Sell on Monday" has been the rallying cry for Castrol's involvement with motorsports for over 100 years. The brand's heritage of proven track performance and its support of winning drivers and teams across all forms of racing proved to be fundamental in building its identity and in fuelling its commitment to technological improvement.

The sentiment still holds true. Castrol is the oil of choice for some of the world's most successful automotive racing teams. From John Force and his 14 NHRA Top Fuel drag racing titles, to the Williams Team in Formula One, Castrol is there with innovative products that help provide a competitive edge.

In Canada, Castrol has long supported CASCAR, both the series and through the #17 Castrol Dodge Charger DJ Kennington team. In 2006, Castrol became the title sponsor of Castrol Raceway in Edmonton, the first time in its history that Castrol has attached its name to a motorsports facility.

These sponsorships along with a comprehensive marketing effort including advertising, consumer promotions, PR and the Internet contribute to the success the Castrol brand has enjoyed in Canada and around the world.

BRAND VALUES

Castrol Liquid Engineering provides a "strength within" that delivers in performance throughout the life of a vehicle and, in so doing, provides peace of mind and security. With more than 100 years satisfying customer needs, Castrol remains committed to its core brand values:

- A **passion** to help consumers get more out of life through their vehicles
- A drive for **performance** and innovation that respects the environment
- **Progress** derived from challenging the status quo and never standing still
- **Honesty** in clear communications with customers and consumers

THINGS YOU DIDN'T KNOW ABOUT CASTROL

- ○ The name Castrol is a derivative of castor oil, an ingredient in the original blend.

- ○ Castrol soared with flight pioneers Alcock and Brown in the first non-stop flight across the Atlantic in 1919.

- ○ The world land-speed record has been broken 21 times by a vehicle using Castrol.

- ○ In July 2005 Wakefield Canada Inc. — named in homage to Castrol founder C. C. Wakefield — was appointed as Castrol's strategic business partner, responsible exclusively for sales, marketing and distribution in Canada. Wakefield, which is independently owned, has its entrepreneurial focus on the Canadian market.

CIRQUE DU SOLEIL ®

THE MARKET

Live entertainment was a $120 billion industry in 2002, and it only continues to grow. North Americans have more entertainment choices than ever, and *Cirque du Soleil*® has risen to the top of this competitive field in record time. In just 21 years, Cirque has become a live-entertainment giant, with a brand recognised by close to 60 percent of North Americans. Cirque currently has seven different shows touring the globe, five resident shows in Las Vegas and a fifth in Orlando, Florida.

ACHIEVEMENTS

Since its creation in 1984, Cirque has produced 17 shows seen by more than 50 million people worldwide. Thirteen of those shows are still going strong today, and new productions are constantly being developed.

Cirque du Soleil has garnered international honours for its artistic and business achievements, including Emmy® Awards, Felix and Gemini Awards, Drama Desk Awards and Clown d'Argent Awards from the Monte Carlo Circus Festival. In 1986, Cirque ventured into television and recording for the first time, and its audio-visual products have garnered more than 20 awards.

HISTORY

Imagine a group of street performers entertaining passers-by in the early '80s — hippies juggling balls, breathing fire and walking on stilts. It seems impossible that in just 21 years, this same group would be at the helm of a multimillion-dollar entertainment organization with more than 3,000 employees on four continents. Yet that, in a nutshell, is the history of *Cirque du Soleil*.

Under the guiding hand of accordion player, fire-breather and stilt-walker Guy Laliberté, Cirque's founder and CEO, the company took its

first steps with small touring shows that quickly became the darlings of audiences throughout Quebec.

Before long, the U.S. came calling, and in 1987 *Cirque du Soleil* took the biggest risk in its brief history by agreeing to perform a show called *We Reinvent the Circus*™ at the Los Angeles Arts Festival. Cirque underwrote its own expenses in exchange for 100 percent of the gate. Failure was not an option: unless they wowed audiences in LA, they didn't even have the funds to get home. They were banking on rave reviews — and that's exactly what they got.

We Reinvent the Circus gave the United States its first taste of the company's innovative approach to circus arts: a masterful blend of acrobatics, theatre, dance and live music. From there, Cirque returned to the East Coast, introducing new live shows every two or three years.

Cirque made its first foray into Europe in 1990 with *We Reinvent the Circus*. Since then, Cirque has toured Europe and ventured into new markets each year with *Saltimbanco*™, *Alegría*®, *Quidam*® and, most recently, *Dralion*™ in 2004. Other regular tour destinations include Japan, Australia, New Zealand, Singapore, Hong Kong, Mexico and South America.

In 1993, Steve Wynn, then president and CEO of Mirage Resorts, approached *Cirque du Soleil* to create a resident show for Treasure Island in Las Vegas. The result was *Mystère*®, whose success blazed the trail for "O®" at Bellagio, *Zumanity*™ at New York-New York Hotel & Casino, KÀ™ at MGM Grand and LOVE™, which recently opened at The Mirage.

A similar agreement was made with the Walt Disney Company, and in 1998 *Cirque du Soleil* premiered *La Nouba*™ in a permanent theatre at *Walt Disney World*® Resort in Orlando. A new resident show at Tokyo Disney Resort is scheduled to open in 2008, making it the first permanent show outside North America.

In 2001, *Cirque du Soleil* thrilled its largest TV audience to date with a gala performance at the 74th Academy Awards® that earned an Emmy Award for its amazing choreography.

THE PRODUCT

The heart and soul of *Cirque du Soleil* is its live shows — spectacular productions that celebrate the beauty and energy of the human body. Every production has its own unique concept and features hand-made costumes, original music and magical lighting.

Each show is created at Cirque's headquarters in Montreal. This one-of-a-kind space houses dance studios, three acrobatics studios, costume and props workshops and Cirque's administrative nerve centre. All told, Cirque employs more than 1,600 people at its International Headquarters.

Creativity has always been at the core of Cirque's business plan, too. The strength of the *Cirque du Soleil* brand has allowed it to become a content provider — in the broadest possible sense of the term — as the producer of television series and the distributor of high-end merchandising and exclusive licensed products.

RECENT DEVELOPMENTS
In the past three years, the multi-media division at *Cirque du Soleil* has come into its own. In 2003, the reality series "*Cirque du Soleil* Fire Within" received a Primetime Emmy Award for Outstanding Non-Fiction Program.

Cirque has founded its own in-house music label, *Cirque du Soleil Musique*™, not only to produce show-related records, but also to showcase emerging talent.

In 2003, *Cirque du Soleil* defied expectations once more by introducing *ANOTHER SIDE OF CIRQUE DU SOLEIL*™ with the launch of *Zumanity*, a sexy and provocative new show for adults.

In 2004, *Cirque du Soleil* premiered yet another thrilling resident production on the Las Vegas strip — a show named KÀ at MGM Grand that has pioneered a new, more theatrical direction both for *Cirque du Soleil* and for Las Vegas entertainment.

In January 2006, Cirque launched DELIRIUM, a new kind of show that show-cases the music of *Cirque du Soleil* remixed and reinterpreted for a multimedia produc-tion that is touring major arenas in North America.

In 2006, *Cirque du Soleil* partnered with Apple Corps Ltd. and The Mirage to present an un-precedented live the-atre production that evokes the musical and cultural legacy of *The Beatles*™. This show marks the first time *The Beatles'* company

has agreed to a major artistic partnership in a joint venture.

Cirque du Soleil hasn't let the Internet revolution pass it by. In 2002, its Web site, cirquedusoleil.com, picked up four Gold Awards at Canada's Digital Marketing Awards.

PROMOTION
Cirque promotes its shows with a varied marketing mix of print, television, radio, public relations and outdoor media. Cirque selects media partners in each of its markets to minimize costs, create long-term relationships with local players and develop promotions adapted to the local community.

In recent years, Cirque has taken advantage of Web-based advertising and now reaches highly motivated customers through its online Cirque Club. In addition to receiving regular updates on Cirque activities, more than a million Cirque Club members worldwide have access to advance tickets, and in North America, Club members account for between 20 and 30 percent of touring show tickets sold.

Since its earliest days, *Cirque du Soleil* has built sponsorship alliances with industry leaders such as IBM, BMW, Audi, American Express, Canon, Vodafone, Celebrity Cruises, Epson, Porsche and Toyota. Sponsors leverage their relationship through advertising campaigns and hospitality programs, which in return increase Cirque's brand recogni-tion in areas outside the reach of its in-house marketing activities.

BRAND VALUES
Cirque du Soleil is a complex and emotion-laden brand — one that touches audiences' hearts and imaginations. The *Cirque du Soleil* name prom-ises a carefully crafted product and the highest levels of entertainment.

Some come to Cirque for an intensely personal experience, while others come for the best in live entertainment, but for all, every Cirque show is an explosive sensory event that encourages the spectator to look within. *Cirque du Soleil* shows address human nature at its best, championing togeth-erness, acceptance and physical strength and beauty.

Creativity is also at the heart of the organization's over-all business plan. There is no room for compromise at *Cirque du Soleil* when it comes to artistic expres-sion or to strong business development. Maintaining the delicate balance between these principles is a continuous process.

Photos: Éric Piché, Norman Jean Roy, Al Seib, Véronique Vial
Costumes: Dominique Lemieux, Marie-Chantale Vaillancourt
© 1998-2004 Cirque du Soleil Inc.

THINGS YOU DIDN'T KNOW ABOUT CIRQUE DU SOLEIL

- The average age of *Cirque du Soleil* employees is 35.
- More than 25 languages are spoken among Cirque artists and employees, who hail from over 40 countries.
- Cirque was rated Quebec's most admired company in 2003 and has been in the top ten since its inception.
- For its 20th anniversary, employees from the International Headquarters in Montreal set the world record for the greatest number of stilt-walkers (544) in the same place at the same time, an achievement noted in "Guinness World Records 2006."
- The pool in the "O" show holds more than 1.5 million gallons of water.
- *Cirque du Soleil* touring shows need a 180,000-square-foot site.
- Each year, Cirque's costume workshop uses more than 20 kilometres of fabric.
- *Cirque du Soleil* headquarters feature a train-ing studio large enough to house a big top.
- More than 300,000 meals are served by tour kitchens every year.
- Each tour has its own fully equipped school for the children on tour.
- One percent of Cirque's revenues is dedicated to social action and community programs.

CN TOWER
CANADA'S WONDER OF THE WORLD

LA TOUR CN
NOTRE MERVEILLE DU MONDE

THE MARKET

Located on the northern shore of Lake Ontario, Toronto is Canada's largest city with a population of 5 million people. Home to a vibrant mix of many different cultures, it is also the country's financial centre and the hub of a thriving arts scene. It's a beautiful, clean city with many distinctive neighbourhoods, green spaces and a spectacular waterfront: a great place to live and a destination with international appeal.

Standing tall as the defining landmark of this cosmopolitan city is the CN Tower, Canada's National Tower. At 553.33 metres (1,815 ft., 5 in.), it is not only the World's Tallest Building but a dazzling symbol of Canadian architectural achievement. A true Wonder of the Modern World, the CN Tower became the iconic symbol of Toronto tourism as soon as it was built in 1975. Today, the Tower is a must-see attraction for visitors to Toronto and a first-class dining and event centre. Looming high above the city's skyscrapers, it is a constant reminder of the world-class experiences that can be found in Canada.

ACHIEVEMENTS

The CN Tower holds a long and distinguished record of achievement in its history.

Over the years, the CN Tower has been recognized by the Guinness Book of World Records as the World's Tallest Building, Tallest Tower and Tallest Freestanding Structure. In 1995, the CN Tower was classified as one of the Seven Wonders of the Modern World by the American Society of Civil Engineers. To this day, 30 years since construction was completed, there is no freestanding man-made structure taller than the CN Tower on earth. A marvel of engineering, it continues to thrill visitors from all over the world.

The CN Tower introduced the world's first Glass Floor to visitors in 1994, providing a dare-to-walk-on-air view 342m (1,122 feet) straight down to the ground. Almost 20 million people have walked on the the Glass Floor since it was built, including numerous celebrities and dignitaries. It's been the setting for numerous high-altitude weddings; and the CN Tower Millennium celebrations transformed the Glass Floor into a one-of-a-kind dance space complete with lighting effects.

On May 13, 1997, *360 The Restaurant at the CN Tower* officially opened its European-style wine cellar in the sky. At 351 metres (1150 ft.), it is a high-altitude magnet for wine lovers. Created to resemble a typical underground wine cellar, it features precision climate and humidity controls and houses one of the most extensive wine lists in Canada.

The CN Tower has earned numerous awards, including: DiRoNA Award (Distinguished Restaurants of North America) for excellence in dining experience (recipient since 1997), Wine Spectator Best of Award of Excellence (since 1999), and other awards, including: Most Romantic Restaurant, Best Tourist Attraction, Best Attraction and Best Restaurant with a View.

The CN Tower has also become a tourist magnet by celebrating its unique assets in innovative ways.

The World's Longest Metal Staircase is available to the public only twice each year for fund-raising stair climbs. This event attracts over 15,000 climbers who raise over $1.5 million for charities annually. And the World's Highest Mailbox, built to Canada Post specifications and standards, provides visitors with an unique opportunity to send mail from the "top of the world."

Whether they be leaders or celebrities or just curious visitors, the CN Tower offers everyone who ventures to the top a thrilling experience. From breath-taking 360-degree views of the city to the best regional Canadian cuisine, the Tower is an unforgettable experience for people of all ages.

HISTORY

Although the CN Tower inspires a sense of pride for Canadians and a sense of awe in visitors, its origins are rooted in practicality. The 1960s ushered in an unprecedented construction boom in Toronto, transforming a skyline characterized by relatively low buildings into one dotted with skyscrapers. The existing transmission towers couldn't handle the demand for clear communications. Downtown Toronto needed a very tall new structure to accommodate its changing cityscape.

With its microwave receptors at 338 m (1,109 ft.) and the antenna some 200 metres higher, the CN Tower brought some of the clearest reception in North America to people living in the city.

The CN Tower was built by Canadian National Railway, which wanted to demonstrate the strength of Canadian industry by raising a tower taller than any other in the world. Building the CN Tower was a vast and ambitious project that involved 1,537 workers who worked 24 hours a day, five days a week for 40 months to completion.

When the 44th and final piece of the antenna was bolted into place April 2, 1975, the CN Tower joined the ranks of 17 other great structures that had previously held the title of World's Tallest Free-Standing Structure. The Guinness Book of World Records was on hand to record the milestone.

THE PRODUCT

Defining the Toronto skyline, the CN Tower is Canada's most recognizable and celebrated icon. At a height of 553.33m (1,815 ft., 5 in.), it is the World's Tallest Building, a Wonder of the Modern World, an important telecommunications hub and the centre of tourism in Toronto.

Each year, approximately 2 million people visit Canada's Wonder of the World to enjoy all the CN Tower has to offer. Three observation levels provide breathtaking views of Toronto at a range of 120 kilometres. Other attractions include a simulator ride, arcade, exhibits and 10,000 square feet of shopping with a wide array of high-quality merchandise. Three restaurants satisfy every appetite include the award-winning *360 Restaurant* with its one-of-a-kind wine cellar in the sky. A leading event venue, the Tower hosts over 300 memorable events each year for 2 to 2,000 for receptions, dinners, themed events, meetings and product and press launches.

Public events have ranged from concert series, exhibitions and seasonal special events. Recent events included the only Canadian stop for *The Secret Life of Sets*, the Academy of Motion Picture Arts and Science's exhibition celebrating the art of set decoration. *The CN Tower Communities in*

Bloom Gardens were conceived as a tourism initiative to promote tourism to Canada, Ontario, Toronto and the CN Tower while enhancing the

visitor experience. *The CN Tower Gardens* are an inspired tribute to a national program committed to fostering civic pride, environmental responsibility and beautification.

RECENT DEVELOPMENTS

The CN Tower has been a technological leader since it was first built and upgrades all systems on an ongoing basis to ensure it is operating at optimum efficiency.

Over the years the CN Tower's legacy has also been supported with numerous enhancements such as the redesign of *360 Restaurant*, building the world's highest wine cellar, adding two new elevators, replacing the Radome (the Teflon-coated fiberglass fabric, which protects the Tower's microwave equipment at the base of the main pod), installing a $2 million leading-edge security system and adding new flexible meeting space to meet the growing needs of event clients — to name a few.

In June 2006, the CN Tower celebrated 30 years as a national icon, an engineering wonder . . . and still the World's Tallest Building.

PROMOTION

As Canada's National Tower and icon, the CN Tower takes a leadership role in the tourism industry. This commitment is demonstrated through active support of tourism associations at all levels — national, provincial and municipal. The CN Tower participates in a number of tourism initiatives reaching a variety of markets including international trade missions annually to promote tourism to Canada.

Ongoing customer satisfaction and demographic research keeps Tower management in touch with the needs and interests of its visitors. In addition to advertising, annual marketing plans reach out to all markets through public relations, promotions and events.

Innovative thinking helps to develop strategic partnerships within the industry. Recently the CN Tower partnered with five major attractions and worked with CityPass® to introduce the

Toronto CityPass®, making Toronto the first Canadian city to offer this convenient value-packaged ticket of six regional attractions.

With pro-active public relations and publicity outreach, the CN Tower assists over 200 print, radio and television broadcast media crews from all over the world each year.

The CN Tower values its role as a tourism ambassador for the city, province and country and believes that the high standards that it maintains and the excellent value it provides to visitors reflect positively on all members of the Tourism industry.

BRAND VALUES

According to a recent Ipsos-Reid poll, when Canadians are asked to name Canada's top three landmarks, it's the CN Tower (44 percent) that tops the list, with Niagara Falls (33 percent), the Canadian Rockies (32 percent) and the Parliament Buildings in Ottawa (26 percent) next in line.

The CN Tower doesn't just dominate the Canadian imagination by virtue of its height. It has maintained its pre-eminence with a brand philosophy that revolves around innovation, value and exceptional service to the public.

Always building on its legacy as an iconic attraction, the CN Tower will continue to be the defining symbol of tourism for Toronto and Canada, and a place to create wonderful memories.

THINGS YOU DIDN'T KNOW ABOUT THE CN TOWER

○ The CN Tower took 40 months to build. 1,537 people worked 24 hours a day, five days a week to complete the job.

○ Lightning strikes the CN Tower an average of 75 times a year. Long copper strips running down the CN Tower feed into massive grounding rods below ground level to ensure public safety.

○ Plans for the Tower included a wind resistance factor of 418 km/h (260 mph).

○ The CN Tower weighs 130,000 tonnes — the same weight as 23,214 large elephants.

THE MARKET

Coca-Cola, the world's number-one brand, is a symbol of refreshment to people around the world. The familiar shape of the Coca-Cola contour bottle and the flowing script of its distinctive trademark are a familiar part of people's lives. In fact, nearly half a million times every minute of every day, someone chooses a Coca-Cola — classic, diet or light, with vanilla, cherry or lemon, with or without caffeine. Soft drinks have been part of the Canadian lifestyle for more than 100 years.

ACHIEVEMENTS

From its birthplace and headquarters in Atlanta, Georgia, The Coca-Cola Company now has operations in 200 countries. Today, the company is a total beverage company with product offerings that extend well beyond carbonated soft drinks to include juice drinks, sports and energy drinks, waters, tea and more.

From the early days, Coca-Cola has been part of major events in North America and around the world. In World War II, the company assured that every member of the U.S. armed services was able to obtain a Coke for five cents, regardless of the remoteness of duty station or cost to the company. To fulfill that pledge, the company assembled bottling plants in 64 locations in Europe, Africa and the Pacific. The effort extended the company's reach beyond North America, positioning the company for postwar worldwide growth.

Significant Coca-Cola milestones over the last 25 years include the opening of the Soviet Union as a market, re-entry of Coca-Cola products into China in 1979 and the launch of the space shuttle in 1985. Coca-Cola celebrated its centennial in 1986 and has sponsored every Olympic Games since 1928.

HISTORY

On May 8, 1886, pharmacist John Stith Pemberton made a caramel-coloured syrup and offered it to the largest drugstore in Atlanta. But first year sales averaged only nine soft drinks a day, and Pemberton was never able to see his product's success. He died in 1888, the same year in which Atlanta businessman Asa G. Candler began to buy outstanding shares of Coca-Cola.

Within three years, Candler and his associates controlled the young company through a total investment of $2,300. The company registered the trademark "Coca-Cola" with the U.S. Patent Office in 1893 and has renewed it ever since. ("Coke" has been a trademark name since 1945.) By 1895, the first syrup manufacturing plants outside Atlanta had been opened in Dallas, Chicago and Los Angeles. Candler reported to shareholders that Coca-Cola was being sold "in every state and territory of the United States."

As fountain sales expanded, entrepreneurs sought additional sales by offering the drink in bottles. Large-scale bottling began when Benjamin F. Thomas and Joseph B. Whitehead of Chattanooga, Tennessee secured from Asa Candler exclusive rights to bottle and sell Coca-Cola in nearly all of the country. They gave other individuals exclusive territories for community bottling operations. Those efforts laid the groundwork for what would become a worldwide network of Coca-Cola Bottling companies.

In 1905, Coca-Cola applied for and received the registration of the Coca-Cola trademark in Canada. In January 1906, Canada became the first country in which Coca-Cola could be bottled and sold outside of the United States.

The company's response to the imitators who quickly arose included the adoption of one of the most famous product containers ever developed — the unique, contour Coca-Cola bottle, created in 1915 by the Root Glass Company of Indiana and approved as standard by the company's bottlers in the following year.

In 1919, a group of investors headed by Ernest Woodruff, an Atlanta banker, purchased The Coca-Cola Company. Four years later, Robert W. Woodruff, Ernest's 33-year-old son, became president of the company and led it into a new era of domestic and global growth over the next six decades.

Since Woodruff's time, Coca-Cola has always placed high value on citizenship. Today, as part of the Coca-Cola Promise to "benefit and refresh everyone who is touched by our business," the company strives to refresh the marketplace, enrich the workplace, preserve the environment, and strengthen communities. Working through The Coca-Cola Foundation and other avenues, the company's lead philanthropic efforts are focused on education and youth achievement. The Coca-Cola Company's recent five-year, $1 billion commitment to diversity through a comprehensive empowerment and entrepreneurship program

offers individuals and small businesses many opportunities as well.

On the corporate side in 2004, E. Neville Isdell formally assumed the position of chairman and chief executive officer of The Coca-Cola Company.

THE PRODUCT

Life is a series of special moments, and each is an opportunity for Coca-Cola to add its bit of magic. From the look and feel of the bottle to the sound of effervescence, the tickle of fizz on the nose and tongue and of course, the unique flavor, Coca-Cola is a sensory experience. But consumer emotions, memories and values are even more powerful.

New graphics are part of what keeps the Coca-Cola brand relevant to today's consumers.

The new visual identity introduced in 2003 offers a contemporary interpretation of traditional elements such as the Spencerian script, refreshing it with a lighter, more open look; a contemporary dynamic ribbon featuring multiple ribbons of white, silver and yellow; and effervescing bubbles. A broad overview of the history, growth and contemporary activities of The Coca-Cola Company is available on the Internet at www.thecocacolacompany.com.

People love to speculate about the secret ingredients in Coke. One secret is indeed locked away in a secured vault. But another is readily available: the consistent quality of Coca-Cola products. And that commitment to quality extends to the company's entire portfolio of brands, including Coca-Cola Classic, Diet Coke, Coca-Cola Zero, Sprite and Diet Sprite Zero, Dasani remineralized water, Full Throttle, TaB energy and a full line of Minute Maid juices and juice drinks.

PROMOTION

Coca-Cola's promotional efforts began with an oilcloth "Drink Coca-Cola" sign on a drugstore awning. Asa Candler then put the newly trademarked name not only on syrup urns at soda fountains, but on novelty items such as fans, calendars and clocks. Since those days, marketing and promotional efforts combined with a top quality product have made the Coca-Cola trademark among the most admired and best known in the world.

One way The Coca-Cola Company reaches its consumers is through affiliations with activities that people enjoy. For example, the company has extensive worldwide sports affiliations that reinforce identification with the brand. As far back as 1903, advertising has featured famous major league baseball players drinking Coca-Cola. One of the most notable and long-lasting sports affiliations is the company's 76-year association with the Olympic Games. The company has a long relationship with FIFA World Cup soccer, the Special Olympics, the Rugby World Cup, NASCAR® and the National Basketball Association.

RECENT DEVELOPMENTS

The Coca-Cola Company continues to connect with people in exciting new ways, including the introduction of successful new products and innovations that give people the experiences they desire.

In the summer of 2005, Coca-Cola Ltd. launched iCoke.ca, an innovative, long-term online loyalty program that was designed to provide Coca-Cola drinkers with fully integrated promotions and events. In the past year, Coca-Cola has developed partnerships with House of Blues, the biggest concert promoter company in Canada, Sony Canada, Cineplex Entertainment and other key suppliers to ensure that iCoke.ca can offer consumers a unique entertainment experience through grand prizing, daily instant wins and redemption towards cool items or entry into sweepstakes.

In the fall of 2005, in response to a growing need for a new entry into the diet category, one that didn't emphasize diet but focused on taste, the Company introduced Coca-Cola Zero — real Coca-Cola taste, zero calories.

Consumers were offered their first taste of Coca-Cola Zero at a launch event featuring the world's largest air hockey game with special

guests former Toronto Maple Leaf players Wendel Clark, Darryl Sittler and Nick Kypreos.

Coca-Cola continues to respond to consumer demands for innovative packaging and design. In 2005, Coca-Cola introduced two new packaging sizes — the mini can, a 237mL can that is one-third smaller than the traditional can and the "shortie," a resealable

355mL plastic bottle. Both new packages allow the company to offer greater packaging variety to the consumer.

BRAND VALUES

The Coca-Cola brand stands for the most successful product in the history of commerce and for the people responsible for its unique appeal. Along with Coca-Cola, recognized as the world's best-known soft-drink brand, the company markets many of the world's top soft-drink brands, including Diet Coke, Fanta and Sprite. Through more than a century of change and into a new era that promises even more change, Coca-Cola remains a timeless symbol of authentic, original and "Real" refreshment.

THINGS YOU DIDN'T KNOW ABOUT COCA-COLA

○ The Coca-Cola trademark was registered in Canada in 1905.

○ The first Canadian bottle of Coca-Cola came off the line in 1906.

○ In Canada, Coca-Cola Ltd. (CCL) is an indirect, wholly owned subsidiary of The Coca-Cola Company, the world's largest beverage company and the leading producer and marketer of soft drinks, juices and juice drinks.

○ Coca-Cola Ltd. has grown from producing a single product to a wide range of hydration choices.

○ The Coca-Cola portfolio now includes Dasani remineralized water, Minute Maid juices and juice drinks, Five Alive, Fruitopia, Nestea, non-colas such as Fresca and Sprite, energy drinks including TaB energy and Full Throttle, and PowerAde.

○ Coca-Cola leads in the following categories: colas, diet colas, iced teas, and total juices and juice drinks.

○ Diet Coke is the number one consumed diet soft drink in Canada.

THE MARKET

The origin of whisky goes back far earlier than the existence of the nation of Canada: nearly a full millennium. The first to create this admirable brew were the Irish, back in the 1200s. Next were the Highlanders of Scotland in the 1400s, who began to produce what they called *uisage beatha* — "the water of life."

As immigrants from Ireland and Scotland descended upon what would become Canada, they brought with them their distilling traditions. Here, they discovered abundant grains, including rye, from which they could produce a unique Canadian (rye) Whisky. Since its birth in 1794, this fine beverage has joined the distinct fabric of this nation's history and risen to become one of the top selling beverage alcohol categories consumed today.

Canadian Whisky is very much a *North American* passion, with 86 percent of all that is produced being sold to the United States. It is, however, much loved by, and exported to, over 150 countries globally. In Canada, the Canadian Whisky market represents 3.6 million 9L cases, with 45 percent of these being sold in the province of Ontario.

Crown Royal DeLuxe is the number one Canadian Whisky brand in Canada, selling over half a million 9L cases annually. Beyond being the top selling Canadian Whisky, Crown Royal is also the most "adored" whisky in Canada, according to Ipsos-Reid Brand Tracking Research, thanks to its rich and deeply rooted history, which underpins its commanding ownership of status, and understated privilege.

ACHIEVEMENTS

When the sixth annual San Francisco World Spirits Competition was held in March 2006, with 19 judges tasting 701 products in over 70 different spirits classifications from 52 countries, Crown Royal achieved Gold Medal honours for the third year in a row. Today, Diageo has the privilege of upholding nearly 70 years of impeccable standards, through the gatekeeping of Crown Royal's equity and stature.

Beyond this individual accomplishment, the 2005 San Francisco World Spirits Competition Gold Medal for "Importer of the Year" went to Diageo, which proudly owns Crown Royal and a number of other premium spirit brands, including Smirnoff, Johnnie Walker, Baileys, Captain Morgan and Tanqueray.

HISTORY

Few man-made creations have legendary power in their very origin, but such is the case for the birth of Crown Royal Canadian Whisky. Samuel Bronfman had read that the King and Queen of England were planning a visit to Canada in 1939, and decided to salute their majesties with his own superior blend, presented in a crown-shaped bottle and a royal purple bag. Bronfman reportedly tried over 600 different blends, before settling on the one which he felt was worthy enough to be called CROWN ROYAL.

Ultimately, Bronfman was allowed to place only one single, precious case of his master blend on the Royal train when it stopped in Montreal, and later, one more case in Toronto, before the royal couple continued West. This was the auspicious birth of Crown Royal Canadian Whisky — and one of the most astonishing marketing coups in modern history.

In July 2000, Diageo Inc. announced a strategic realignment behind its premium drinks business, which led to the acquisition of 60 percent of the Seagram's spirits and wine business. Included in this acquisition were the brand jewels of Crown Royal Canadian Whisky and Captain Morgan Rum.

In Canada, the Crown Royal franchise includes the flagship brand Crown Royal DeLuxe, as well as Crown Royal Limited Edition and Crown

Royal Special Reserve. And the future looks to hold new gems on the horizon for the growing Crown Royal family.

THE PRODUCT

Today, Andrew Mackay is the master whisky blender for Crown Royal, with the task of guaranteeing its majesty and consistency. "The distinctiveness of Crown Royal comes from the insistence on excellence that can be seen in the attention to **every detail** from the ground up: quality grains, exact processes, expert distillation, careful maturation, appraisal and small batch blending, and over 61 different quality checks." Mackay will tell you that the family of whiskies to which Crown Royal belongs is quite distinct from all other Canadian distilleries in production today, since the aim is to "consistently make balanced, creamy, fruity and spicy whiskies that are blended in a manner where the sum adds up to *more* than the individual parts." So, while all men are created equal, all whiskies are NOT.

Just outside Gimli, Manitoba, an hour's drive north of Winnipeg, stands a proud sign that reads, "WELCOME TO CROWN ROYAL GIMLI PLANT." It seems a strange place to put this important centre, until one realizes that it's all about the clear and pure water supply that is tapped from an endless underground river running between Lake Winnipeg and Lake Manitoba. Gimli is Diageo's only remaining distillery, replacing six others, including the long-revered "Joseph E Seagram and Sons," which thrived in Waterloo, Ontario, between 1857 and 1992.

Aside from the rich history and superior liquid blend, another attribute that truly makes Crown Royal one of a kind is the crown cut glass bottle, and the legendary purple bag loved by virtually every Crown Royal drinker, young and old. Crown Royal is proudly bottled in Amherstburg, Ontario, producing just over 4.2 million 9L cases annually. Crown Royal's Canadian-based team of dedicated experts, from coast to coast, is truly passionate about bringing the superiority and worthiness of Crown Royal to whisky aficionados everywhere.

RECENT DEVELOPMENTS

With a company that has been around for nearly 150 years, and a magnificent blend nearly half that old, "recent developments" can mean decades — or days. Crown Royal has introduced a number of new "offspring" over the past two decades. In celebration of the 50th anniversary of the birth of Crown Royal Deluxe, a noble blend was developed to commemorate this milestone — Crown Royal Limited Edition. This unique blend is a distinguished collection of "batch distilled" whiskies which yield a robust taste sensation for flavour-seeking whisky connoisseurs. In the mid-'90s, master blender Arthur Dawe created Crown Royal Special Reserve, an ultra-premium version of its parent. Early in the maturation process, the best of the young whiskies are hand selected and reserved for this blend. The additional aging gives the product maximum richness, mellowness, and more complexity.

In 2006, Crown Royal will yet again set discerning taste buds alight with a monumental

Ever see a grown man cry?

It's about quality, not quantity. • *Visit crownroyal.com*

luxury blend, which at the time of publication of this book could not yet be divulged. Stay tuned for rarity that could come only from the Kingdom of Crown Royal.

PROMOTION

In 1938, when Crown Royal was still being blended — **and blended!** — to be fit for a King

and Queen, its distilling company won a "first place among advertisers in all fields of industry," by wisely directing its sales messages to the upper end of the drinking scale. "This company . . . recognizes that confidence is the dominant influence in liquor buying," announced the advertising magazine presenting the award. These inspired promotions have continued over the decades, with such magnificent, memorable ads as a dropped and shattered bottle of Crown Royal with the caption below, **"Have you ever seen a grown man cry?"** Originally developed in the early '80s and spanning three decades, its unprecedented longevity is a testament to the power and effectiveness of great advertising.

The renowned advertising agency Grey Worldwide has been working with the Crown Royal brand for many years, delivering inspired and iconic advertising that has helped to maximize the power of its magnificent assets.

Of course, there is more to promotion than magazine and TV ads. One of the most compelling promotional vehicles is the

Crown Royal Web site (www.crownroyal.ca). Loyal consumers tap into this site for new and exciting information and rewards from Crown Royal and its sponsorship platforms. In terms of sponsorship, two very prominent platforms have been supported by Crown Royal — the CFL (Canadian Football League) and more recently, NASCAR, via sponsorship of the Roush Nextel Cup Racing #26 racing team. This motorsports platform allows Crown Royal the opportunity to deliver communications around the responsible use of beverage alcohol. Crown Royal and Diageo are passionate about social responsibility.

A great brand, a great product and a close affiliation and identification with two of the most popular professional sports in North America today — football and motorsport racing. This is what successful promotion is all about.

BRAND VALUES

Crown Royal owes its unparalleled success to its rich heritage and status, unwavering product quality and a passion for delivering **only the best**. All this, while never forgetting what the brand and its consumers both value most: Genuineness, Approachability and Excellence.

THINGS YOU DIDN'T KNOW ABOUT CROWN ROYAL

○ During its inception in 1939, Sam Bronfman reportedly tried over 600 different blends, before settling on the one which he felt was worthy enough to be served to a king — and a queen — and to be blessed with the name **Crown Royal**.

○ Six million gallons of water and 10,000 bushels of grain are used each day in the production of Crown Royal.

○ Crown Royal is poured — or, rather, regally served — over 119 million times every year across Canada.

○ Crown Royal has long been, and continues to be, the number one spirit gifting option during special holidays.

THE MARKET

Canadians are unplugged. They play, communicate, calculate and plan all with the help of portable power. Energizer batteries power the lifestyle of this on-the go society. In fact, the average Canadian household owns more than 22 battery-operated devices. In a technological game of leapfrog, devices evolve as battery power improves, and battery power improves to make way for the next evolution of gadgets and gizmos.

More devices with added bells and whistles are certainly one trend that drives the category. Smaller devices are another. For example, music machines once the size of a small suitcase fit in the palm of your hand. This trend toward miniaturization has made AA and AAA-size batteries the workhorses of the category. Of the more than 5 billion batteries sold each year, 80 percent of them are AA or AAA sizes, according to A. C. Nielsen.

In short, there is an ever-increasing demand for reliable batteries that can keep pace with today's mobile lifestyles. Energizer continues to be the leading premium alkaline power source that keeps families going . . . and going . . . and going.

ACHIEVEMENTS

Energizer invented alkaline batteries in the late 1950s and has continued to enhance them over the years. Since 1960, the service life of an Energizer battery has improved dramatically. Anticipating the trend toward high-tech devices, Energizer led the industry, designing batteries to meet the needs of these sophisticated devices. The company continues to innovate in all segments of the battery category.

Energizer was the first company to design and introduce a super-premium Energizer e^2 titanium battery, harness the power of lithium in a AA and AAA cell size and revolutionize the rechargeable battery category by introducing a full line of high-powered Nickel Metal Hydride (NiMH) batteries.

Energizer is the world's largest manufacturer of batteries and portable lighting products. Energizer products are distributed to more than 160 countries. Nearly one out of three batteries sold in the world is an Energizer.

HISTORY

The country was alive with the spirit of discovery in the 1890s when Joshua Lionel Cohen began selling his latest invention, a tiny battery-and-bulb device used to illuminate flowers in a pot. Conrad Hubert, who operated a New York City restaurant, was so impressed that he quit his job to sell the devices for Cowen. When the power failed in a restaurant where Hubert had just installed the flower pots he had an inspiration: put the "flowerpot lights" in people's hands. And the seeds for the Eveready Battery Company — and portable power — were planted.

Hubert acquired the patent for the first Eveready "electric hand torch" in 1898. His first flashlights were handmade, consisting of a dry cell battery, a bulb and a rough brass reflector inside a paper tube. By 1900, his flashlights were sold in London, Montreal, Paris, Berlin and Sydney, Australia.

Hubert's company, the American Electrical Novelty and Manufacturing company, became American Ever Ready in 1905 to emphasize the dependability of its flashlight products. American Ever Ready merged in 1914 with the National Carbon Company, whose six-inch-tall Columbia battery was the first to power home telephones. The newly formed company merged with Union Carbide three years later.

Today Energizer Holdings Inc. is a publicly held company traded on the NYSE. Energizer purchased the Schick Wilkinson Sword brands of men's and women's grooming product in 2003.

THE PRODUCT

Energizer offers a unique, complete portfolio of products designed to meet the distinct needs and expectations of different consumer groups. The flagship brand, Energizer, offers premium, long-lasting battery performance fueled by continuous commitment to product improvement.

On the high end, Energizer e^2 Lithium batteries last seven times longer than alkaline in today's high-drain digital still cameras. Energizer e^2 with titanium technology and Energizer Nickel Metal Hydride batteries round out the high-performance line-up. The company also offers value brands under the Eveready name. For consumers looking for a lower price and a dependable brand name they can trust, Eveready can't be beat.

In addition to primary household batteries, Energizer manufactures miniature batteries for hearing aids, watches and other electronics.

Also they are one of the world's largest manufacturers of flashlights, including several award-winning designs.

RECENT DEVELOPMENTS

Over the course of several decades, the company continued to grow, focusing upon its strong reputation as the dependable battery that you can trust. The batteries were certainly reliable, but one young, persistent scientist knew they could be better and his work launched a new era for the company.

Assigned to an existing Eveready division in 1957, Lew Urry soon began to focus on an entirely new chemical system — a system known today as alkaline. Urry made a mock-up of an alkaline battery from an empty flashlight shaft, inserted it into a toy car and tested it on the cafeteria floor. The vice president of technology at the time brought the two flashlights to the then head of the consumer products division and asked him to leave both on overnight. One light, containing carbon-zinc batteries and the other, alkaline batteries. To their surprise, the alkaline powered flashlight was "still going" in the morning, while the carbon-zinc–powered light had gone dead. The rest, you could say, is history. Alkaline batteries now make up over 90 percent of all batteries sold in North America. And that is one of the reasons the company began using Energizer as its trade name to emphasize the alkaline focus and the flagship brand.

Lew Urry, a 40-year-veteran at Energizer, was a highly respected fellow at the company where he is still known as "the father of Alkaline." Lew was born in Canada and graduated from the University of Toronto. He has held over 50 patents covering battery designs and systems, but his invention of the alkaline battery remains a shining success story to Energizer, which brought the first alkaline batteries to the world. Urry's proto-

type cell is displayed at the Smithsonian Museum of Natural History.

PROMOTION

Energizer — the battery with the power to keep you going and going. This long-lasting power is embodied by the Energizer Bunny, the likeable, infamous, battery-operated toy, one of the most recognized symbols of perseverance and determination. The pink, furry Energizer Bunny with flip-flops and oversized sunglasses began marching across television screens in 1989 and drumming up quite a "bang" for Energizer batteries.

He first appeared in a parody of a competitor's "Toys" campaign in which he not only lasted longer than toys powered by the competitor's batteries but "kept going and going" right off the commercial set as an off-camera voice yelled "stop the Bunny!" Since that time, he has appeared in more than 110 TV spots always with an element of surprise and a message of long-lasting power. The campaign has generated billions of consumer impressions since it was introduced.

Today, the Energizer Bunny has earned pop-culture status and is a favourite character to millions. The Energizer Bunny is so popular he has been invited to appear at weddings, class reunions, birthday parties and even church services. His photo sits by the bedside of critically ill patients as a symbol of encouragement to keep going.

The Energizer Bunny's tagline "keep going" has become so popular that it is used to describe

perennially successful sports, entertainment and political figures. The Energizer Bunny campaign itself ranks among the top 10 favourite advertising campaigns of all time.

The Energizer Bunny not only uses his notoriety to promote the brand, he also uses it to advance causes. He leads the crusade for home fire safety through the company's "Change Your Clock, Change Your Battery" program through sales promotion and the Web, and in classrooms across the country, where he takes the message directly to children, who are five times more likely to be severely hurt in a home fire.

BRAND VALUES

Energizer has a unique approach to the marketplace. Its goal is to match consumer wants and needs with the most meaningful, reliable, long-lasting product offerings. As a result, Energizer offers the broadest product lineup in the industry.

THINGS YOU DIDN'T KNOW ABOUT ENERGIZER®

○ Energizer manufactures nearly one out of every three batteries sold in the world.

○ More than 25 chemical reactions take place within an Energizer battery to turn on a device and have it start working.

○ The year 1999 marked the 40th anniversary of Energizer's invention of the alkaline battery.

○ Since its creation in 1989, the Energizer Bunny has appeared in more than 110 television commercials, generating more than 119 billion impressions.

○ Former Prime Minister Jean Chretien compared himself the Energizer Bunny because he kept on going . . . and going . . . and going.

"The difference between day and night"
EVEREADY
FLASHLIGHTS & BATTERIES
NATIONAL CARBON COMPANY, INC.
Unit of Union Carbide and Carbon Corporation

†

THE MARKET

Ever stopped to wonder how many millions of kilometres of streets and highways there are in Canada? In a land as vast as ours, it's no surprise that driving is a necessary part of life for most of us. Whether travelling to work, taking kids to hockey practice or to a doctor's appointment, visiting relatives or vacationing in another city or simply doing the grocery shopping, we are indeed a society on the run.

According to the most recent figures, there are 17.4 million cars in Canada, driving over 300 billion kilometres per year. Fuelling those cars — and meeting a growing range of other convenience needs for their drivers — is where the Esso brand comes in. Without gasoline, everyday life in Canada would be profoundly different.

"Service stations have come a long way over the past century," says Simon Smith, vice-president and general manager, Fuels Marketing at Imperial Oil, the organization behind the Esso brand. "The simple shed with a manual pump out front has become a sophisticated retail operation, with many of the newest locations boasting a large convenience store with a foodservice offer, an automatic car wash and a spacious canopy to shelter motorists from the weather as they fill up." As of 2004, there were over 14,000 retail gasoline outlets operating across Canada, making this one of Canada's most competitive retail sectors.

The convenience store is a newer phenomenon, but plays an increasingly vital role in the shopping habits of time-starved urban and suburban Canadians, Smith notes. Industry research shows that over half of those people who shop at c-stores do so at least five times per week.

"Many people view gasoline as a commodity product," says Smith. "From our worldwide

research, we know that people *love* their cars but *hate* life on the road. They relish the privacy of their cars, the space, the chance to be alone with their thoughts. But they can't stand the traffic, the noise and, mostly, the other drivers! To win in the marketplace, the Esso brand strives to delight customers and continually earn their business by providing a superior experience that enhances their busy life on the move," Smith says.

ACHIEVEMENTS

"Since the very beginning, Imperial Oil and the Esso brand have been leaders in meeting the evolving needs of Canadian drivers," explains North America brand manager Alex Roth.

"Back in 1907, we opened Canada's first gas station in Vancouver. During the 1930s, we pioneered innovative fuel blends like 3-Star gasoline, and also incorporated new design trends when building our service stations," Roth says.

In 1970, Esso opened its first self-serve station, and eight years later was the first petroleum company operating in Canada to sell premium unleaded gasoline that helped protect the environment.

In 2003 — a year ahead of the legislated deadline — Esso introduced low-sulphur gasoline that reduced sulphur content by 90 percent. And, in tandem with Exxon Mobil Corporation, Imperial Oil Limited conducts ongoing research to take on the world's toughest energy challenges.

HISTORY

At the time of Imperial's founding in London, Ontario in September 1880, gasoline was considered a relatively useless by-product in the petroleum refining process. However, this soon changed as the horseless carriage made its way onto Canadian roadways.

"Back in 1903, there were fewer than 200 cars in all of Canada," says Roth, adding that the number of cars mushroomed to a quarter-million by 1920. "Gasoline had become essential to daily life and Imperial was there to help supply the fuel to keep Canadians on the move."

The actual Esso brand name first appeared at Imperial service stations in the mid-1940s, although the term "Esso" was coined earlier as a reflection of the majority ownership position in Imperial acquired in 1898 by the Standard Oil Company ("S-O") of the U.S., today known as Exxon Mobil Corporation.

Imperial began its long association with hockey in 1936 by sponsoring live radio broadcasts. When hockey broadcasts moved to television in 1952, the company seized this new opportunity to promote itself with memorable "Happy Motoring" TV commercials that featured a friendly neighbourhood Imperial-Esso dealer. "Most people actually

believed that the actors in the ads were real dealers, and many of them wrote us letters asking which station they worked at!" Roth says.

In the 1960s, to help promote the power of its Esso Extra blend of gasoline, Esso retailers handed out free tiger tails to customers. "We gave out 800,000 of them in just four months, and made the slogan 'Put a tiger in your tank' a memorable part of Canadian advertising history," says Roth.

In 2001, Esso built its first On the Run store — ExxonMobil's global convenience-store brand — and recently opened its 300th On the Run store in Canada. In Quebec, these stores are known as Marché Express.

With nearly 2,000 locations across the country — about one-third of them company-owned — Esso is proud of operating the largest retail

Life. On the Run

gasoline network in Canada, as well as having more c-stores and car washes than any of its gasoline retailing competitors.

THE PRODUCT

"Gone are the days when a tank of gas or a new set of tires was all you could buy at Esso," says Smith. "Nowadays, what we're really selling is a comprehensive retail convenience experience that not only fuels the vehicle, but the driver as well."

Esso sells its fuel and car washes under its own brands, carries the leading convenience product brands in its stores and has alliances with other well-established organizations to further satisfy its customers' daily needs. For instance, at many Esso locations, customers can grab a fresh Tim Hortons® coffee or baked good, or get cash from an RBC® Royal Bank automated teller machine. Esso is currently conducting a test with Loblaw Companies Limited in which President's Choice® frozen meals, beverages and snacks are available in selected On the Run stores.

"In any retail business, customer service is the ultimate key to success," says Smith. "That's why

we work closely with our diverse population of Esso-branded retailers to help them and their staff deliver a helpful and friendly experience to every customer, every time, everywhere. After all, an energetic, enthusiastic and caring site staff is what really keeps customers coming back."

RECENT DEVELOPMENTS

After making significant investments in its retail facilities in major markets over the last five years, Esso is now benefiting from the upgraded stores and better trained staff that are capable of delivering the best customer experience.

Loyalty programs are a ticket to the game in retailing today, so Esso offers its customers two loyalty programs to choose from: Esso Extra or Aeroplan®. Customers can swipe their Esso Extra card — or pay with their Royal Bank Esso *Visa** card — to earn Esso Extra points that are redeemable for free gas, car washes, snacks, auto accessories and other products. They may also exchange their Esso Extra points for Hbc Rewards points or RBC Rewards points, to further broaden their choices. Or customers can earn Aeroplan Miles at Esso and redeem them by visiting aeroplan.com for free travel or other rewards. And, thanks to *Speedpass* — ExxonMobil's transponder-based payment option that's linked to a credit card or an RBC Royal Bank Client Card — customers can simply point to pay and earn their choice of rewards automatically.

Inside the c-store, Esso continues to delight customers of all ages with a growing assortment of products that include the latest candy bars and beverages, popular magazines and DVDs, gift cards and even seasonal casual clothing.

PROMOTION

"Esso relies on a range of approaches to tell customers about its products and programs," says Roth. "Since many Esso customers are behind the

wheel, we use signage at the roadside to grab their attention, then other signs by the pumps and in the store to talk about our products and promotional offers. Our advertising is focused on radio and out-of-home media to reach customers while they're on the go," he explains.

Sponsorships and other community programs are also vital means of promoting the Esso brand while demonstrating good corporate citizenship. "We're a leading sponsor of hockey right across Canada, from boys and girls minor leagues right up to the pros," Roth says. Away from the rink, Esso retailers regularly raise funds for local community projects and, once a year, the company raises funds in major cities with Esso United Way Day.

BRAND VALUES

"At the heart of the Esso brand is our passion for providing each and every customer with the best experience to enhance life on the move," says Smith. "We know customers are busy, so whether it's at the pump, in the car wash or in the c-store, we strive to create a safe, clean and friendly environment where they can quickly and easily get what they need and carry on with their day. How do we know? Because we're drivers too."

THINGS YOU DIDN'T KNOW ABOUT ESSO

○ The original "three-star" selection on hockey broadcasts was first inspired by Imperial's 3-Star brand of gasoline in 1936.

○ A number of the country's leading men's and women's hockey players received Esso Medals of Achievement as youngsters.

○ Back in the 1940s, Esso founded its Touring Service program that provided roadside assistance to drivers in distress, and also helped motorists plan their trips. The program continues today as Esso Auto Club.

○ Esso uses an online customer survey system that awards $1,500 to several respondents each month.

THE MARKET

In only two decades, wireless has changed the way Canadians live. Half of the Canadian population have made wireless products an integral part of their daily lives.

Even as prices become more competitive and minutes-of-use increase, the Canadian industry grows more than 10 percent annually. A growing number of households now rely exclusively on wireless for their overall telephone services. Canadians currently use more than 17 million wireless devices on a daily basis.

The Canadian wireless industry currently generates more than CDN$9 billion in annual revenues and employs 25,000 people. Despite steady double-digit growth, the wireless market in Canada has greater scope for further expansion than markets in most other developed nations. Compared with current Canadian usage of one wireless device for every two people, countries like Italy have penetration rates of 100 percent or one wireless device per person.

The phenomenal growth of mobile telephone service in Canada began in 1985, when licenses were issued to regional wireline incumbent monopolies and to Rogers Cantel Inc., which was awarded a national license. Microcell Telecommunications Inc. — the originator of the Fido brand — received a license to provide wireless service in 1996.

ACHIEVEMENTS

From a standing start in November 1996 — and pitted against much larger, more established and better financed competitors — the story of the Fido brand has been one of remarkable growth. Overnight, the brand became a personality.

In its first year of operation, Fido built a base of 66,000 subscribers, exceeding its target by 10 percent. By 1999, Fido had attracted 500,000 subscribers, reaching that milestone faster than any player in the Canadian wireless market. By 2001, the number of subscribers had doubled again to more than 1 million — once again, growing faster than any other competitor in the Canadian market.

It was an amazing achievement: the Fido brand had attracted this large customer base despite being a complete newcomer to the scene, with more limited network coverage and fewer distribution outlets than its competition.

November 1996, Fido is unleashed onto the mobile market

What were the secrets to this remarkable success?
- Fido offered more flexible billing options for customers.
- It became a leading-edge innovator.
- It launched an award-winning program of advertising and promotion.

HISTORY

Fido came as a breath of fresh air in a market long-dominated by complex offerings. Eliminating contracts and introducing billing by the second, Fido quickly became the new transparent, innovative and simple wireless provider. It offered fair cost — with no hidden charges.

Although still a young brand — Fido is celebrating its 10th anniversary this year — it has become associated with simplicity and the democratization of wireless. Fido ensured that wireless became a mass-market product for everyday use rather than a niche technology.

When it was first introduced, the Fido network was the only one in Canada to operate on the Global System for Mobile communications (GSM) standard. As a result, from the very beginning, Fido customers could use their wireless devices and their same Fido phone number all over the world, in many more countries than subscribers to other services. As roaming agreements were signed, Fido was soon able to offer coverage in more than 180 countries on five continents. That is 78 percent of the world's digital mobile market.

Among many other pioneering initiatives, Fido was the first wireless operator to introduce messaging and two-way e-mail service on a mobile phone and to introduce fast mobile wireless data service (GPRS) across Canada. It also launched a groundbreaking and soon-to-be-imitated Fido-to-Fido package, allowing customers unlimited local calling, text messaging and instant messaging between Fido subscribers. Fido was also the first in the Canadian wireless market to set up a loyalty program enabling customers to earn rewards that can be applied toward the purchase of a new handset.

In 2003, City Fido™ — Canada's first home and mobile service, featuring unlimited anytime local calling — was launched in the Greater Vancouver area, and because of the company's Competitive Local Exchange Carrier (CLEC) status, customers were allowed to transfer their home landline number to Fido wireless service.

THE PRODUCT

The hardware and other equipment offerings of wireless service providers are often very similar. The goal for the Fido brand was to differentiate

Travel with Fido in over 180 countries

itself in the market by offering simplified, flexible billing options and advanced technological features — all supported by an award-wining advertising and promotion program.

Fido style meant attractive pricing "per-second" billing and freedom from lengthy service contacts.

On the technological front, Fido products were clearly differentiated from those of competitors because they could operate around the world, unlike most of its competitors at that time, which were restricted to use within North America.

Award-winning advertising and promotion campaigns were also highly successful in associating Fido products with the attributes that people find most admirable in their canine cohorts — namely, that they are friendly, loyal companions who will follow you anywhere.

RECENT DEVELOPMENTS
In November 2004, Microcell Telecommunications Inc., the company that created the Fido brand, was acquired by Rogers Wireless Inc. The resulting amalgamation of the Fido brand with Rogers Wireless created Canada's largest wireless service provider, with 5.7 million subscribers.

As a result of combining forces with Rogers, Fido's network coverage area is now eight times larger than before and covers 94 percent of the Canadian population.

Operating with a dual-brand strategy, the combined organization offers a wide range of wireless products and services, ranging from text,

Fido Rewards Program
Only from Fido

picture and video messaging, downloadable games and MP3-quality ring tones, to wireless Internet and desktop access, to fully customized business solutions.

The organization also operates Canada's only GSM/GPRS network, the world standard for wireless voice and data telecommunications technology.

PROMOTION
A key element of the strategy of the new organization is to offer products and services that are attractive to young adults as well as small and medium-sized businesses. With its high recognition and strong appeal to these target groups, Fido is viewed as an important factor in carrying out that strategy.

Why pay a full minute for a 12 second call?

A major contributor to the growth and success of the Fido brand was a unique and consistent program of advertising and promotion.

Energizer had its rabbit, Michelin had Bibendum, and Fido found its powerful brand identity with its gallery of loyal, happy dogs.

Perhaps the most important branding decision was the choice of the name itself — Fido — which invokes images of friendliness, simplicity and loyalty in a market often dominated by technological jargon. The brand name also worked well in both English and French — an important consideration for a founding company that was head-quartered in Montreal.

The launch of the Fido brand took place in Montreal in late 1996. Early the following year, the brand was unleashed in Toronto, then in major centers across the country during the balance of 1997 and 1998. Each launch followed a consistent three-phase pattern.

The first phase was aimed at creating a "buzz" about the new brand. This was achieved through the use of a Fido-branded airship hovering over the target city. Teaser commercials were also used to increase interest in the soon-to-be-introduced wireless product.

In phase two, a full-scale advertising campaign was launched in the target city. The campaign relied on longer-than-average 90-second broadcast messages and on full double-page print ads. The objective was to reflect an open, honest organization that was fully disclosing the details of its product offering and had nothing to hide.

In the final phase, a multimedia program was used to provide continuing support for the brand, as needed, over time.

And of course, one of the most prominent visual features of the advertising and promotional materials was dogs — dogs of all colours and breeds, shapes and sizes.

An important strategic decision in establishing the brand so quickly and completely was that Fido branding would dominate every ad — rather than giving prominence to specific messages and offers.

BRAND VALUES
From its inception, the Fido brand has made its name by delivering simplicity, value and innovation.

Many features launched by Fido have now become the industry standard. It was the first Canadian wireless carrier to offer service without a contract and billing by the second, and is still acknowledged for offering Canadian customers "more from their Fido."

Fido started out by democratizing wireless, and continues its role as the customer advocate. From its customer loyalty program to earlier starts for evenings and weekends, Fido continues to put customers first.

THINGS YOU DIDN'T KNOW ABOUT FIDO

○ In addition to the Fido airship that hovered over Canadian cities prior to service launches, Fido also toured on the ground in the Fidomobile, a refurbished art deco–design bus that was originally built in 1942 by General Motors. Only 12 of these buses were ever built.

○ Some of the best Fido ad campaigns use employees and their own pets.

○ Year after year, people contact Fido wanting to put their dogs in our ads.

○ Fido customers often refer to their phone by its brand name: "Call me on my Fido."

FISHERMAN'S FRIEND ®

THE MARKET

With a market share of over 38 percent, Fisherman's Friend is the top-selling medicated throat lozenge in Canada. Originally sold only in pharmacies, the market for Fisherman's Friend lozenges soon expanded beyond the traditional pharmacy distribution base as a result of their high rate of sale and widespread popularity. Today, this distinctive product is also available in a broad array of retail outlets including convenience stores, grocery and gas bar outlets.

ACHIEVEMENTS

For the first 98 years of its existence (until 1963), Fisherman's Friend was only available in a single pharmacy outlet in Fleetwood, England. Today Fisherman's Friend is marketed in over 120 countries worldwide with sales of over 5 billion lozenges per year.

Fisherman's Friend lozenges are still produced exclusively in Fleetwood, England, by Lofthouse of Fleetwood Limited. The company has received three Queen's Awards for Export Achievement from the British government, in recognition of the brand's worldwide success and positive economic impact.

In the highly competitive Canadian market, Fisherman's Friend has exhibited an impressive volume growth over an 18 year period. Although major corporate and brand competitors have introduced many new products in the lozenge and cough drop category during that time, Fisherman's Friend has continually expanded its market share and maintained an extremely loyal consumer following.

HISTORY

In the 1860s, the town of Fleetwood in Lancashire on the northwest coast of England was a thriving community and the centre of the United Kingdom's fishing industry. Fishermen would depart from Fleetwood on long voyages through the North Sea and Arctic Circle. Given prolonged exposure to freezing winds and rough seas, the men would often suffer from coughs, colds and bronchial problems.

In 1865, pharmacist James Lofthouse created a new recipe for lozenges in his chemist shop on East Street in Fleetwood. It was designed to solve the problem of liquid syrups stored in glass bottles which broke when accidentally dropped at sea in rough weather. His special blend of liquorice, capsicum, eucalyptus and menthol was highly effective and quickly became popular amongst not only the fishermen, but also the townsfolk of

Fleetwood. They would come into the shop and ask for a packet of the "fishermen's friends" or "the fishermen's lozenges" — which is how the brand name "Fisherman's Friend" originated.

The lozenges continued to be sold exclusively in the family pharmacy until 1963 when Doreen Lofthouse, the wife of James Lofthouse's grandson, began selling the lozenges to stores in the surrounding area. The business grew so quickly that in 1969 a separate factory was opened in Fleetwood in order to keep pace with increasing consumer demand.

National distribution was achieved in the United Kingdom when the Boots pharmacy chain noticed a high volume of Fisherman's Friend sales in one of its shops and placed the lozenge into all their outlets. In 1974, the company received its first export order from a distributor in Norway. From that point on, the export business grew dramatically and quickly outpaced sales in the home market.

In Canada, TFB & Associates Limited was appointed the distributor for Fisherman's Friend in 1988 and started by selling the Original Extra Strong and Regular Strength lozenges to pharmacies for placement in the medicated lozenge section. The variety of Fisherman's Friend lozenges labeled as "Regular" in Canada are marketed as "Aniseed" or "Licorice" flavour in virtually all other international markets. Health Canada would not permit labeling the original lozenges as "Extra Strong" unless there was another variety designated as the "Regular."

THE PRODUCT

Perhaps the most important factor in the success of Fisherman's Friend lozenges is their effectiveness. Simply put, they work! They provide highly effective relief from sore throats, coughs and nasal congestion. This winning formula, combined with strategic brand promotion, has created a strong and ever expanding base of loyal consumers.

The Original Extra Strong Fisherman's Friend lozenges are still formulated exactly as they were in 1865 with capsicum, liquorice powder, eucalyptus and menthol. Each lozenge still takes at least one week to produce, with every step in the production cycle checked and double-checked for consistency and quality under conditions carefully controlled for temperature and humidity.

The lozenges are no longer produced with a pestle, mortar and rolling pin as they first were in the Lofthouse pharmacy. The Fisherman's Friend factory is a gleaming pharmaceutical-grade manufacturing facility with state-of-the-art mixing, forming and packaging equipment which produces millions of packets per day. Skilled technicians and quality-control personnel use the latest laboratory techniques to monitor every batch, and make sure each packet leaves the factory in perfect condition.

Today, Fisherman's Friend lozenges are available in a variety of flavours including Cherry, Lemon, Mint and Apple/Cinnamon. The new flavours don't taste as strong as the Original recipe — but they work just as effectively, and almost all are sucrose free. As a result, the brand now has a broader consumer appeal, and more customers than ever.

The Fisherman's Friend packaging is every bit as unique as the product. The lozenges are sold in distinctive paper packets which must be torn to open, and consumers often write and e-mail about the package. Some comment that the lozenges fall out of the packet into their pockets and suggest the product should be sold in a re-sealable container. A separate re-usable tin pack is now available for fans who desire a more permanent home for their supply of Fisherman's Friends, but that is the only solution!

The paper packet is one of the brand's hallmarks, and there are no plans to change the long-standing

and successful tradition. The packet is economical and effective without any excess bells and whistles . . . a straightforward package for a straightforward, true-to-its-roots brand! Some lighthearted advice for those who might prefer a more substantial package: If a lozenge should fall out into the depths of your purse or pocket, just consider it a "reserve" for a sore throat emergency!

RECENT DEVELOPMENTS
The most recent addition to the Fisherman's Friend product line in Canada was the launch of the Cherry Sucrose Free flavour in 2003. Developed specifically for the Canadian market, it has been the most successful new flavour introduction in the history of Fisherman's Friend in Canada. Cherry Sucrose Free has subsequently been introduced successfully in other Fisherman's Friend markets around the world.

The Cherry flavour was also introduced in a unique merchandising shelf box which was designed specifically to fit into front checkout racks in retail stores, right beside competitive cough drop products. The new display box is now also available for the Original Extra Strong variety so Canadian retailers can capture extra sales with two top-selling flavours of Fisherman's Friend at their front checkouts.

PROMOTION
Fisherman's Friend in Canada is supported by a wide range of brand-building consumer promotion activities.

Trial generation is a key objective, and consumer trial generation programs continue on a year-round basis targeting specific consumer groups including young adults and diabetics who can benefit from the sucrose-free varieties. Trial generation activities also target medical and pharmacy professionals to ensure they are familiar with the product and provide them with trial-size packets to recommend to their patients and clients.

Consumer advertising targets heavy cough drop and lozenge users in the Canadian market. The current Canadian TV commercial titled "Dancing

Cherries" is building consumer awareness that the Cherry flavour is an effective and pleasant tasting alternative to the Original Extra Strong.

Fisherman's Friend has also developed a strong following among professional and amateur singers, choir members, auctioneers, radio and TV announcers and all sorts of voice professionals. These relationships are nurtured with targeted promotions and relationship building programs on an ongoing basis.

To strengthen relationships with Canadian consumers, Fisherman's Friend promotion also includes participation in community events and the lending of support to numerous charity and nonprofit organization events throughout the year.

BRAND VALUES
Fisherman's Friend has built its reputation as the best throat lozenge in the world. It consistently provides superior performance and quality at a price that is affordable to all. Fisherman's Friend respects its consumers and never over-promises . . . it delivers!

THINGS YOU DIDN'T KNOW ABOUT FISHERMAN'S FRIEND LOZENGES

○ If all the Fisherman's Friend lozenges sold in a year were placed end to end, they would circle the globe two times.

○ Fisherman's Friend lozenges are 100 percent gluten free.

○ Fisherman's Friend lozenges are 100 percent peanut and nut free.

○ Fisherman's Friend lozenges are 100 percent vegetarian and do not contain any milk or egg ingredients.

○ Fisherman's Friend lozenges are both Kosher and Halal approved.

○ "Sucrose Free" Fisherman's Friend flavours can be easily identified by the diagonal stripes on their packets.

Built for life in Canada

THE MARKET

The automotive marketplace is in a constant state of change. The continuous evolution of technology and the ongoing move towards globalization have put the heat on international competition. Today, products come from all over the world, making it more difficult to identify competitive threats and predict the trends that will impact the industry for years to come. Consumers face an endless array of choices, and buying a new vehicle in this crowded environment can be a confusing and overwhelming experience. As a result, consumers now demand the perfect mix of value, styling, product quality, performance and customer service.

The Ford Motor Company of Canada sees the new realities of the automotive marketplace as an arena of endless opportunity. Propelled by a dedication to innovation and imagination, Ford produces and delivers the cars and trucks that Canadians want and need — in a way that inspires continuing brand loyalty.

ACHIEVEMENTS

The Ford Motor Company was responsible for the great invention that essentially created the modern automotive industry. The moving assembly line, first implemented in Michigan in 1913, was a revolutionary idea that meant individual workers could stay in one place and perform the same task repeatedly on multiple vehicles that passed before them. The result of this process was that vehicles could be produced in mass quantities, so quickly and efficiently that vehicle ownership soon became an affordable luxury to the working class. The rest, as they say, is history — and few companies have been as much a part of modern life as the Ford Motor Company.

More recently, Ford has contributed to both the automotive industry and the environment through its ongoing commitment to environmental vehicle technology. In early 2006, Ford set an industry precedent by announcing it will be the first manufacturer to build hybrid vehicles in Canada.

Consistent with Ford's commitment to the environment, Ford introduced the world's first full hybrid SUV — the Ford Escape Hybrid. The Ford Escape's Full Hybrid Technology results in an 81 percent reduction in smog-forming emissions and can travel over 600 kilometers on a single tank of gas.

The Escape Hybrid is a tremendous success and a real example of Ford's Environmental Pledge, which states that "Ford Motor Company is dedicated to providing ingenious environmental solutions that will position us as a leader in the automotive industry of the 21st century. Our actions will demonstrate that we care about preserving the environment for future generations."

Ford of Canada has had remarkable success with a number of vehicle lines. In particular, Ford F-Series trucks have been the best-selling full-size pick-up truck in Canada for the past 40 years. The F-Series line of trucks is not just used in rugged work situations; many people just appreciate the distinctive and rugged styling of a Ford truck and drive one for pleasure on a daily basis. In addition to the truck line, Ford has also created such legendary vehicles as the Mustang and the Thunderbird, which have captured the spirit of the times for many generations of car lovers.

HISTORY

Ford Motor Company produced its first vehicle over a century ago in 1903. Henry Ford insisted that the company's future lay in the production of affordable cars for the mass market.

The Ford Motor Company of Canada began producing automobiles a year later in 1904. A total of 117 cars were produced in the first year. The Model T made its way onto Canadian assembly lines in 1908. Although the Canadian-made Fords were similar to the American models, Ford of Canada made it a priority to maintain a high level of Canadian-made parts in its lineup of cars and trucks.

Nineteen years later, Ford had produced 15 million cars and had expanded to become a true global power in the automotive industry. The company established its North American Automotive Operations in 1971, consolidating its U.S., Canadian and Mexican operations more than two decades ahead of the North American Free Trade Agreement.

Canada has always maintained its own distinct identity with regards to vehicle lines. Historically, some body types were sold under different names in Canada. When the American "T Runabout" was renamed the "Roadster" in 1923, Ford of Canada continued calling it the "Runabout." Ford of Canada also called their four-door sedan of the time a "Fordor" — it was another five years before that name was adopted in the United States. After the Canada-U.S. Auto Pact came into effect in 1965, many Mustangs and Thunderbirds that were shipped from the United States to

Canada were outfitted with Canadian-made engines and imported duty-free from the States.

Throughout its history, Ford of Canada has always had a long standing tradition of building strong vehicles and finding ways to improve product design to further develop product capabilities.

THE PRODUCT

Henry Ford drove the company's success by looking beyond the norms of the current reality and instead imagined what could be. He once quipped, "The man who will use his skill and constructive imagination to see how much he can give for a dollar instead of how little he can give for a dollar is bound to succeed." Throughout history, Ford product has illustrated the essence of that statement by providing outstanding value through faster innovation, superior organization and greater imagination.

Ford vehicles have ignited the passion of automotive enthusiasts and attracted scores of consumers. Vehicles like the GT40, Explorer, F-150 and, of course, the Mustang, have become ingrained as icons in our culture.

An equally impressive array of vehicles including the Focus, Fusion, Escape, Freestyle, Freestar, E-Series and Ranger round out the Ford product offering. In their own unique and distinctive way, each of these vehicles embodies the Ford passion for value, innovation and style.

RECENT DEVELOPMENTS

Ford dubbed 2004 "The Year of the Car." Having recently redesigned the F-Series pickup, already a segment leader, Ford was set to tackle the various sedan segments where Asian competitors had been gaining ground. The first new arrival was the Five Hundred. Ford engineers were challenged to imagine just how remarkable a sedan could be and succeeded in creating a sophisticated and affordable car that provided excellent fuel economy and all-wheel-drive capability while proving to be one of the safest cars in North America. The arrival of the family-friendly Freestyle further demonstrated Ford's dedication to imaginative design. Combining the best attributes of a car, an SUV and a minivan, the Freestyle now defines the crossover segment in Canada.

Next to arrive was the redesigned Ford Mustang. With what was described as "retro-futurism" styling, the Mustang was an instant hit with car lovers.

The Ford Fusion rounded out the new car product lineup. Arriving at dealerships late in 2005, the Fusion delivered style and substance to the mid-sized sedan segment, traditionally dominated by bland cars with little personality. The Fusion combined a sleek young look with exciting driving dynamics at an attractive price. It soon became very popular with consumers and captured an exceptionally healthy share of category sales.

The year 2006 saw a major redesign of the Ford Explorer, with improved power, comfort, safety, styling and possibly most impressive — better fuel economy.

Ford of Canada was very pleased to announced in 2006 that the Oakville, Ontario plant would be responsible for building two of its newest and most exciting vehicles — the Ford Edge and the Lincoln MKX. The Edge is an all-new entry into the increasingly popular crossover segment featuring modern styling, AWD capability and precise handling dynamics. The MKX represents Lincoln's first volume vehicle to be built in Canada.

PROMOTION

With over a century of production in Canada, Ford of Canada has become part of the Canadian experience. The company has made a solid commitment to community involvement, and with an incredible history behind it, Ford will continue to be an integral part of the fabric of Canada. This sentiment is evident in all aspects of its marketing, advertising and sponsorships.

The tagline "Built for Life in Canada" is a true reflection of the Ford brand across the country. But at Ford, being Built for Life in Canada means much more than producing cars and trucks that can withstand Canada's extreme weather conditions.

For Ford, life in Canada also means understanding that we are a country fanatical about sports. Sports are an essential part of the Canadian experience, and Ford is proud to support activities at all levels across the country. Ford of Canada is a proud sponsor at many NHL arenas, and equally important is their presence at many community rinks across the country. Canada's hockey hero, Wayne Gretzky, is a Ford partner who shares similar community-focused values and helps reinforce Ford's enduring connection with all things Canadian. In addition, each year, Ford partners with many charitable organizations, including the Wayne Gretzky Foundation, the Canadian Breast Cancer Foundation, the Juvenile Diabetes Foundation and the United Way to raise money and build awareness.

Beyond vehicle technology, Ford of Canada's commitment to new technologies and innovations

is evident in its support of new media in the marketplace. Some examples include Canada's largest billboard in Calgary, Alberta, the Escape Living Billboard, which featured over 800 living plants, and the Escape Birdhouse Billboard, which housed and fed countless thousands of birds throughout its posting. These were not only firsts in innovative media thinking, but also supported Ford's stated Environmental Pledge.

BRAND VALUES

Ford is a customer focused, forward thinking, imaginative company that combines global strengths and resources with an understanding of the unique Canadian marketplace to provide customers with a relevant, diverse lineup of vehicles to meet their needs. Ford Motor Company believes that technology, innovation and environmental awareness are key factors to serving their customers today and in the future.

THINGS YOU DIDN'T KNOW ABOUT FORD

○ The automotive brands owned by the Ford Motor Company include Ford, Aston Martin, Jaguar, Land Rover, Lincoln, Mazda, Mercury and Volvo.

○ Ford F-150 has been Canada's best-selling pick-up truck for 40 years in a row.

○ Ford is Canada's largest automotive recycler. Being a leader in automotive recycling is part of Ford of Canada's commitment to serving customers and the environment throughout the entire lifecycle of a vehicle. All Canadian-built Ford vehicles exceed the industry average of 75 percent vehicle recyclability.

○ The first modern car chase is generally seen as that in 1968's *Bullitt*, featuring a "Highland Green" 1968 Mustang GT 390 Fastback.

○ Spraying champagne after racing victories has become a tradition. This tradition began when three Ford GT40s placed 1-2-3 at Le Mans in 1966.

○ America's first commercial airlines used 199 Ford Tri-Motor airplanes in 1925.

THE MARKET

As Canadian society has changed, so has Hudson's Bay Company, Canada's oldest company. As a world-class retail organization, Hbc responds to the needs of Canadians through its diversified family of stores: the Bay, Zellers, Home Outfitters, Fields and Designer Depot. Each format provides customers with a unique shopping experience, tailored to meet their needs by providing value, quality, choice and service they can trust.

ACHIEVEMENTS

Hbc contributes nearly $11 million annually to international, national and community-based organizations across Canada in the areas of health, wellness and inspiration for young Canadians.

Hbc is a Canadian retail leader in ethical sourcing and social compliance. The company introduced its Code of Vendor Conduct in 1998 and rolled out a program to monitor and audit vendor factories in 2001.

Hbc was named Best Corporate System at the sixth annual Retail Systems Achievement Awards held in Chicago on May 17, 2004. These awards honour outstanding examples of systems and interactive applications that have resulted in more effective customer service and improved business processes.

BC Hydro designated Hbc a Power Smart Certified Customer for its achievements in energy efficiency. Since 2000, these efforts have reduced Hbc's emissions by over 100,000 tonnes, the equivalent of the emissions from more than 23,500 cars.

Hbc was awarded a 2005 Excellence in Retail Marketing Award from the Retail Council of Canada for their work on *Belle* magazine.

HISTORY

Hbc's history is as rich and diverse as our nation. As the country's oldest retailer, Hbc started as far back as the fur trade when, two centuries before confederation, a pair of resourceful Frenchmen

named Radisson and des Groseilliers discovered a wealth of fur in the interior of the continent accessible via the great inland sea that is Hudson Bay. Prince Rupert, cousin of King Charles II, acquired the Royal Charter which, in May 1670, granted the lands of the Hudson Bay watershed to "the Governor and Company of Adventurers of England trading into Hudson Bay."

Its first century of operation found Hbc firmly ensconced in a few forts and posts around the shores of James and Hudson Bays. Natives brought furs annually to these locations to barter for manufactured goods such as knives, kettles, beads, needles and blankets.

In 1820, Hbc merged with its most successful rival, the North West Company based in Montreal. The resulting commercial enterprise now spanned the continent. The merger set the pattern of Hbc's growth, being the first of a series of notable acquisitions.

By the end of the 19th century changing fashion tastes contributed to the fur trade losing importance. Western settlement and the Gold Rush quickly introduced a new type of client to Hbc — one that shopped with cash and not with skins. With the Deed of Surrender in 1870, Hbc yielded sovereignty over its traditional territories to the new country. The retail era had begun. The company's focus began to shift as it concentrated on transforming trading posts into saleshops, stocked with a wider variety of goods than ever before.

In 1912, Hbc began an aggressive modernization program. The growth of retail spurred Hbc into a wide variety of commercial pursuits, such as wholesale, real estate and natural resources, particularly oil and gas.

The economic downturn of the 1980s caused Hbc to rethink its priorities and, like many other firms, return to its core business. Non-retail businesses were sold off. The pace of retail acquisition increased with takeovers of Zellers (1978), Simpsons (1978), Fields (1978), Robinson's (1979), Towers/Bonimart (1990), Woodwards (1993), and K-Mart Canada (1998), following in the tradition of Cairns (1921), Morgan's (1960) and Freiman's (1972).

The 21st century finds Hbc well into its fourth century of retailing in Canada. The newly launched Hbc.com, along with its major retail channels — the Bay, Zellers, and Home Outfitters — together provide more than two-thirds of the retail needs of Canadians. Proof positive, if any were needed, of

the aptness of Hbc's proud claim: **Canada's Merchants since 1670.**

THE PRODUCT

Hbc Banners

The Bay is the department store division of Hbc, offering quality merchandise at mid-to-upper price points. The Bay concentrates on exclusive fashion merchandise in apparel, accessories and soft home categories. Bay stores are located in suburban and urban markets, along with a dominant position in the downtown cores of Canada's major cities.

Zellers is the mass merchandise division of Hbc, with locations in communities nationwide. The chain offers customers stylish brands at competitive prices.

Home Outfitters is Hbc's kitchen, bed and bath specialty superstore chain with unbeatable selection and service. With locations across Canada, Home Outfitters offers customers more choices, more brands and great ideas.

Fields is a chain of small, value-priced general merchandise stores located in western Canada. Fields focuses on great value and everyday merchandise for the entire family.

Designer Depot is the off-price banner of Hbc, offering designer and better-branded men's, women's and junior's apparel, accessories and home merchandise at "depot" prices.

Hbc Brand Offering. Through its credit card and loyalty programs, Hbc offers Canadians a simple, rewarding shopping experience throughout its retail banners. In addition, Hbc offers ease of shopping through Gift Cards, gift registries, an online shopping portal and a charitable foundation that enables Hbc customers to benefit their communities every time they shop.

RECENT DEVELOPMENTS

In late 2004, Hbc successfully negotiated the rights to outfit the Canadian Olympic Team for the next seven years (Torino 2006, Beijing 2008, Vancouver 2010 and London 2012). During that period, Hbc will be a Premier National Partner of the Canadian Olympic Team. Hbc also negotiated the rights as an official supplier and key corporate sponsor Premier National Partner of the Vancouver Organizing Committee for the 2010 Olympic and Paralympic Winter Games. This long-term partnership is based on Hbc and the Canadian Olympic Movement's shared vision of a proud, strong Canada, highlighting the beauty of our country, the warmth of its people and its strength, on and off the field of play. The Hbc mantra "The Spirit of Hbc" will be the driving force over the next seven years, to make the people of this country proud in every way when they see our nation's official uniform on centre podium, beneath a gold medal.

PROMOTION

Exclusive brands are a large component of Hbc's promotions. Promoting product created through exclusive partnerships with well-known Canadians such as Lynda Reeves (House & Home), Brian Gluckstein (GlucksteinHome) and Alfred Sung (Sung Home) provides the opportunity for all Canadians to purchase affordable trend-right products. Hbc leverages these partnerships through contests, tradeshows and in-store appearances across the country.

Hbc strategically plans sales events that are attractive and seasonally relevant to Hbc customers, including Bay Days, Storewide Sale, Lowest Price of the Season, Scratch & Save and Dollar Daze, to name a few.

Recently, Hbc launched the "Great things for Canada" campaign in November 2005, unveiling the 2006 Canadian Olympic Team apparel and Hbc's commitment to amateur sports. The success of the campaign was due to strong integration

between public relations, advertising, the Hbc Foundation and Hbc.com.

BRAND VALUES

The Hbc brand stands for more than its banners; it is built on an emotional connection between the iconic retailer and its customers. Based on the common values Hbc shares with Canadians, like community, innovation, citizenship and diversity, Hbc seeks a better way to run its businesses, support its associates, serve its customers. Hbc respects and enhances the integrity and diversity of the communities in which it operates. In both its philosophy and everyday operations, Hbc will strive to be a model of the highest integrity.

Over the past 335 years, Hbc the brand has evolved and changed to better reflect the company it has and the company it wants to be. The new Hbc logo was developed to communicate its vision of the future and to acknowledge its rich history in Canada.

THINGS YOU DIDN'T KNOW ABOUT
Hbc

○ Established in 1670, Hudson's Bay Company is Canada's largest department store retailer and oldest corporation. With nearly 70,000 employees, Hbc serves Canadians through over 500 locations.

○ Hbc has a long tradition of supporting the Olympic Movement. Those famous Hbc multi-stripe coats were the official uniform of the Canadian Winter Olympic Team at a number of Games: 1936 in Garmish-Partenkirchen, Germany; 1960 in Squaw Valley, California; 1964 in Innsbruck, Austria; and 1968 in Grenoble, France.

○ Most Canadians live within 20 minutes of an Hbc store, and those who don't can shop at the online store, Hbc.com.

○ Hbc's loyalty program, Hbc Rewards, has over 8 million members.

○ Over the next seven years, Hbc has committed to raising $20 million to help fund Canadian Olympic athletes, their training facilities and their national sports organizations.

HEART & STROKE FOUNDATION

Finding answers. For life.

THE MARKET

The Heart and Stroke Foundation of Canada (HSFC), a volunteer-based health charity, leads in eliminating heart disease and stroke and reducing their impact through the advancement of research and its application, the promotion of healthy living and advocacy. HSFC is a federation of 10 Provincial Foundations, led and supported by a force of more than 134,000 volunteers.

The mission of the Foundation has three major aspects — research, health promotion and education (both consumer and professional) and advocacy.

On the research front, in 2005 alone, the Foundation invested nearly $54 million into peer-reviewed heart disease and stroke research. In addition, the Foundation is providing over $8 million annually to support the training of young Canadian heart and stroke researchers. Since 1956, the Foundation has invested close to $950 million in research support.

Through health promotion and education, the Foundation encourages Canadians to lead healthier lives — to be active each day, to eat a balanced diet, to live smoke-free — in order to reduce their risk of developing heart disease and stroke. The Foundation also promotes training guidelines that help Canadians save lives by learning cardiopulmonary resuscitation (CPR).

Advocacy is a top priority. In the past year, the Foundation advised the government on issues such as the review of *Canada's Food Guide to Healthy Eating*, food labeling, food fortification guidelines and the elimination of trans fats from the food supply. Foundation-based advocacy has helped pave the way towards tobacco control and smoke-free spaces and is making Canadians aware of the danger of untreated high blood pressure.

ACHIEVEMENTS

When Heart and Stroke Foundation research, health promotion and advocacy combine, the results benefit everyone. The Ontario Stroke Strategy is an example.

Research showed a drug called tPA could dissolve the blood clots that cause the most common type of stroke; **health promotion** geared up to teach Ontarians the warning signs and symptoms of stroke; **advocacy** persuaded the provincial government to back a new stroke care system bringing diagnosis, treatment and rehabilitation into a series of specialized centres. Building on this success, the Heart and Stroke Foundation is a leader in

developing a Canadian Stroke Strategy, which will ensure that all Canadians have access to coordinated and integrated stroke prevention, treatment, rehabilitation and community re-integration by 2010.

In partnership with federal, provincial and municipal governments, HSFC is working to expand the presence of automated electronic defibrillators (AEDs) in public spaces. AEDs use electric shocks to restore normal heart function when the heart stops beating — a cardiac arrest. AEDs are part of a major emphasis by HSFC to make every Canadian aware of the Chain of Survival™, in which some of the critical links are: call 9-1-1 or emergency services, use CPR and have a trained person use an AED as soon as possible.

HSFC is leading the way in helping the federal government warn Canadians about the health impact of trans fatty acids (trans fat). Trans fat consumption significantly increases the risk of coronary heart disease. The federal government asked the HSFC to co-chair, with Health Canada, a national Trans Fat Task Force to find ways to practically eliminate trans fats in Canadian foods. The Task Force's recommendations were submitted to the Minister of Health in June 2006, and the Foundation will continue to press for action on this issue.

To deal with the problem of overweight and obesity, the Foundation launched *Target*

Obesity — over $1 million in research funding to examine the biological, social, behavioral and environmental aspects of this deadly epidemic.

The Foundation's *Action Plan on Obesity* recommends removing "junk" food from vending machines in schools and increasing physical activity in schools, workplaces and communities.

HISTORY

At the Heart and Stroke Foundation, history is very much a living presence. The Foundation has come so far in so short a time that the past is a living reality, a tradition that today's young researchers can all but reach out and touch.

Only 40 years ago, diagnosis of high blood pressure was a death sentence and heart attack and stroke patients were told to go to their beds and spend the rest of their lives there. Dr. Michael Sole remembers that in the 1960s, as a young emergency physician, he bled patients to treat acute congestive heart failure — a treatment straight from the 18th century.

Today Dr. Sole anticipates the day that every Canadian will have their genome on a compact disc — the blueprint for lifetime prevention of heart disease and stroke.

Take another example. In 1963, a very sick 23-month-old child named Maria made medical history. Maria Surnoski was a "blue" baby. Blue babies are born with congenital defects that cause blood from the lungs to flow back to the lungs rather than to the body. Such babies look blue because insufficient oxygen is circulating in their bodies. Eighty percent of blue babies died within the first year of life.

All that changed when surgeon Dr. William Mustard reversed the direction of the blood flow in Maria's heart. She was his first patient. Today she is married with grown children of her own.

And that's only part of the story. Heart and Stroke Foundation funding made possible the first-ever cardiac critical care unit, helped fund some of the earliest research into the cardioprotective qualities of acetylsalicylic acid (ASA), commonly referred to as Aspirin® and pioneered the transplantation of heart cells to boost heart function.

THE PRODUCT

Each year HSFC publishes more than 200 information products on heart disease and stroke.

In addition, all Canadian cardiopulmonary resuscitation (CPR) training materials published in Canada, whether by the Foundation or other organizations, are based on international guidelines developed by HSFC and other experts.

Health Check™, the Heart and Stroke Foundation's food information program, is a well-recognized and trusted symbol for healthy food choices on over 700 products in the grocery store.

The Health Check symbol on the package means that the product's nutrition information has been reviewed by the Foundation's dietitians and meets specific nutrient criteria based on *Canada's Food Guide to Healthy Eating*.

Visit http://www.healthcheck.org.

RECENT DEVELOPMENTS

Across Canada, provincial Heart and Stroke Foundations are taking action at a community level to boost heart health.

In Newfoundland, over 1,000 students in five schools have been running, jumping and playing as part of the school curriculum. This daily exercise program was piloted by the Heart and Stroke Foundation of Newfoundland. The Foundation hopes to bring this program to all elementary schools in the province.

Halifax, Nova Scotia is about to become a more active, walker-friendly city thanks to the Heart and Stroke Foundation of Nova Scotia's input into a 25 year regional growth plan.

Prince Edward Island kids are increasing their exposure to heart-healthy foods thanks to the Heart and Stroke Foundation of PEI. A school healthy eating policy was officially adopted by the province in September 2005.

In Quebec, development of a provincial stroke strategy is well under way, guided by input from the Heart and Stroke Foundation of Quebec.

In Ontario, the Heart and Stroke Foundation continues to be instrumental in leading public education campaigns to build support for smoke-free legislation and to improve public access to AEDs.

People in Manitoba are now better informed about the warning signs of stroke thanks to a robust and informative campaign by the Heart and Stroke Foundation of Manitoba. It's the first step in establishing a province-wide stroke strategy.

It's getting more difficult to light up and a lot easier to butt out in Saskatchewan. The Heart and Stroke Foundation of Saskatchewan (HSFS) played a key role in the development of the province's Tobacco Control Amendment Act. Public places in Saskatchewan have been smoke-free since January 1, 2005.

Thanks to advocacy efforts led by the Heart and Stroke Foundation of Alberta, NWT & Nunavut (HSFA), the government of Alberta has dedicated $20 million for stroke care delivery throughout the province over the next two years. HSFA's goal is that every Albertan, regardless of where they live, has timely access to high-quality stroke care.

The Heart and Stroke Foundation of British Columbia & Yukon's advocacy program is ambitious. It seeks to influence public policy and regulatory change to decrease the impact of tobacco, increase physical activity, encourage heart-healthy eating and address the needs of heart patients and stroke survivors.

PROMOTION

The HSFC Web site (www.heartandstroke.ca) is a much-visited resource. It is widely recognized as one of most comprehensive sources of information on heart disease and stroke in Canada. Over 80,000 Canadians receive Heart&Stroke He@lthline, a free, online monthly e-newsletter that can be subscribed to or viewed online at www.heartandstroke.ca.

In schools across Canada, exercise-based fund-raising programs such as Heart&Stroke Jump Rope for Heart promote active, healthy living for today's and future generations.

Heart&Stroke Big Bike and Walk for Heart also combine good healthy fun with fund-raising, while creating awareness that heart disease and stroke are the leading cause of death in Canada.

Heart&Stroke lotteries in Ontario and British Columbia are huge successes in generating funds for research. Over $110 million has been raised since 1997.

BRAND VALUES

In 2003, HSFC developed a new tagline: "Finding answers. For life." That tagline identifies and celebrates our strengths and unique characteristics: caring, knowledgeable, responsible and innovative.

THINGS YOU DIDN'T KNOW ABOUT THE HEART AND STROKE FOUNDATION

○ Heart and Stroke Foundation cookbooks have sold more than 1.5 million copies.

○ The Heart and Stroke Foundation "Hearts in Motion" walking clubs provide a list of great walks to keep the whole family on the trail to heart fitness.

○ The Heart&Stroke Big Bike was built to an Alberta design and seats 30 pedallers.

○ From 1952 to 2003, the cardiovascular death rate in Canada was reduced by 70 percent.

HITACHI
Inspire the Next

THE MARKET

Hitachi offers a wide range of systems, products and services in a variety of market sectors that include information systems, electronic devices, power and industrial systems, consumer products, materials and financial services. Consolidated sales for fiscal 2006 totaled USD$80.9 billion.

Hitachi takes its commitment to the customer seriously, which means delivering the best products for the best value.

ACHIEVEMENTS

Hitachi has always been at the forefront of technological evolution and innovation in each of its market segments.

The company's home electronics products are sleekly packaged technological masterpieces. Hitachi's core technologies mesh perfectly with each other, resulting not just in superior performance and features but in more efficient use of interior space.

Hitachi was at the forefront in the marketing of solid-state colour television in Canada, and the brand's outstanding achievements have continued over the years. For example, Hitachi developed the first DVD camcorder that could record videos onto an 8cm disc rather than on a tape — an ingenious invention that won an Emmy for the company. Hitachi also leads the way in plasma screen technology because of exclusive features like ALiS and pixel-pixel mapping that offers full 1080 vertical resolution, resulting in outstanding picture quality unsurpassed in the industry. As the market leader in LCD home theatre projectors, Hitachi's innovative technology allows for a superb home theatre experience, regardless of ambient light conditions and room sizes.

In the medical field, Hitachi not only engineers but also manufactures a remarkable array of low-impedance, five-frequency wideband ultrasound

probes, infusing Hitachi quality into every step of this demanding process for maximized sensitivity and clinical flexibility. Other cutting-edge medical equipment includes proton beam therapy systems and intraoperative magnetic resonance systems. Hitachi's new MercuRay Cone-Beam CT is changing the standard of care in orthodontistry and maxillo-facial surgery.

Hitachi's achievements in its optical and security products field are numerous as well. Opnext, formed in 2000 by Hitachi, is the first to develop a semiconductor laser for undersea fiber cable transmission and the first to demonstrate a fully functional 40Gbit/s transmitter and receiver. Hitachi/Opnext's optical engines are the core of an extensive portfolio of active optical components (laser modules, optical receivers, transponders, etc.) and subsystems for applications of communication networking and industrial measurement equipment. Opnext received the Cisco Technology Award in 2001.

Companies and governments have in recent years expressed a growing need for biometric authentication, which offers an inherently higher level of security. Seeing this need, Hitachi pioneered and developed an authentication system that reads a finger's vein pattern. The use of a vein pattern makes forgery, falsification or impersonation practically impossible, affording a high level of security. Applications are wide-ranging, including access control and PC login as well as ATMs and more.

On the power and industry side of the business, Hitachi supplied and constructed advanced power generating stations across Canada for over 35 years. These plants provide enough safe and reliable power to meet the needs of a city of over 5 million people.

HISTORY

The founder of Hitachi, Ltd., Namihei Odaira, designed the Hitachi logo even before the company was established in 1910 as the electrical machinery repairs shop of a copper mine. He believed that a logo was necessary to win the trust and confidence of the people as a symbol of quality products. Odaira used two Chinese characters — hi, meaning "sun," and tachi, meaning "rise" — to form the mark by superimposing one character on the other and enclosing them in a circle.

Now headquartered in Tokyo, Japan, Hitachi is a leading global electronics company, with more than 350,000 employees worldwide. Hitachi, Ltd. has almost 1,000 subsidiaries, including more than 400 overseas companies.

Hitachi Canada, Ltd., established in 1971, is a subsidiary of Hitachi America, Ltd. and Hitachi, Ltd., Japan.

THE PRODUCT

Four distinct divisions manufacture or market products that contribute to many aspects of Canadian society.

Digital Media Division. Hitachi home entertainment products have enriched the lives of Canadians for nearly 30 years. The brand's products are renowned for their quality and durability. Over the years Hitachi has developed products that are superior in original technology and regarded as among the industry's best.

Today the Digital Media Division markets plasma, LCD and projection TVs; DVD camcorders; LCD home theatre projectors; and LCD presentation projectors. These products are sold to the Canadian consumer through a vast dealership network comprising local independent retailers as well as large national chains.

Medical Solutions Division. While conventional wisdom dismissed open magnetic resonance imaging as a niche modality, Hitachi continued to rethink and innovate. Today the company's Altaire High Field Performance Open MR is delivering daily what many said could not be done: advanced high-field clinical capabilities in a truly open system. Hitachi has made many of those capabilities available in the mid-field range as well, in the AIRIS family of Open MR systems, creating a new value equation for a variety of clinical situations.

Optical and Security Products Division. OSPD was established within Hitachi Canada, Ltd. in 2003 to focus on the sales and marketing in Canada of Hitachi's optical products, finger vein (FV) biometrics and radio frequency identification (RFID) security product solutions, and small LCD products to the high-tech, telecom and datacom industries, as well as user communities that have high security requirements.

Power and Industry Division. Hitachi's Power and Industry Division provides innovative and proven solutions to meet today's energy challenges and society's growing needs for safe and reliable power generation and industrial systems.

RECENT DEVELOPMENTS

The Hitachi plasma TV series speaks eloquently to a sleek design and performance aesthetics that define elegance, with a roster of proprietary technologies including ALiS that provides a seamless, filmlike picture with more detail than ever before. The company's line of Director's Series plasmas elevates this product to an unsurpassed level of quality.

Hitachi's invention of the DVD camcorder revolutionized the camcorder industry and today the company is continually enhancing the product's features and cosmetics. Super Multiformat, R3 Rapid Record and Photo Frame Grab are tucked into the smallest case ever.

Since first popularizing the concept of Open MR over a decade ago, Hitachi has contin-

Hitachi Canada Ltd. is a proud sponsor of the NFL.

™NFL and the NFL Shield are registered trademarks of the National Football League, 2006.

ued to provide its customers with magnetic resonance imaging (MRI) systems that combine cutting-edge technology with patient-comfort design. The company's newest scanner, the 1.5T compact Echelon, continues this tradition. Echelon's standard imaging suites provide an impressive array of sequences, tools and features that promote scan efficiency and excellent image quality. Advanced techniques, such as radial scans and fluoro-triggered bolus MRA, position Hitachi's imaging centre at the forefront of MR applications.

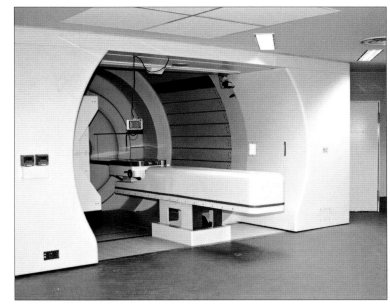

Hitachi high-resolution digital ultrasound system features HI VUE, a design and engineering philosophy that optimizes each component for individual high performance while integrating them to work more efficiently in concert. The result is more consistent high-quality imaging on a more productive, user-friendly ultrasound system. More than 30,000 Hitachi ultrasound systems are installed worldwide.

Hitachi recently completed the construction of the power island for Canada's most advanced and environmentally friendly coal-fired power plant. The Genesee Phase 3 Project located near Edmonton, Alberta features state-of-the-art technologies and received the prestigious "Coal Project of the Year" award at the PowerGen International conference in 2005. The plant was built in a record 36.5 months and produces 450 megawatts of electrical energy, enough power for a city of 350,000 people.

PROMOTION

Hitachi is the official sponsor of the National Football League in Canada. This sponsorship sets Hitachi in a rather enviable position through an alliance with the most dominant sports league in North America. The NFL's Super Bowl is the highest-rated televised sporting event in Canada. Moreover, the week prior to the Super Bowl is the strongest week in North America for the purchase of large-screen televisions.

Hitachi recently conducted a five-week radio campaign promoting its new line of DVD camcorders as well as a massive print campaign supporting plasma TVs. Ads appeared in major Canadian publications such as *Macleans, House & Home, Nuvo, Here's How, The Globe & Mail, L'Actualite* and *La Presse*.

In the medical field, Hitachi is actively involved in bringing more advanced technologies to Canadian clinicians. Its offerings include high-end imaging systems for dentistry, and on the therapeutic side, Hitachi is one of the few developers of proton-beam therapy systems for cancer treatment.

BRAND VALUES

The basic credo of Hitachi is to further elevate its founding concepts of harmony, sincerity and the pioneering spirit, to instill a resolute pride in being a member of society and thereby contributing to it through the development of superior and original technology and products.

Hitachi strives to be a good corporate citizen and to contribute toward the community and to this end to conduct its corporate activities in a fair and open manner, promote harmony with the natural environment and engage vigorously in activities that contribute to social progress.

THINGS YOU DIDN'T KNOW ABOUT HITACHI

○ Hitachi turbine generators produce over 40 percent of the base electrical generation in Alberta and Saskatchewan.

○ With Hitachi's finger vein authentication technology, your fingers essentially become your keys (password), allowing you to gain access and to verify identity.

○ The four barbs protruding at the four points of the compass in the Hitachi logo signify the sun's rays. The mark was designed to capture Odaira's vision of a man standing before the rising sun, planning a better future for all.

HONDA
The Power of Dreams

THE MARKET
Canada is a huge country, an enormous land mass that stretches to the horizon and beyond in every direction. It is divided by mountain ranges, bisected by rivers, dotted with lakes and punctuated by a handful of urban centres that are connected by thousands of kilometres of road. It's the perfect market for Honda.

No other brand has as many product lines as Honda. Honda makes almost every conceivable mode of transportation to tackle Canadian terrain. There are automobiles, trucks, motorcycles, all-terrain vehicles and even marine engines. Plus there is a line of power equipment to tame the land in between those times Canadians are not on the move.

Honda's trump card has always been the ability to anticipate the consumer's need and then to satisfy it through product innovations. In the case of Canadian consumers, one desire stands above all others: Canadians like things that work. They need their cars to start on cold mornings. They want a boat engine that starts on every pull. They can't afford to waste time with power equipment that doesn't finish the job. Honda products, across all lines, give Canadians what they desire most: reliability.

ACHIEVEMENTS
Through the years there have been many bright moments for Honda in Canada, including

numerous Automobile Journalists Association of Canada (AJAC) awards. The most recent include AJAC's Canadian Car of the Year and Best New Sports Car, received by the Civic Sedan/Coupe and the Civic Si, respectively; AJAC's Best New

Alternative Power, received by the Civic Hybrid; as well as AJAC's Canadian Truck of the Year, won by the Ridgeline.

But the one story that best epitomizes Honda's success in Canada is the Civic. There is something very special about the relationship Canadians have with their Civics. Perhaps it starts with the character of the car. Like Canadians themselves, the Civic is about substance. And in addition to its affordable price, the Civic delivers everything one would need in a car: safety, fuel efficiency, style and peppy performance that make it loads of fun to drive.

So it is understandable that Canadians have embraced the Civic. So much so, Civic has been the number one selling car in Canada for eight consecutive years; more than one million of them have been bought by Canadians since it was first introduced. On the strength of the Civic, and other successes, Honda recently became the third largest automobile manufacturer in Canada.

HISTORY
In its early years in Japan, Honda was a local company with a global vision. Today, Honda is a global company with a local vision. It's a philosophy Honda

calls "glocalization." What it means is that all around the world Honda builds products close to its customers. This allows the company to become part of the communities where Honda products are used. It helps Honda make products that serve local needs and conditions.

Great examples of "glocalization" are the TRX 400 and TRX 500 Canadian Trail Edition all-terrain vehicles. After extensive research, Honda discovered that the way Canadians ride ATVs is different from anywhere else in the world. Canadian trails are rougher and longer and frankly, Canadians just ride their machines harder. So Honda designed the two Canadian Trail Edition ATVs with uniquely calibrated suspension systems. And both models are available only in Canada. This focus on customer satisfaction at the local level has helped Honda reach the position of trust it enjoys in Canada today.

A brief history of Honda Canada:

1969 Honda Canada is founded. Early activities include the sales and distribution of motorcycles, power equipment and a few cars.

1973 The Civic launches in Canada.

1976 The Accord launches in Canada.

1986 Honda opens an automobile manufacturing facility in Alliston, Ontario.

1999 A second facility is added to increase production capacity.

2000 Honda Insight, North America's first gasoline-electric hybrid, is launched in Canada.

2001 The two-millionth Honda vehicle is sold in Canada.

2005 Honda introduces the world's first production motorcycle airbag system.

2006 Canadian-made Civic wins *Motor Trend*'s Car of the Year award and AJAC's Canadian Car of the Year.

Canadian-made Ridgeline wins *Motor Trend*'s Truck of the Year award and AJAC's Canadian Truck of the Year.

Civic and Ridgeline win North American Car and Truck of the Year.

PRODUCT
Whether it's a car, a motorcycle, a marine engine or power equipment, the hallmark of a Honda product has always been reliability. But there is another side to Honda products that is equally impressive — namely how innovative they are.

Back in 1972, Honda introduced the CVCC engine. The company researched low-emission engine technology in the belief that clean air wasn't just a company issue, but a duty to which the industry at large was obliged. The CVCC engine was the first standard-bearer of the lean-combustion concept and the first engine to pass the stringent 1975 emissions requirements of the 1970 Clean Air Act in the United States. The CVCC engine is just one example of Honda's environment-friendly innovations. Today, Honda continues to pursue cleaner engine designs with its lineup of hybrids. There is the Honda Insight, Canada's first hybrid car; the Civic Hybrid, Canada's most affordable hybrid car; and the Accord Hybrid, which is Honda's most powerful hybrid car. The pursuit of cleaner engines has resulted in multiple Natural Resources Canada EnerGuide awards.

Another example of innovative thinking is Honda's "Safety for Everyone." Honda is committed to providing the highest level of safety protection on all their vehicles, regardless of size or price. This means features such as Advanced Compatibility Engineering™ (ACE™) body structure; front and side curtain airbags and unibody frames are being incorporated into more and more Honda designs as standard equipment. Features that protect pedestrians are also built into all models — such as impact-absorbing hoods and fenders.

RECENT DEVELOPMENTS

Canadians will soon see earth-friendly hybrid technologies adapted to motorcycles and they are already seeing them on selected power equipment. Honda's fuel cell car, the Honda FCX, has already reached the stage of development where it has been leased to a family for trial use. And a fuel cell motorcycle will be ready for release in 2009.

More recently, Honda developed the world's first production motorcycle airbag system. This breakthrough system, which inflates in approximately 0.0601 seconds, helps lessen the severity of injuries caused by frontal collisions. It will be available in Canada on the new Gold Wing motorcycle in the fall of 2006.

And Honda has just introduced the 2006 Honda Civic. This new Civic is a complete redesign of the popular model, and it will complete Honda's transition to the next-generation i-VTEC® engine — a new series of engines that achieve a 20 percent improvement in fuel economy. The new Civic offers Honda customers more of everything. More power. More control. More space. More wind-cutting aerodynamics. More leading-edge technology. In short, more driving fun.

PROMOTION

One of the many strengths of Honda is its diversity of product. From motorcycles to snowblowers, and from cars to generators, consumers have the opportunity to use a Honda on a daily basis. This frequent interaction between consumer and product has shaped Honda's approach with its customers. Rather than telling consumers what to think and feel about Honda products, the promotion objective has been to complement the already positive experience Canadians have with their Hondas.

BRAND VALUES

One of Honda's core philosophies is something called "The Three Joys." Simply stated, it means that every person who comes in contact with a Honda should feel joy as a result. By getting a product that exceeds their expectations, Honda customers experience the Joy of Buying. By forming meaningful relationships with their customers and servicing excellent products, Honda dealers experience the Joy of Selling. And by making innovative products that surpass customer expectations, Honda associates experience the Joy of Creating.

Another pillar of Honda's brand values is the notion of dreams. Honda is a company built on dreams. The company founder, Soichiro Honda, had the dream of bringing the joy of mobility to all people. Today, that dream is still alive and it manifests itself in a startling array of products. Honda is presently developing a corporate jet that will increase cabin space and fuel efficiency through innovative design. Honda is also continuing to

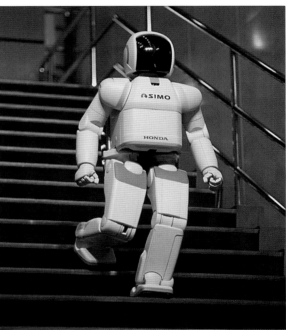

work on a robot called ASIMO (Advanced Step in Innovative Mobility), which one day could be employed as a personal helper and companion. Every Honda product, from the NSX supercar to the simplest lawn mower, in some way is the result of a dream. Dreams fuel the imaginations of Honda engineers. Dreams give shape to the Honda products of tomorrow — products that will bring the joy of mobility to Honda customers. See our dreams at honda.ca.

THINGS YOU DIDN'T KNOW ABOUT HONDA

- ❍ In what could be considered the first Honda product, Soichiro Honda used a small generator engine designed for a wireless radio to power a bicycle.

- ❍ Honda became the first Japanese manufacturer to produce cars in Canada when it established a manufacturing facility in Alliston, Ontario.

- ❍ Honda and Nagoya University in Japan teamed up to successfully isolate a gene that dramatically increases the crop yield of a rice plant.

HunterDouglas

THE MARKET

Not so long ago, window fashions were nothing more than just a way to dress a window. Then Hunter Douglas embarked on a long conversation with its customers, and from that dialogue a new idea was born. Window fashions must be more than window dressing; they should be a way to change the dynamics of a room.

Hunter Douglas provides everything the consumer needs in order to change the light in a way that best suits their needs. There are a number of key elements in the selection process – light source, privacy issues, style options and window shape. And with increased consumer awareness, energy efficiency, UV protection and child safety have also become important considerations for homeowners.

Hunter Douglas is the world market leader in window coverings and a major manufacturer of architectural products. With a head office in Rotterdam, the Netherlands, the Group comprises 161 companies in more than 100 countries. In 2005, the Hunter Douglas Group had sales of euro $1,920 million.

Hunter Douglas employs over 16,000 people worldwide, with more than 9,000 in North America, which accounts for about one-half of total worldwide sales. Hunter Douglas operates in a highly decentralized mode to better serve each individual country and market.

Hunter Douglas Canada is the country's leading resource for custom window fashions and serves more than 2,000 dealers nationwide. The company operates two plants, one in Brampton, Ontario and the other in Edmonton, Alberta in order to provide outstanding service to all markets.

ACHIEVEMENTS

Hunter Douglas has garnered numerous industry accolades and annual product awards that celebrate innovative style and design. Five notable introductions have assured the company's dominance as the world leader in superior window coverings, and all were developed in North America, primarily for the Canadian and U.S. markets.

- **1985** — Duette® honeycomb shades were launched, revolutionizing the window covering industry. By the end of 1988, Duette shades enjoyed a 60 percent share of the pleated shade market. The patented honeycomb construction provides the consumer with the ultimate choice in light control, privacy options and energy efficiency.
- **1991** — Silhouette® window shadings were introduced and achieved rapid success. Unlike any other product on the market, Silhouette window shadings give the consumer the ability to transform harsh light into gentle, diffused beauty and create a sense of luminous calm, while still providing a view.
- **1994** — Vignette® Modern Roman Shades brought another innovative product into the marketplace. A unique and dramatically improved innovation on the traditional Roman shade, Vignette shades had an immediate impact and continue to enjoy strong sales.
- **1996** — Luminette® Privacy Sheers were introduced and provided a new option for a traditional window covering. They were created to completely manage the light in the home on large window expanses. The graceful folds recall traditional draperies but with a lighter and softer feel.
- **2003** — Alouette® LightLouvers product was launched. When fully opened, the elliptical louvers offer the consumer a virtually unobstructed view of the outside and make an impressive architectural statement.

These top quality products are all backed by consistently superior service and a commitment to not only satisfy, but delight today's consumers.

Hunter Douglas is also a company that is committed to the highest safety and environmental

standards in its manufacturing processes. In addition, it offers employees outstanding benefits as well as platforms for growth through training and education initiatives. Employee retention is a priority and key employees boast an average of 17 years experience with Hunter Douglas.

HISTORY

The origins of the Hunter Douglas Group go back to 1919, when Henry Sonnenberg started a machinery distribution company in Düsseldorf, Germany. He later expanded his operations into machinery manufacturing and opened facilities in Holland and the United Kingdom. At the outbreak of WW II, he moved to the United States, where he founded the Douglas Machinery Corporation.

In 1946, Sonnenberg established the Hunter Douglas Corporation in association with Joe Hunter, a gifted inventor. Together, they developed a revolutionary continuous casting process for aluminium. With this manufacturing technology, they produced and commercialized the modern aluminium venetian blind. This revolutionary new product quickly gained leadership in the American market.

In 1956, policy differences led to the sale of the U.S. assets, but not the Hunter Douglas brand, and Henry Sonnenberg moved the company headquarters to Montreal, Canada.

In 1969, the Hunter Douglas Group headquarters were transferred from Montreal to Rotterdam, and Hunter Douglas N.V. became the worldwide Group holding company. In 1976, Hunter Douglas reacquired its former North American business, which is now Hunter Douglas Inc.

Over the last 25 years, Hunter Douglas has exploded in growth — with sales in North America increasing exponentially. The company's commitment to innovation has made it an unrivalled leader in new product development, continually meeting — and exceeding — the expectations of today's discriminating consumer for on-trend style and superior functionality in home fashions.

New product innovations have gone hand in hand with a commitment to the highest standards in custom manufacturing and the development of a first rate network of fabricator partners.

Hunter Douglas also provides excellent service to its customers. Strategic investments in marketing and communications infrastructure as well as IT have made Hunter Douglas a company that effectively supports window fashions retail dealers and drives consumers to them.

Hunter Douglas has repeatedly won industry acclaim for its extensive dealer training and education programs — the first of their kind — as well as its merchandising initiatives and its ongoing communications and advertising to consumers. In fact, the company is the leading advertiser in the field and has been for over 20 years.

In the last quarter century, thanks to the efforts of Hunter Douglas, window coverings have been transformed from a commodity into fashion for the home.

THE PRODUCT

The company's strength is in its ability to develop and market innovative, high quality, proprietary window fashions targeted primarily to the upscale consumer and supported by outstanding customer service.

Exclusive Hunter Douglas fabric window coverings are consistently recognized for excellence in design, styling, features, quality and breadth of selection: Duette® honeycomb shades, Silhouette® window shadings, Vignette® Modern Roman Shades, Luminette® Privacy Sheers and Alouette® LightLouvers.

Hunter Douglas also offers additional fashion-forward and colour-coordinated window coverings at various price points. These include horizontal and vertical blinds, roman, roller and woven wood shades, pleated shades, wood and alternative wood blinds.

Each product is custom-made for each consumer's specific needs and tastes and delivered within days.

The proprietary operating systems are equally innovative and unique. They offer ease-of-use,

reliable performance and convenience, with essential child safety elements built into each product.

RECENT DEVELOPMENTS

The Alustra™ Collection. In 2004, The Alustra™ Collection was launched in Canada to a network of Hunter Douglas dealers who met certain sales and support criteria. This collection is a new line of high-end custom window coverings based on the company's best selling product categories. From luminous sheers to elegant woven textures at the window, The Alustra Collection offers the highest standard of style for discriminating homeowners.

This exclusive collection was recently named product of the year by the Window Covering Manufacturer Association (WCMA), the eighth consecutive year that Hunter Douglas products have won this prestigious award.

The Hunter Douglas Gallery. In 2006, the Hunter Douglas Gallery® program was introduced to a host of loyal and dedicated retailers across the nation. Gallery dealers are committed to Hunter Douglas products and receive extensive marketing support and sales training to ensure they are completely focused on the goal of providing consumers with a thoroughly satisfying shopping experience.

The Gallery program provides the consumer with a showroom featuring the full line of Hunter Douglas products showcased in a compelling display environment. The trained professionals in Hunter Douglas Gallery stores help guide the consumer to a solution and a choice that is distinctly theirs in a way that makes shopping and selecting a product stress-free.

Direct Connect. In late 2005, Hunter Douglas offered its dealers an online order entry system to place their custom orders. This Internet-based system allows them to access tools that enhance the selling process and helps them to effectively manage their business.

Direct Connect offers everything from flexible product option comparisons at the click of a button, to automated prospective client follow-up, to the flexibility of being able to order 24/7.

PROMOTION

Hunter Douglas strategically positions itself to the retail dealer and the consumer alike as a manufacturer of quality, high-end product for the home. Television and consumer print ads featuring the *Light Can Change Everything*™ commitment captivate a homeowner's imagination with the idea that they can change the dynamics of their living spaces by using Hunter Douglas custom window coverings that "paint" rooms with light.

BRAND VALUES

Light Can Change Everything. The brand promise is the cornerstone of the company's commitment to the consumer. To shape the light as it enters, creating a mood, reflecting an attitude, personalizing the home with a luminous signature. In short, it is the company's belief that the product should bring not just beauty and privacy to the surroundings, but feelings of contentment and serenity as well.

Hunter Douglas products require the hands-on involvement of true artisans, piece-by-piece attention and a true pride in craftsmanship through every step of the production process. And that is exactly what goes into all Hunter Douglas custom window fashions.

THINGS YOU DIDN'T KNOW ABOUT HUNTER DOUGLAS

- ❍ Duette honeycomb shades can increase the energy efficiency of a single pane of glass by almost four times and more than double the energy efficiency of a double-glazed window.

- ❍ Every Habitat for Humanity house built in Canada includes custom window fashions donated by Hunter Douglas.

Hush Puppies®

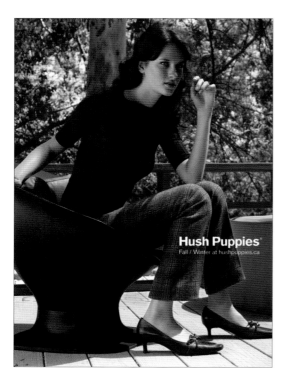

THE MARKET

Since the mid 1990s, North America has been the center of a worldwide casual boom in fashion. Khaki trousers and comfortable knit shirts have replaced more tailored European fashions. Businesses established "Casual Friday" dress codes that soon extended to the rest of the week. "Uniform" business attire has given way to a relaxed, more individual style of dress. And Hush Puppies — the footwear brand that "invented casual" — has kept pace with relevant product styling that supports its brand values of Relaxed, Confident, Youthful and Modern.

ACHIEVEMENTS

Since its introduction in 1958, Hush Puppies has become the world's best loved shoe brand. Sold in 120 countries around the world, Hush Puppies enjoys a brand recognition of over 90 percent in Canada and nearly that high in most of the countries in which the brand is sold. Somewhere in the world, a pair of Hush Puppies is sold every two seconds throughout every day!

HISTORY

Hush Puppies is a subsidiary of Wolverine World Wide Inc., which also owns many of the world's best known shoe brands.

The company that would become Wolverine World Wide Inc. was founded in 1883, by G.A. Krause. Ten years later, G.A. and his sons built a shoe factory in Rockford, Michigan, and were soon producing 300 pairs of horse leather shoes a day. G.A. Krause was a true visionary who ran his business like a modern tycoon: he recognized opportunity where no one else did; he was a risk taker and an innovator. By 1919, G. A. Krause took his business to the next level with an advertising campaign and one of the earliest national sales forces in the U.S. Krause never rested on his laurels, and was always a step ahead of his time. As horses began to disappear from the American landscape, Wolverine's engineers created a new leather: pigskin suede — a soft material that lead to a breakthrough in 1957 — with the design of soft, casual shoes which were called Hush Puppies after a treat that Southerners used to quiet their barking dogs.

In an era when footwear choices were limited, Hush Puppies provided the world with a new alternative — a modern shoe which offered authentic style, casual flair, as well as comfort. Hush Puppies — fashioned of pigskin suede and light crepe soles — were an innovation that would ultimately change the kind of shoes we wear.

The Hush Puppies brand was launched in 1958 with a heavy marketing and advertising campaign, marked by the beloved basset hound that soon embodied the easygoing Hush Puppies style.

Introduced during a time of new freedoms and changing lifestyles, the Hush Puppies brand name and mascot quickly became symbolic of the emerging optimism of mid-century America.

Hush Puppies were an amazing success from day one. As soon as the shoes hit retail stores, Greb Shoes of Canada signed up as the first licensee. Plans for international expansion were soon under way.

By 1963, one in ten American adults owned a pair of Hush Puppies, and sales continued to expand. The brand never got stale and continued to attract consumers around the world for the next three decades. In 1990, Wolverine World Wide created a dynamic new image for Hush Puppies: "We invented Casual" and five years later, Hush Puppies Shoes were voted Fashion Accessory of the Year by the Council of Fashion Designers of America. Although Wolverine World Wide would go on to acquire many prestigious shoe brands, Hush Puppies are still the jewel in the crown of a company that began as a little shoe factory at the turn of the 20th century. They keep evolving with the times: relaxed and classic in design, they continue to define what it means to be both modern and casual.

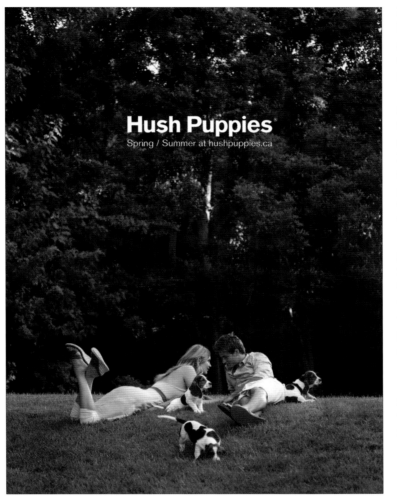

THE PRODUCT

Today, Hush Puppies offers a lot more than the original suede shoe that made the brand famous. Hush Puppies produces complete collections of contemporary casual footwear for men, women and

children. There are styles appropriate for work, play and for all aspects of today's busy lives.

In December 1989, Hush Puppies Canada Ltd. was formed to create new product ideas in the casual segment of the footwear market. The goal was to provide the consumer a uniquely Canadian perspective on footwear while encompassing the Hush Puppies philosophy of "Relaxed, Confident, Youthful and Modern" shoes for the entire family.

In order to deal with Canadian winters, the logical extension of the classic Hush Puppies suede oxford was a casual winter boot. Therefore Hush Puppies Canada went about establishing itself as a premier manufacturer of waterproof casual Hush Puppies winter boots in smooth leather and suede. Hush Puppies boots are now viewed as the footwear of choice for people looking for quality and comfort combined with stylish fashion.

The Hush Puppies brand name can also now be found on accessories from handbags to watches, eyewear, socks and even plush toys.

While styles may change, one thing remains the same with today's Hush Puppies: their comfort. Hush Puppies have long been known as "the world's most comfortable shoes," and designers and technicians continually work to ensure comfort is a top priority. Wolverine World Wide has received over 120 proprietary design patents over the course of its history.

RECENT DEVELOPMENTS

Today, Hush Puppies offers a wide range of comfort technologies, from "ZeroG" — lightweight footwear built to athletic specifications — to "WaveReflex," a uniquely designed outsole, with reverse-action waves that combine to provide extreme flexibility for immediate comfort.

In fall 2001, Hush Puppies introduced its new Float FX cushioning — a nitrogen oxide filled heel bubble, ABS stabilizer and non-liquid forefoot gel pad to customize the entire walking motion from heel-strike through toe-off.

PROMOTION

The Hush Puppies basset hound remains one of the world's great icons. It is as well known as "the Hush Puppies dog" as it is by its breed. Basset hounds were first introduced in many countries around the world soon after the introduction of the Hush Puppies shoes.

It was one of the first nationally advertised shoe brands, appearing on the *Tonight Show* with Johnny Carson and the *Today* show with Hugh Downs. There have been many memorable Hush Puppies moments in advertising — from shoes that "make the sidewalk softer" in the 1960s to "We Invented Casual" in the 1990s. In 1988, Hush Puppies won the prestigious Gold Lion at the Cannes Festival for a television commercial showing the basset hound on a subway grate with its ears flapping in the air as a train passed below. The ad was later named one of the top 100 television commercials of all time by *Entertainment Weekly* magazine.

Today, the Hush Puppies spirit is reflected in its contemporary imagery, which positions the brand as relaxed, modern, and confident. The image conveys that Hush Puppies understands fashion and has the right shoes for today's modern consumer.

BRAND VALUES

Hush Puppies was built on the foundation of innovation, its reputation for comfort and a style distinctly its own. The brand is authentic, as it was the first casual shoe made in America. It is established as one of the most recognizable names in footwear throughout the world. And while the roots of the Hush Puppies brand are firmly planted in a relaxed and casual lifestyle, the shoes always express a fresh new style, which keeps them looking youthful and modern. They are classics, but also completely modern and up to date.

THINGS YOU DIDN'T KNOW ABOUT HUSH PUPPIES

○ Nearly 40,000 pairs of Hush Puppies shoes are sold every day around the world.

○ In 1959, just one year after being introduced in the United States, Hush Puppies began its globalization with its entrance into the Canadian marketplace.

○ Many celebrities have worn Hush Puppies, including Tom Hanks, Sharon Stone, Nicolas Cage and Susan Sarandon.

○ Hush Puppies shoes have been featured in many major movies, including a recent appearance in *Austin Powers in Goldmember*.

○ The actress Rene Russo appeared in a Hush Puppies catalog in the 1970s, early in her modeling career.

○ Hush Puppies Canada has been a proud supporter of the Canadian Breast Cancer Foundation since 2002.

THE MARKET

Intel is the world leader in silicon innovation, developing technologies, products and initiatives to continually advance how people work and live.

This year, 100 million people around the world will discover digital for the first time; 150 million additional people will become part of the wireless world. The living room will grow more interactive, and the digital divide will shrink. More people will use technology in more fascinating ways than ever imagined. And behind all of this progress you'll find innovative Intel® technology.

ACHIEVEMENTS

Intel set a broad corporate re-alignment in motion in 2005, creating six new business groups to better meet the needs of the marketplace and to drive growth by delivering platform solutions. These platform solutions — which integrate hardware, software and supporting technologies — enable thrilling new capabilities, enhance system performance and improve the overall user experience.

Designing and manufacturing the spectrum of technologies necessary to bring platforms to life requires Intel's unparalleled breadth and depth of expertise. Intel backs this with billions of dollars and tens of thousands of person-hours in industry investment, validation, software services and programs, tools and joint marketing programs for audiences from developers to CIOs to consumers.

At the heart of Intel's platform approach is the ability to consistently deliver architectural innovation. At the end of 2005, Intel introduced the Intel® Core™ Duo processor as the centerpiece of Intel client platforms. This new dual-core technology rewrites the rules of computing, delivering breakthrough performance with amazingly low power consumption. It's changing the PC landscape and fostering a revolution in computer product designs from the world's most innovative PC manufacturers.

HISTORY

For nearly 40 years, Intel has been committed to driving unparalleled technology innovation that advances life. From the introduction of the first microprocessor in 1971, Intel has been the catalyst behind the digital revolution and has played a fundamental role in shaping the way the world lives and works.

Intel continues to create state-of-the-art, market-driving technology and solutions; to inspire the industry to support these solutions with innovative products and services; to seed the next generation of technology entrepreneurs; and to donate more than $100 million each year to help young people develop critical math, science and engineering skills.

THE PRODUCT

Intel has been driving a fundamental shift in the company's approach to the market. The focus is now on four key market segment opportunities: mobile, digital home, enterprise and health.

Intel® Centrino® Duo mobile technology redefines mobile computing, paving the way for innovative laptop designs that are even thinner, lighter and more battery efficient. New features enable amazing digital entertainment experiences, flexible connectivity and revolutionary performance for responsive multi-tasking on the go.

At the 2006 Consumer Electronics Show in Las Vegas, Intel announced the arrival of Intel® Viiv™ technology, a platform that is taking the entertainment PC to new heights and enabling people to enjoy their digital music, movies and photos as never before. With Intel's help, the home is becoming an entertainment complex; Intel is not only developing the underlying technologies to enable this experience, but is also working across the technology and media industries to help establish the industry standards and the collaboration needed to deliver the entertainment people want.

Intel's breakthrough enterprise solutions help global businesses, large and small, become more secure, manageable and productive — built on open architecture that increases flexibility and reduces costs. Intel platforms — from servers and clients to communications platforms and storage

ingredients — provide organizations of all sizes with better technologies to grow effectively and manage their operations well.

Intel is drawing on its heritage as a technology innovator to improve cost, quality and access by helping patients, hospitals and health-care systems around the world in thrilling new ways. Intel's strategy to drive technology-enabled continuous health is focused on improving acute care in the institutional setting; empowering patients and caregivers to better track and manage chronic conditions; accelerating progress of the biomedical research enterprise and advancing standards and policies that enable innovation and interoperability across the health-care ecosystem.

RECENT DEVELOPMENTS

On January 3, 2006, Intel Corporation formally unveiled a new brand identity that represents a significant milestone in the company's history and further signifies the company's evolution as a market-driving platform solutions company.

"Intel has one of the most valuable brands in the world, and we intend to grow the value of our brand as we evolve the company," said Eric Kim, Intel senior vice president and general manager of the Sales and Marketing Group. "This evolution will allow Intel to be better recognized for our contributions, establish a stronger emotional connection with our audiences and strengthen our overall position in the marketplace."

Intel's new brand identity involves changes to the widely recognized Intel Inside® logo created in 1991, and the original Intel "dropped-e" logo, which was created when Silicon Valley pioneers Robert Noyce and Gordon Moore formed their "integrated electronics" company in 1968. Intel's new logo combines the essence of both of these powerful symbols — building on Intel's rich heritage, while signaling the direction in which the company is headed today.

A new branding system simplifies and unifies the look and feel across Intel products and platforms in an effort to better communicate important characteristics and value to consumers. The system includes new logos for Intel Viiv technology and Intel Centrino mobile technology, and redesigned logos for individual processors, chipsets, motherboards and other Intel technologies.

PROMOTION

In 2006, the Intel communications group adopted an integrated marketing model to maximize synergy and efficiency across communications. This strategy was evidenced in two iconic consumer campaigns that were launched to support the company's leadership platform brands: Intel Centrino Duo mobile technology and Intel Viiv technology.

The "Laps" campaign for Intel Centrino Duo taps into the increasing interest of consumers worldwide to use their laptop PCs as all-in-one entertainment systems. It creates a compelling

metaphor for the amazing and lifelike entertainment experiences Intel makes possible by putting celebrities, such as Mariah Carey, Tony Hawk and Lucy Liu, on the laps of actual users.

Media-based Intel Viiv technology was launched in a similar fashion — with users demonstrating how this exciting new PC technology can transform the living room. People featured in the ads hold up their fingers in a "V" shape to

reinforce the new brand name, while extolling the virtues of digital entertainment in the home.

In addition, Intel continued to demonstrate business marketing leadership through its case study based "Success built in" campaign. The 17 country campaign highlights how Intel products and technologies help business of all sizes and from many different industries realize compelling benefits.

Another 2006 landmark was the announcement of Intel's first major sports sponsorship. Through a comprehensive partnership agreement, Intel has become the Official Corporate Partner of the BMW Sauber F1 Team. During the team's inaugural 2006 season, the Intel brand will reach hundreds of millions of passionate fans worldwide — fans who appreciate the critical role that technology plays in Formula One.

BRAND VALUES

Intel's employees share a common mission: to deliver platform and technology advancements that become essential to the way people work and live. This mission and Intel's brand promise are embodied in Intel's new tagline, "Intel. Leap ahead.™" Leap ahead declares who Intel is and where the company is going. According to Intel's Eric Kim, "These two words capture what drives us, inspires us, galvanizes us into action and unites us in purpose and practice. It is the simple embodiment of what Intel makes possible for people everywhere."

Leap ahead drives focus, ensuring that every idea, product, decision and action is considered in the context of Intel's mission as a company. Intel is committed to finding and driving the next Leap ahead — in technology, education, culture, social responsibility, manufacturing, environment and more — to continuously challenge the status quo, and to encourage others to join them as Intel continues to take exciting leaps forward.

For Intel, in the end, it's not just about making technology faster, smarter and cheaper. It's about using that technology to make life better, richer and more convenient for everyone it touches.

THINGS YOU DIDN'T KNOW ABOUT INTEL

○ It is estimated that, on average, the five-note Intel sonic brand is heard somewhere in the world at least once every 40 seconds.

○ Intel is the fifth most valuable brand in the world, according to *BusinessWeek* and *Interbrand* (July 2005).

○ The Intel Inside® Program is one of the world's largest cooperative marketing programs.

○ Since 2000, Intel has trained more than 3 million teachers worldwide as part of the Intel® Teach to the Future professional development program.

○ During the manufacturing process, a silicon wafer moves through 250 process steps and it runs through clean rooms that are 10,000 times cleaner than a hospital operating room.

JAGUAR

THE MARKET

With the all new XK now in the market, 2007 will be an exciting year for Jaguar as the company gears up for the future. On the heels of the overwhelmingly positive response to the naturally aspirated XK, the company is preparing for the launch of the super-charged XKR, which debuted at the London Motor Show in July 2006. The X-TYPE, S-TYPE and XJ also continue to improve and receive enhanced packaging and equipment levels.

Like all great Jaguar sports cars, the focus of the XK is firmly on the future, while acknowledging the marque's rich history. It heralds a new era for Jaguar in terms of both design and engineering and is the most technically advanced Jaguar ever built.

The all new sports car delivers on performance, dynamics, safety, exterior and interior design. All the quality expected of a brand which is a leader in the international market.

Jaguar's long standing commitment to creating beautiful, contemporary, fast cars is reinforced once again with the unveiling of the new, special edition 400bhp XJR Portfolio. This super-charged performance sedan continues the evolution of the design cues first seen on the striking Concept Eight show car, which starred at the New York International Auto Show in 2004, which were taken forward on the limited edition production model produced in 2005.

The Concept Eight was the first time that Jaguar had shown its new performance styling to the public, and the reaction was so positive that many of its key design details, such as the eye-catching polished wheels, side power vents and Satin American Walnut trim, were soon to grace the long wheelbase XJ Super V8 Portfolio, a special edition XJ produced for the Canadian and other global markets.

Now, the new XJR Portfolio continues the successful theme of exclusive, sporting sedans with attitude, power and a modern character.

ACHIEVEMENTS

Jaguar has received the 2006 World Traffic Safety Symposium's Traffic Safety Achievement Award in the Automaker Category for the new XK's Pedestrian Impact Safety System. The World Traffic Safety Symposium recognizes organizations that are creating a safer environment for motorists and pedestrians.

Jaguar achieved a remarkable quadruple success in the latest J. D. Power and Associates Initial Quality Study released in 2006 in the United States.

The company improved to second position overall in the survey and was the highest ranked European nameplate.

The J. D. Power Study ranks new vehicle quality after 90 days in the hands of customers.

This major achievement for Jaguar was led by

its best-performing model, the X-TYPE saloon, which improved 35 percent over last year's results.

In addition, Jaguar's Halewood plant, where the X-TYPE is manufactured, received J. D. Power's Gold Award for European plant performance. This state-of-the-art facility is now a centre of excellence for lean manufacturing, a discipline that focuses on elimination of waste, while driving high quality, continuous improvement.

HISTORY

For 50 years, the Jaguar story was the story of one man, founder Sir William Lyons, who built up one of the world's greatest automotive names: renowned for captivating style, breathtaking performance and a commitment to quality.

Since the company was founded in 1922, Jaguar has evolved from the production of motorcycle sidecars to become one of the world's leading designers and manufacturers of premium sedans and sports cars. The company's vision is simple: to produce beautiful, fast cars that are desired the world over. The company operates three manufacturing plants in the United Kingdom.

THE PRODUCT

The Jaguar X-TYPE: Jaguar's best-selling all-wheel-drive X-TYPE moved up to become Jaguar's best quality model with its impressive showing in the latest J. D. Power and Associates' Initial Quality Study in 2005. For 2007, Jaguar's X-TYPE adopts more standardized equipment including Dynamic Stability Control, moonroof, split/fold rear seats (sedan only), reverse park control (Sportwagon only) and a premium package for the Sportwagon. Also, while the Sport package is discontinued, a new luxury package replaces the VDP Package and Premium Package on the sedan.

There are quite a few impressive things about the X-TYPE's performance, including the innovative aluminum suspension that provides improved handling, or the all-wheel-drive system, a Jaguar first that provides smooth traction in any road condition.

The Jaguar XK. In April 2006, Jaguar launched the all new 2007 Jaguar XK to overwhelmingly positive reviews from media, dealers and customers alike. Engineered to exceed the high demands that consumers rightly expect from a Jaguar sports car — complete with advanced aluminum chassis, sophisticated transmission and exquisite exterior and interior design — the all new 2007 XK Coupe and Convertible mark an exciting new era for Jaguar in terms of both design and engineering.

In July 2006, Jaguar unveiled the R Performance supercharged version of the XK Coupe and Convertible. Built using the same aluminum construction as the naturally aspirated XK, the supercharged 4.2-liter V8 will produce 420 bhp and 413 lb. ft. of torque, making this the fastest production Jaguar to date. The XKR will also feature unique styling geared toward power and performance.

The Jaguar S-Type is characterized by its distinctive appearance and instinctive performance. The premium mid-sized Jaguar S-TYPE sports sedan continues to tone its appearance and appeal with styling changes, and the addition of new

features and value-added packaging. Referring to the S-TYPE as a mere luxury vehicle misses the point. While Jaguar S-TYPE does feature uniquely sensual styling, reflecting its celebrated predecessors of the 1960s, its breathtaking combination of performance, technology and high-grade interior appointments make an S-TYPE literally impossible to mistake for anything else.

For 2007, Jaguar's premium mid-sized sports sedan — the S-TYPE — gains an additional ultra-luxurious package option for the S-TYPE R model — the "SV8." The S-TYPE R "SV8" comes complete with soft-grain leather seating with contrast piping, Burl Walnut veneers, chrome exterior trip and Adaptive Cruise Control. Also for 2007, the S-TYPE 3.0 and 4.2 get an increase in standard features, making them better equipped than ever.

The Jaguar XJ, the flagship of the Jaguar line, is the rare automobile that needs no calling card. A truly modern update of a timeless classic, the XJ range has undergone dramatic change over the past two years, expanding from three to five distinct derivatives to three new Long Wheelbase models — XJ Portfolio, Vanden Plas and Super V8 in 2005. And in 2006, all XJs are further refined with the addition of acoustic laminated side glass and a radio frequency based tire pressure monitoring system as well as being joined by

the most exclusive and luxurious production Jaguar ever built: the Super V8 Portfolio.

RECENT DEVELOPMENTS

Over the past several years, the Jaguar product range has gone through a period of remarkable change. There have been continuous developments, including revised versions of the compact X-TYPE and distinctive S-TYPE and the beautiful XK sports car range. Jaguar has also launched the all new aluminum XJ, and the beautiful XJ Long Wheelbase models, and now the all new aluminum Jaguar XK sports car.

Jaguar's 2007 XK is the most tested Jaguar ever. It will have been frozen at a bone-chilling minus 40 degrees in the icy wastes of Northern Canada, and cooked in the 120 degree furnace that is Death Valley, California. Its performance at maximum speed will have been tested on Italy's famous Nardo high-speed bowl, while its handling abilities will have been honed around Germany's legendary Nürburgring race track. And to ensure that it protects those inside, it will have been crashed and analyzed at Volvo's Safety Center, in Gothenburg, Sweden — acknowledged as the world's most advanced safety testing facility.

Like any of the great Jaguar sports cars of the past fifty years and more, the all new XK pushes the boundaries of sports motoring. It is the most technically advanced Jaguar ever and undoubtedly, one of the most beautiful.

PROMOTION

In May 2005, Euro RSCG/Fuel Worldwide was hired by Jaguar to launch a global campaign. The new "Gorgeous" campaign's purpose is to reposition the brand image and make it more attractive to consumers of all ages and backgrounds.

New-Fashioned Luxury is the powerful strategic platform from which Fuel and Jaguar can communicate the brand image and personality across all consumer touch points. The Jaguar creative expression of New-Fashioned Luxury is "Gorgeous." Everything Jaguar does to engage, entice and communicate the brand worldwide will be Gorgeous.

Furthermore Jaguar puts a slant on the unique and distinctive characteristics of all its products. Indeed, they particularly paid attention to the design of their cars, making it seductive. They

also kept their sporting luxury aspect, focusing on their use of various materials to enhance their feel and making cars that feel alive, rewarding all the senses. These cars stimulate the senses with precise, responsive and refined performances.

Euro RSCG/Fuel strives to craft the Jaguar brand to be imaginative, innovative and uncompromising, with a rich, colorful story. They give the brand a unique tone of voice, spoken in a warm, confident, exciting, highly individual way. They communicate in a way that breaks the codes of the automotive category.

BRAND VALUES

At the heart of Jaguar's product philosophy is a firm commitment to emotional engineering: the production of beautiful, fast cars that combine intelligent, relevant technologies and contemporary luxury. While modernization is part of this commitment, they do not lose sight of traditional values.

As a responsible international corporate citizen, Jaguar is fully engaged in environmental programs, community work and brand awareness exercises. For example, Jaguar Cars were named National Champion in the Green Apple Awards in 2003 — the sixth consecutive year that Jaguar won a Green Apple Award in the national campaign to find Britain's greenest companies.

In 2005, Jaguar introduced a new campaign to assist in the effort of preserving the company's namesake, the jaguar. The Jaguar Conservation Trust provides grants and funding for projects that promote the preservation of the jaguar and its habitat, with actress and conservationist Stephanie Powers leading the development as advisor.

THE MARKET

Land Rovers sell in 140 countries. With such an extraordinarily high international presence, they are as likely to be seen in a small African village as they are in London or Toronto. Completely at home both in rugged landscapes and sophisticated urban settings, Land Rovers capture the imagination of discriminating, worldly consumers who value quality, timeless style and a sense of adventure.

Since the very first design appeared in 1948, the Land Rover name has become universally identified with definitive four-wheel drive vehicles. Year after year, Land Rover models have redefined the world's 4x4 categories.

Over the past 58 years, Land Rover has meticulously engineered eight iconic models. Today, Land Rover's innovation is taking on bold new shapes and gaining rapid momentum. Over the next six years, Land Rover plans to release five new groundbreaking models.

In 2006, Land Rover's global sales set new records each month. Range Rover itself has seen a 34 percent increase during the first quarter of 2006. This represents the best continuous period of sales success since Land Rover was acquired by Ford Motor Company in 2000. Since then, Ford has made significant investments allowing Land Rover to revitalize the entire model lineup.

From the very first Land Rover to the futuristic concept vehicle, Range Stormer, Land Rover remains faithful to the core values engineered into each and every vehicle: authenticity, adventure, guts and supremacy. Land Rover is not just an SUV, it is a lifestyle — a lifestyle that represents a spirit of adventure and a zest for life.

ACHIEVEMENTS

Land Rover has won two Queen's Awards for Enterprise — for Innovation and for International Trade.

In 2002, the Range Rover won *4x4 Magazine*'s overall SUV of the Year Award and *Top Gear Magazine*'s Car of the Year Award.

The Range Rover Sport has racked up an impressive list of awards as well. It was named SUV of the Year by *Top Gear Magazine* in 2005, 4x4 of the Year by *4x4 Magazine* in 2006 and SUV of the Year by the Association of Scottish Motoring Writers in 2005.

Since its introduction in 2005, the LR3's powerful on-road performance, unparalleled off-road standards and state-of-the-art technologies have set new industry standards. LR3 has earned more than 20 North American awards, including the 2005 Motor Trend Sport Utility of the Year, a record amount for any SUV in its introductory year.

HISTORY

The first Land Rover, built by brothers Spencer and Maurice Wilks for British car company Rover, rolled off the production line in 1948. Over the last 58 years, the Land Rover range of vehicles has evolved to become a byword for toughness, durability, comfort and elegant style.

Land Rover Canada is part of Aston Martin Jaguar Land Rover with headquarters in Bramalea, Ontario. Land Rover established operations in Canada in 1991 and now imports and distributes Range Rover, Range Rover Sport and LR3 vehicles manufactured by Land Rover in Solihull, England. Land Rover's worldwide operations are wholly owned by Ford Motor Company based in Dearborn, Michigan.

THE PRODUCT

Range Rover, Land Rover's flagship vehicle, is more powerful than ever. With the choice of a 305 horsepower HSE or the 400 horsepower Supercharged, the Range Rover for 2007 has extraordinary all-terrain ability. It is Land Rover's most refined, most luxurious and most complete SUV.

Range Rover Sport is the best performing and best handling vehicle that Land Rover has ever built in its class. Designed to complement the renowned Range Rover, the Range Rover Sport is a completely new vehicle, a more compact, more agile and more performance oriented SUV.

It combines invigorating dynamic ability with outstanding comfort and refinement. This reflects its ability to effortlessly cover long journeys quickly and comfortably and yet also to deliver sharp handling and exhilarating performance.

LR3. Since its introduction in the 2005 model year, LR3's powerful on-road performance,

unparalleled off-road standards and state-of-the-art technologies have set a new industry standard.

In addition to the existing 4.4 liter 300 bhp V8 engine, LR3 offers the new 4.0 liter V6 engine. All V6 models come equipped with a long list of four-wheel-drive technologies including the innovative Terrain Response™ system, and four corner electronic air suspension.

RECENT DEVELOPMENTS
For 2007, the Range Rover gains Land Rover's patented Terrain Response system™ for exceptional off-road performance as well as reduced driver effort, providing the finest blend of performance and refinement ever offered on a Land Rover vehicle, making it the world's most complete luxury SUV.

The Range Rover Sport's top-line version uses a 390 bhp Jaguar-derived supercharged V8 engine and has a top speed of 225 km/h electronically limited. It is the fastest and best accelerating vehicle that Land Rover has ever made.

Land Rover is showcasing a catalog of innovative technologies — collectively known as the e-Terrain System — that are designed to reduce both fuel consumption and harmful tailpipe emissions while also improving the outstanding breadth of capability of Land Rover's SUV vehicles.

They are designed to contribute to a potential improvement in fuel economy — of up to one-third over a current vehicle of similar size and

performance. And many of the technologies will be available on Land Rover production models in the next few years — all without compromising the breadth of on and off-road capability that defines all Land Rover products.

LR2. The fourth new model from Land Rover in just four years, LR2 joins the impressive line-up of Range Rover (2002), Land Rover LR3 (2004) and Range Rover Sport (2005) that together have seen record breaking sales performance around the world.

New from the ground up, LR2 delivers outstanding on-road performance as well as the class-leading off-road ability of a Land Rover. A dynamic design, purposeful stance, smart and spacious interior and an abundance of advanced technologies complete the LR2 package. The all-new LR2 will be available at retailers mid 2007.

PROMOTION
In June 2006, women's tennis superstar Maria Sharapova was in London attending a pre-Wimbledon party where she gave on-lookers a sneak preview of the all-new LR2. Sharapova is an official Land Rover ambassador in North America, where she promotes the vehicles.

Land Rover's LR3 accepted its mission in Paramount Pictures' action movie *Mission: Impossible III*, which opened in May 2006. In one of the film's most incredible action sequences, Ethan Hunt gets assistance from the LR3 as he makes a courageous escape from his enemies.

Land Rover presented a glimpse of its future environmental technology at the 2006 New York International Auto Show. The concept — called Land_e — showcases some of the alternative technologies that Land Rover is considering adopting on its vehicles in the near future.

Land Rover also used the New York show as an opportunity to announce

details of its Go Beyond TV — the industry's first broadband television station offered by a single auto manufacturer. Go Beyond TV will feature Land Rover–dedicated footage along with lifestyle and adventure content via external partners.

Land Rover Canada along with its sister company Jaguar Canada is the Official Vehicle Sponsor of the all-new Four Seasons Centre for the Performing Arts, Canada's new opera house.

BRAND VALUES
Land Rover is committed to addressing the challenges of sustainable development and operating as a responsible company. It promotes sustainability by integrating and balancing economic, environmental and social responsibilities within all of its activities.

Environmental responsibility is a major part of the business philosophy of Land Rover, as it is one of their core brand values. They set improvement goals and targets and monitor progress. They aim to produce as economical and clean a car as possible. The policy considers the wider environment and produces recyclable vehicles in a pollution-free production process. Every Land Rover is designed to be at least 85 percent recyclable.

THINGS YOU DIDN'T KNOW ABOUT LAND ROVER

○ Land Rover has supplied the Royal Geographic Society with vehicles for more than 20 years, assisting in some of their most exciting research expeditions.

○ Land Rover has joined up with Born Free, renowned animal conservation charity. It provides essential support vehicles in the countries where the charity works to keep wildlife in the wild.

○ Land Rover supplies Biosphere (a research organization that aims to protect species and the environment) expeditions with fully equipped vehicles, permitting access to the most difficult and remote locations.

THE MARKET

Canada's snack food industry is booming. According to A. C. Nielsen, the snack food category — comprising potato chips, corn chips, tortilla chips, pretzels, and nuts and seeds — has surpassed more than $1 billion in sales and counting. Potato chips account for 50 percent of the savory snack world, representing more than $500 million in sales annually. As Canada's number one potato chip brand, Lay's® plays an integral role in category growth and performance by driving consumers to the snack food aisle.

ACHIEVEMENTS

The brand's focus on product quality and innovation has generated positive attention from consumers, industry and retail customers alike. Celebrating the brand's flavour innovation, the Lay's® Sea Salt & Pepper flavour was chosen by consumers for the 2005 Best New Product Awards. Appealing to regional and emerging consumer taste preferences, Lay's® continues to develop exciting flavours like Lay's® Roast Chicken, Lay's® Fries & Gravy, Lay's® Old Fashioned BBQ, Lay's® Wasabi and Lay's® Spicy Curry.

HISTORY

Lay's® has a rich history as one of the first brands of Frito Lay Canada. The evolution of the brand from its humble beginnings in Nashville, Tennessee to its present day success as Canada's favourite potato chip brand is a story of entrepreneurial growth and constant innovation.

In 1932, Herman W. Lay started a small business in Nashville, Tennessee, distributing potato chips made by a company in Atlanta, Georgia. Six years later he bought the Atlanta potato chip maker to launch H. W. Lay & Company.

By 1942, H. W. Lay & Company was producing potato chips on a continuous potato chip machine, which enabled a huge surge in sales. Two years later, the company changed its product name to Lay's® Potato Chips and became one of the first snack food companies to advertise on television. It also became known as a leader in innovation when it opened a research lab to develop new products.

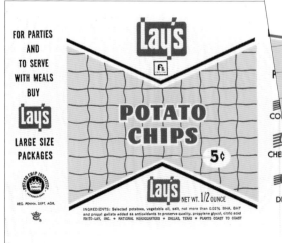

In 1961, Lay's® potato chips arrived in Canada.

Lay's® Canadian business grew slowly at first, but in 1992, its merger with Hostess created a Canadian snack food icon. Ironically, at the time, Hostess® potato chips were actually a more popular brand.

The pivotal moment in the history of Lay's® was in 1996. At this time, The Hostess Frito-Lay Company decided to re-launch the Lay's® brand as its flagship potato chip.

In 1997, within eight weeks of the re-launch of Lay's® brand by The Hostess Frito-Lay Company, Lay's® replaced Hostess® as the number one potato chip in Canada, and the rest is history!

Today, Lay's® are still Canadians' favourite potato chip brand.

THE PRODUCT

Lay's® is Canada's favourite potato chip brand and is proud to be made in Canada with four plant locations — Lévis, QC; Taber, AB; Cambridge, ON and Kentville, NS. Two of Lay's® plants recently reached an impressive milestone, each celebrating more than 50 years of service making Lay's® potato chips.

Lay's® top quality is known for being consistently fresh-tasting, crispy and irresistible. Each bag of Lay's® potato chips is made with specially selected potatoes and to the highest quality standards. Lay's® potato chips are made with 100 percent pure sunflower oil and are low in saturated fat and contain zero trans fat.

Available in many delicious flavours, sizes and formats to meet the wide range of consumer snacking needs, Lay's® potato chips offer one-of-a-kind, irresistible great taste.

The brand continues to build on its ongoing commitment to quality products with consumers. Lay's® brand freshness assurance program was launched in 1998 by printing two dates on every bag: "Made Week Of" and "Fresh Until."

Flavour innovation was a focus in 2000 and 2001 when the Lay's® Cheddar and Lay's® Hot BBQ were launched.

The Lay's® Tastes of Canada™ program kicked off in 2003. New flavours were introduced twice a year, each representing a different Canadian region and its unique flavour profile. Tastes of Canada™ flavours include Lay's® Quebec City Four Cheese, Lay's® Wild Stampede BBQ, Lay's® P.E.I. Loaded Baked Potato, Lay's® Toronto College Street Pizza and Lay's® Cape Breton Sea Salt & Pepper. Canadians voted and today Lay's® Sea Salt & Pepper is a permanent Lay's® flavour.

In January 2004, the brand's innovation continued with the launch of Lay's® STAX™ — a great-tasting, stacked chip for on-the-go snacking.

RECENT DEVELOPMENTS
In 2005, Lay's® potato chips made the transition to 100 percent pure sunflower oil, reducing the saturated fat content by 60 percent while keeping the same great taste of Lay's® potato chips. As a result, all of Lay's® flavours are trans fat free and celebrate that Lay's® is made with three simple ingredients: specially selected potatoes, 100 percent pure sunflower oil and just the right amount of seasoning.

In 2006, Lay's® potato chips introduced Lay's® Lightly Salted. The new chips offer the irresistible taste of Lay's® Classic with 50 percent less sodium. Lay's® Lightly Salted joins Baked! Lay's®, and Lay's® Natural — all sensible choices for consumers looking for snacks that are lower in sodium and/or calories. Most importantly, these snacks do not compromise on taste.

Embracing Canada's multicultural diversity through product innovation, Lay's® brand launched its new Asian-Inspired Flavours, Lay's® Wasabi and Lay's® Spicy Curry, in Toronto and Vancouver in 2006. Designed to offer authentic flavours with strong crossover appeal, Lay's® Asian-Inspired flavours received positive reviews from Canadian consumers and media alike.

In 2006, the Lay's® brand adopted the tagline, "Get Your Smile On!™" to communicate the brand essence and reinforce the brand's light, crispy and irresistibly fresh taste.

PROMOTION
Lay's® advertising and promotional activity has evolved in recent years:

Hockey superstar Mark Messier was introduced as the celebrity spokesperson for Lay's® when the "BETCHA Can't Eat Just ONE®" campaign launched in 1996.

Two years later, that irresistible message evolved to include the new freshness claim. Freshness dating creates a competitive point of difference, which is reinforced through the "Viktor" and "Rookie" Canadian TV campaign and out-of-home activity.

Building on consumer excitement for the popular Star Wars franchise, in 1999, a cross-promotion, "Can You Resist?" features Lay's® potato chips.

During the 2001 Super Bowl, Lay's® unveiled the "Battle of the Sexes" and "Hockey Dads" TV spots with Mark Messier appearances. Building on this success, the 2002 Super Bowl was used to launch further Messier ads, "Hot Shot" and "How About" featuring the Lay's® Classic flavour.

Continuing the brand's link to Canada's favourite sport, in 2004 the "Be There to Cheer" World Cup of Hockey promotion featured Lay's® potato chips. Also on-air were the final three Messier TV spots highlighting the Lay's® Ketchup, Lay's® Dill Pickle and Lay's® Quebec City Four Cheese flavours.

To raise consumer awareness of the brand's switch to sunflower oil in 2004, Lay's® reached out to Canadians through radio and newspaper advertisements. This was extended to TV in 2005 with the "Jenny" Super Bowl spot, reinforcing the message that Lay's® are Canada's best tasting potato chips and they are made with 100 percent sunflower oil and contain zero trans fat.

"Get Your Smile On!™" TV and radio spots launched in early 2006 reinforced the idea that Lay's®, made with sunflower oil, are the best potato chips in Canada. This campaign extended into flavour messaging through the Super Bowl ads supporting the Lay's® Ketchup and Lay's® Dill, as well as Lay's® Wasabi and Lay's® Spicy Curry.

Lay's® is also proud to celebrate the relationships it has with promotional partners such as the Canadian Football League (CFL), the Toronto Maple Leafs, the Montreal Canadians, Hockey Canada and the Hockey Hall of Fame — exciting partnerships that allow one-of-a-kind consumer promotions to come to life.

BRAND VALUES
To potato chip lovers, Lay's® is the brand of potato chips that lets you experience simple joy because of its light, crispy and irresistibly fresh taste. The essence of the brand can be captured in one statement, "Lay's® makes everyday moments a little more joyful." The Lay's® moment is a real moment, whether it's spending downtime with family, watching the big game on TV or attending a sporting event with your kids.

The brand identity is characterized as "light-hearted, dependable and uncomplicated." These unique values represent the core elements of the Lay's® brand. A high quality product with fresh taste you can count on, Lay's® appeals to consumers of all ages and demographics.

THINGS YOU DIDN'T KNOW ABOUT LAYS®

- It takes about one kilogram of specially selected potatoes to make a bag of Lay's®.
- Lay's® classic potato chips are made from three simple ingredients: specially selected potatoes, sunflower oil and salt.
- Over 3,000 pounds of Lay's® potato chips can be made in one hour.

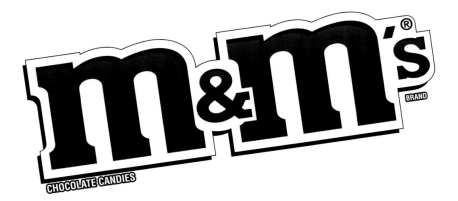

THE MARKET

Canadians love their chocolate. The Canadian chocolate market is $1.3 billion strong, with more than 5 percent compound growth over the last several years. Canadians love their chocolate so much that they consume an average of 5,410 grams annually.* That's the equivalent of everybody eating a chocolate bar every three days. And that's just the tip of the iceberg. The bagged chocolate pieces category has been outpacing the total chocolate market growth for several years. Canadians aren't just buying chocolate for their own consumption; they are buying large-pack chocolate piece candy that they can share with others.

ACHIEVEMENTS

And it's no surprise what brand is leading the pack. The M&M's brand is the largest piece chocolate brand in Canada, with a compounded annual growth rate (42 percent) that outpaces all the top 10 chocolate brands in the country.

The M&M's Brand is sold in more than 100 countries and is the most popular confectionery brand in the world. In North America, retail sales of M&M's candies have topped $1 billion. The famous M&M's spokescandies have been integral to establishing the M&M's Brand as one of the greatest product icons ever. In fact, *Advertising Week* in New York recently crowned M&M's North America's favourite product icons and slogans of all time.

The M&M's Brand has maintained its leadership in the category through an unwavering commitment to making the essence of "colourful chocolate fun" fresh and relevant to its millions of loyal and new consumers.

HISTORY

M&M's Chocolate Candies started in one man's kitchen and grew into an international brand. As the story goes, Forrest Mars Sr. was visiting Spain during the Spanish Civil War and encountered soldiers who were eating pellets of chocolate in a hard, sugary coating which kept the chocolate from melting. Inspired by the idea, Mr. Mars went back to his kitchen in America and invented the recipe for M&M's Plain Chocolate Candies. They were introduced in 1941 and immediately became part of American GI's rations during World War II.

During the 1950s, M&M's Chocolate Candies quickly became a North American household staple, with the help of the now famous advertising slogan "The Milk Chocolate Melts in Your Mouth — Not in Your Hand."

In the 1980s, M&M's Chocolate Candies broadened their horizons by becoming part of the American space program. In 1984, M&M's Candies made their first trip on the space shuttle and have been part of shuttle missions ever since.

Aside from venturing into space, M&M's Chocolate Candies also began establishing an international presence, sponsoring the 1984 Olympic Games in Los Angeles.

As the twentieth century came to an end, the M&M's Brand characters proclaimed themselves the official candy of the new millennium.

THE PRODUCT

M&M's Chocolate Candies are a unique blend of the highest quality milk chocolate with a flavour that is not too sweet or satiating. Individual candies are covered with a thin, crisp, colourful sugar shell that imparts the M&M's Candies texture. The shell colours are bright, shiny and lustrous. The milk chocolate inside and the crisp outside sugar shells provide all the taste; the colour is actually flavourless.

M&M's currently come in five permanent varieties: Milk Chocolate Candies, Peanut Chocolate Candies, Peanut Butter Candies, Almond Chocolate Candies and MINIS Milk Chocolate Candies.

RECENT DEVELOPMENTS

Over the years, M&M's Brand has grown into an icon, while continually adapting to changing times. New developments keep the brand fresh and fun for chocolate lovers.

In Canada, sharing M&M's colourful, chocolate fun is a big part of its success. In 2004, Canada led the North American market by launching M&M's in an innovative Stand up Pouch, making it even easier to share M&M's with a crowd. This step change in the Canadian piece chocolate market yielded 70 percent growth in the first year alone.

Sharing is a big part of every holiday season, and M&M's have helped fuel this sentiment through the seasonal launch of Red and Green Holiday M&M's each Christmas, and the pastel colours of the Easter/Spring special editions.

PROMOTION

The M&M's Brand began its television advertising in 1945, and the M&M's Brand Characters were also introduced that year. Over the decades, Red and Yellow

continued to evolve, eventually becoming one of the most recognized cartoon characters in North America. Green (the first female character) was introduced in 1997, and Orange arrived in 1999.

In 2005, M&M's Brand began an ongoing promotion with the Canadian Breast Cancer Foundation. Special M&M's Chocolate Candies in two shades of pink help further the Foundation's cause; a donation from the sale of the product goes towards the Foundation's goal of realizing a future without breast cancer. Green, the only female character, will act as "spokescandy" for the cause in 2006, which is greatly anticipated by consumers and retail customers across the country.

The characters have also lent their star power to movie promotions. In 2004, *Shrek 2* was celebrated in M&M's "style" with the introduction of swamp-coloured "ogre-sized" M&M's. In 2005, M&M's capitalized on the dark chocolate trend by launching special-edition dark chocolate M&M's in conjunction with the last installment of the Star Wars series, *Revenge of the Sith*. M&M's challenged consumers to "go to the dark side" with the latest variety of M&M's. In 2006, M&M's followed up with the *Pirates of the Carribean* limited edition, with Pirates Gold (yellow Peanut M&M's) and Jack's Gems (Milk Chocolate).

Exciting product news continued in 2006 with the launch of "Mega" M&M's available in Peanut and Milk Chocolate varieties. The new, richer colours are, on average

55 percent bigger in size, delivering against consumers' desire for "Bigger M&M's, Bigger chocolate taste!"

BRAND VALUES

The M&M's Brand has represented superior quality and enjoyment to customers since Mr. Mars developed the brand in 1940. The appeal of M&M's Chocolate Candies is universal, crossing age, gender, national and cultural boundaries, bringing colourful chocolate fun to everyone.

---

* Quote cited from The International Cocoa Organization — 1996.

THINGS YOU DIDN'T KNOW ABOUT M&M'S CHOCOLATE CANDIES

○ The original M&M's Brand colour mix contained brown, yellow, red, orange, green and violet candies.

○ The "M" imprint was not added to M&M's Chocolate Candies until 1950 — in black. Today's white "M" imprint was introduced in 1954.

○ A special machine imprints the "M" onto each M&M's Chocolate Candy. The machine is carefully calibrated so as not to crack the candy shell.

○ Four to eight hours are needed to make an M&M's Chocolate Candy depending on the variety — Milk Chocolate, Peanut, Almond or Peanut Butter.

○ The original M&M's chocolate candies were somewhat larger than today's product and were sold in a tube for five cents.

○ Red M&M's were discontinued in 1960 over a controversy about a specific red food dye that wasn't even used for M&M's. In 1987, Red came back, and is now the spokescandy for the brand.

○ Today more than 400 million M&M's candies are produced each day, totalling more than 146 billion per year!

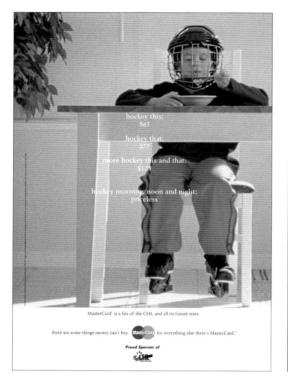

THE MARKET

Question: What's it take to make a lasting brand connection with Canadian consumers in the relentlessly competitive payments category?

- A category in which four big brands compete for more than $74 billion in annual consumer spending . . .
- A category in which a *single share point* in Canada is bigger than the *entire* toothpaste category, the *entire* soap category, the entire bottled water category and the entire coffee, ice cream, snack, laundry detergent and facial tissue categories combined . . .
- A category in which the major players invest more than $60 million in advertising annually...
- A category in which the global growth opportunity exceeds more than $80 trillion — which is more than twice the size of the combined GDP of all the countries in the G8 . . .

Answer: It takes a campaign that taps into universal human truths — and yet speaks simultaneously to uniquely Canadian passions and pursuits.

It takes a campaign that not only *reflects* popular Canadian culture — but also reframes it.

It takes a campaign that builds buzz. Changes behaviour. Galvanizes key constituencies. And drives measurable results.

A campaign that is relevant and resonant. Meaningful and memorable.

And what do you call a campaign that does *all that?*

Priceless, of course.

ACHIEVEMENTS

The Priceless campaign is one of Canada's — and the world's — most recognized and lauded campaigns.

It has won virtually every creative and effectiveness award in the industry.

In 2005, MasterCard was named to *Marketing Magazine*'s "Marketers That Mattered" list and won "Best of Show" honours at the CAPMA PROMO! Awards.

Globally, Priceless has won Gold EFFIE Awards for effective advertising in the "Payments," the "Sustained Campaign Success" and the "Multinational Campaigns" categories. Not to mention more than a dozen AME International Marketing Effectiveness awards.

On the creative front, the campaign has won Clio awards, ADDY awards, One Show awards, Beacon awards, Cresta awards, Creativity awards, Epica awards, Midas awards, Financial Communications Society awards, a Nikkei Advertising award and a Cannes Lion.

In 2004, Priceless was named to the "Viral Marketing" Hall of Fame and the Financial Communications Society "Slogan" Hall of Fame.

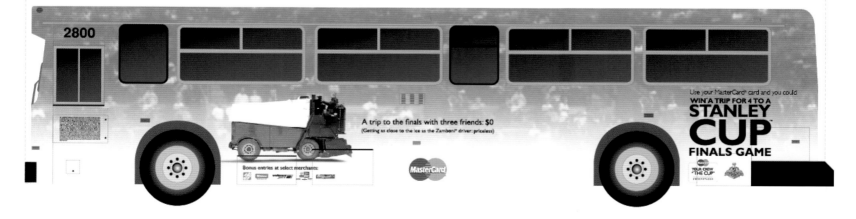

HISTORY

The Priceless campaign was launched during the World Series in the United States in October of 1997.

A year later, the campaign made its international debut, with the launch of the campaign in Canada in April of 1998.

To date, more than 70 Priceless television spots have aired in Canada, many of them created solely for use not only in the English Canadian marketplace but also for the French Canadian marketplace.

Today, the Priceless campaign is not just a landmark Canadian advertising campaign. Priceless is also the world's largest singular campaign, running in 105 markets and 47 different languages globally.

THE PRODUCT

MasterCard serves simultaneously as a trust mark for millions of Canadian consumers — and a payments fulfillment network for many of Canada's largest financial institutions.

In this dual role, MasterCard gives Canadian consumers access to quick and convenient payment at millions of locations in every corner of Canada. In fact, today there are more MasterCard credit cards in Canadian wallets than any other credit card.

What's more, MasterCard's expertise extends far beyond credit cards. MasterCard is a full-service payments brand — leading the way in the

online; to point of sale; to bus wraps; to restaurant tent cards; to credit card statements; to inserts; to Zamboni t-shirts, Zamboni hats, Zamboni NHL arena events and an integrated Zamboni promotional offering.

PROMOTION

MasterCard recently walked away with the highest honors at the 2005 CAPMA PROMO! Awards — the industry's premier showcase for promotional effectiveness.

MasterCard's "We're At Your Service" Holiday Shopping Experience Program won gold for the "Best Activity Generating Brand Awareness & Trial Recruitment" category; gold for the "Best Brand-Building Campaign" category; gold for the "Best Event Marketing Campaign" category and gold for "Best In Show."

The program leveraged MasterCard's partnership with more than 40 shopping malls across Canada, offering shoppers who used their MasterCard cards free services such as coatcheck, gift-wrapping, and mall porters. The program was, of course, supported with integrated Priceless communications.

BRAND VALUES

MasterCard has a unique understanding of what is truly valuable and meaningful to today's consumers.

In a major cultural shift that's taken place over the course of the last two decades, consumers across Canada have altered their collective definition of what signifies "success" in life.

Twenty years ago, success was signified by *material goods* (a fancy car, designer clothes, etc.). Today, *meaningful experiences* (quality time with loved ones, a sense of control in life) are the new symbols of success.

Because MasterCard understands this, it has become the brand's mission to provide Canadian consumers with access to "what truly matters" in life.

So whether it is an airline ticket to Alberta to visit your best buddy from university or a tank of gas for the trip to the cottage with your husband, the kids and the new puppy or a simple cup of coffee on the way to the first hockey practice of the season — MasterCard will be there for Canadians with the payment solutions that lead to priceless moments.

a future in hockey:

a future in hockey: priceless

industry with innovations such as contact-less payments and CHIP technology.

RECENT DEVELOPMENTS

Most recently, MasterCard Canada has taken marketing communication integration to new levels with the launch of the "I Wanna Drive The Zamboni" campaign. This program consists of a series of engaging, slightly offbeat and very Canadian TV spots that launched in MasterCard's NHL partner programming for the '05-'06 season.

The "Zamboni" theme is further extended with integrated communications that span everything from

THINGS YOU DIDN'T KNOW ABOUT MASTERCARD CANADA

○ With nearly 400 commercials since 1997, Priceless has gone on to become one of the most beloved, most lauded and most effective campaigns in the world.

○ Grammy Award winning musicians Wyclef Jean, Frank Sinatra and Paul Simon have all been featured in a MasterCard television spot.

○ Mastercard advertising campaigns have included the FIFA World Cup, the Stanley Cup and the Memorial Cup.

○ Homer Simpson, Miss Piggy and Kermit the Frog have all appeared in MasterCard ads.

A better way forward

THE MARKET

Michelin's tires are recognized for their quality, durability, reliability and performance.

Michelin North America (Canada) Inc. began production for the North American market in 1971 in Nova Scotia's Pictou County, followed by Bridgewater (1971) and Waterville (1982), Nova Scotia. Today, the company's Canadian operations also include the sales and marketing division in Laval, Quebec.

Michelin employs about 3,500 people across Nova Scotia alone. It is the third largest private-sector employer in the province, and with exports second only to that of the oil and gas industry. In fact, 75 percent of Michelin's manufactured products in Nova Scotia are exported.

The company manufactures tires for every type of vehicle, including airplanes, automobiles, bicycles, earthmovers, farm equipment, heavy-duty trucks and the space shuttle. It also publishes travel guides, maps and atlases in Canada and throughout the world.

ACHIEVEMENTS

Michelin is committed to protecting the environment, saving raw materials and energy, reducing emissions into the air and water, reducing vehicle fuel consumption, increasing tire life, reducing waste and devising new solutions for recycling. Michelin applies its Environmental Quality System at all stages in the life of the tire (design, material choice, manufacturing, use and enhancing its recycling potential). As far back as 1946, the quantity of raw materials required to make a tire was cut by 30 percent when Michelin invented the radial tire. Progress has been continuous ever since.

While rolling on the road, a tire has an internal rolling resistance and is, consequently, one of the factors contributing to the fuel consumption of the vehicle. To reduce fuel consumption, Michelin has explored new frontiers both in the fields of material and architecture. The recently developed "green" tire technology lowers rolling resistance by 20 percent and brings substantial reductions in fuel consumption. The energy saved will be almost the equivalent of the energy required to manufacture all the tires on the vehicle.

On a more competitive note, the J.D. Power and Associates 2005 Original Equipment Tire Customer Satisfaction Study shows that Michelin topped the rankings in the luxury/sport tire, mass-market/non-luxury tire, pickup/full-size van tire and SUV tire ratings. Consumers continue to voice their appreciation and support for the technology, quality, performance and value of Michelin's

product lines. These latest awards bring Michelin's total to 45 for J.D. Power and Associates Original Equipment and Replacement Tire Awards in North America, more than doubling the combined total of all other competitors.

In 2005, Michelin was triumphant in the three most prestigious motorsports championships, securing world titles with its partners in Formula One, the World Rally Championship and the MotoGP World Championship. Michelin today has a strong presence in most disciplines thanks to the development of products which set the technical standard for the world in the Competition field. At Michelin, the race doesn't end at the finish line; it ends on the production line. The company's goal is to take what's learned on the track and put it to use developing world-class performance tires for the cars people drive every day.

HISTORY

The Michelin story begins in Clermont-Ferrand, in the Auvergne region, at the end of the 19th century. In 1886, brothers André and Édouard Michelin were called in to help rescue the family business, then in dire straits. In 1889, "Michelin & Cie" was established. In 1891, a detachable bicycle tire was patented by Michelin. Repairs took just a few minutes, instead of the three-hour repairing and overnight drying time usually

required. In 1895, Michelin equipped the very first motor car to use pneumatic tires: *L'Éclair*. A year later, the first cars with pneumatic tires were marketed. Michelin set out to perfect a tire that would absorb the shocks, making it more suitable for motor cars. The company knew it was on the right track when their car, *L'Éclair*, with pneumatic tires won the Paris-Bordeaux-Paris race in 1895. This was when André Michelin confidently predicted, "In 10 years, all motor cars will be fitted with pneumatic tires." In five years, his prediction had come true.

THE PRODUCT

Michelin boasts a diverse and plentiful product line. Since its very existence, Michelin has never been just a tire company. The company continues to lead the industry by constantly expanding horizons with the latest in technology in a variety of products. Here are just a few examples that show innovation is a part of the Michelin culture.

Michelin Maps and Guides®. The company's reputable line of maps and guides has been a part of its travel assistance mission for more than 100

years. Michelin offers a complete range of products and services to make traveling easier, such as maps, atlases, travel guides and hotel and restaurant guides. Michelin publishes more than 650 publications. Nearly 20 million maps, plans and atlases are sold every year in more than 90 countries.

Michelin® Pilot® series. The right tire can make a world of difference when it comes to a vehicle's handling and performance. That's why Michelin engineers often work side by side with

automotive development teams to create original equipment tires that are customized for specific vehicles. Michelin Pilot series performance tires utilize cutting-edge technology — from specialized rubber compounds to computer-optimized tread patterns — to harness the full potential of a high-performance car. They deliver extreme grip, stability and reliability. But, most importantly, Michelin Pilot tires deliver the confidence a driver needs to experience the ultimate in performance — and the sheer exhilaration of driving.

Michelin® HydroEdge®. For drivers who demand only the best, Michelin is proud of its premier passenger car and minivan tire — the HydroEdge®. The Michelin® HydroEdge® tire excels in many performance categories, scoring top marks in wet traction, maximum tread life and quiet ride, while delivering outstanding hydroplaning resistance, exceptional everyday handling and the sleek "look" of a sporty, high-performance tire.

Michelin® X-Ice™. The Michelin® X-Ice™ features a new generation of winter rubber compounds that help deliver predictable grip and performance in challenging winter driving conditions without compromising tread life. Designed specifically for passenger cars and minivans, the Michelin Latitude X-Ice also features Cross Z-Sipes Technology (CZST) to help bite through snow and ice.

Michelin® X-One™. The Michelin® X-One™ wide single tire line is a revolution in truck tire design, delivering significant fuel and weight savings to trucking fleets in North America and Europe. Michelin® X-One™ tires replace dual tires with one wide single tire, converting 18 wheel tractor-trailer rigs to 10 wheelers. When used in both drive and trailer positions, X-One™ tires can save 4 to 10 percent in fuel costs and increase payloads from 800 to 1,300 pounds.

RECENT DEVELOPMENTS

Michelin Airless™ and Michelin Tweel™: Tires without air

Michelin Airless enables vehicles to run safely and comfortably because its elastic characteristics are controlled longitudinally, transversally and vertically. A car doesn't have to stop even if one or more of the radial bands break or become damaged. The Michelin Airless is being tested on passenger cars and motorcycles, but could be fitted to other vehicles as well.

Michelin Tweel is the fusion of the tire and the wheel with the potential to transform mobility. Available now for lower-speed, lower-weight-carrying vehicles, Tweel is in the prototype stage for passenger car applications. Tweel delivers the benefits of pneumatic radial tire performance while dramatically increasing lateral stiffness, which affects handling, cornering and responsiveness. Additionally, Tweel has suspension-like characteristics that can simplify, and in some applications eliminate, the need for a separate vehicle suspension.

PROMOTION

Bibendum — the "Michelin Man"— embodies Michelin's visionary spirit for Better Mobility. Bibendum is the symbol of the Michelin brand and has been its standard-bearer all over the world since 1898. His enduring popularity, his presence among his audience and the spirit that has always been his driving force led him to be voted the Century's Best Symbol in 2000 (panel convened by the *Financial Times*).

BRAND VALUES

Making a contribution to progress in terms of mobility through all modes of transport is now more than ever at the very heart of its corporate strategy. Michelin's mission goes far beyond that of a tire manufacturer: Michelin is a key player in the progress of the automotive and transport industry. In other words, it sees its mission today in the following terms: Contribute to improving the sustainable mobility of goods and people by facilitating the freedom, safety, efficiency and enjoyment of travel.

THINGS YOU DIDN'T KNOW ABOUT MICHELIN

○ The green tire enables 0.26 liters of gasoline to be saved (1) per 100 km, which means approximately 35 liters of fuel per year.

○ If every car in the world was equipped with green tires, nearly 19 billion litres of gasoline would be saved per year.

○ Michelin Canada produces more than 300 different tires in Nova Scotia.

○ Michelin Canada anticipates production of its 200 millionth tire early in 2007.

MOEN

Buy it for looks. Buy it for life.®

THE MARKET

In recent years, the plumbing industry has become a major player in home design and manufacturers have responded by creating new products to meet the changing needs of consumers. New styles, functions and innovations are leading home owners to replace faucets not because they have worn out, but because something new on the market promises to make their homes more distinctive and more comfortable. In this increasingly diversified and competitive marketplace, Moen is the established Canadian leader in the wholesale and retail markets.

ACHIEVEMENTS

More Canadians choose Moen faucets for new home construction, renovation, repair and replacement than any other brand. Moen understands that design is a critical element in the home and is trusted by homeowners for producing collections of premium bath and kitchen faucets that combine distinctive style and function with durable craftsmanship and innovation.

Moen's industry partners have also shown appreciation for Moen's style and innovation. The company has earned several Partner of the Year, Prestigious Partner, Award of Merit and Supplier of the Year awards from the likes of The Home Depot, RONA, Canadian Tire and Reno Depot. Moen's ongoing support of local charitable organizations resulted in the company's selection as United Way of Oakville's Corporation of the Year, and the company is a major sponsor of Habitat for

Humanity through the Canadian Institute of Plumbing and Heating. Moen has also earned a number of high profile North American industry awards. Most recently, the Vivid™ powder room faucet from ShowHouse™ by Moen was selected as a top trend for 2006 by the Kitchen/Bath Industry Show, and *Business Week* magazine recognized Moen's Revolution Showerhead with a Design Research Gold Award in the 2005 Industrial Design Excellence Awards.

HISTORY

In 1937, Al Moen changed the course of plumbing history — literally by accident. One day while trying to wash his hands with a conventional, two-handle faucet, he scalded them under the hot water. This incident led him to invent the world's first single-handle mixing faucet.

Although many plumbing equipment manufacturers appeared uninterested, Al Moen convinced Ravenna Metal Products of Seattle to produce his design. Soon afterward, the first single-handle mixing faucet was sold in San Francisco, retailing for approximately $12. Production at that time was about 5,000 faucets per year. But with its growing popularity, the single-handle faucet caught the attention of Standard Screw of Chicago, which was looking for a major new product line and which purchased Ravenna Metal products.

The rest of the story is plumbing history, and over the years, the Moen brand has remained synonymous with innovation and design and many other plumbing firsts.

Today, homeowners value Moen's product features that make every day tasks a little easier,

including a patented, one-piece washerless cartridge, LifeShine® finishes, pressure-balancing shower valves, the industry's only fingertip-controlled pause button and several filtering faucet options — ChoiceFlo™, AquaSuite® and Pure-Touch®, the patented Hydrolock™ installation system and M•PACT® common valve architecture.

THE PRODUCT

Moen offers residential and commercial faucets, and showering products in a wide assortment of styles and finishes. The company also offers coordinating bathroom accessories and plumbing repair parts. All Moen faucets feature a one-piece, washerless cartridge design that has fewer parts than competitive faucets, which means fewer things can go wrong.

Today's faucets go beyond functionality to be truly distinctive design elements for the home. Moen products provide complete coordination of faucets and accessories in the kitchen and bath. A wide range of faucet styles and finishes allow consumers to coordinate their faucets with their décor, such as dramatic high-arc kitchen faucets in stainless finishes to match appliances. Moen also offers innovative Old World finishes such as oil-rubbed bronze, pewter, antique nickel and wrought iron to create an authentic vintage look.

Moen increased functionality in the kitchen with innovations such as pullout and pull-down faucets. Each Moen faucet brings its own unique design, from traditional Colonnade® to clean,

modern Camerist™. The added convenience of a fingertip-controlled pause button on Moen's high-arc, pull-down Aberdeen™ faucet allows the user to interrupt the flow of water — like a second on-off button in your hand.

In the bathroom, Moen offers coordinating suites of faucets, showering products and accessories. There is a Moen design to suit every homeowner's personal style, ranging from the sleek and sophisticated Eva™ and Icon™ collections, to the classic looks of the Kingsley™ and Castleby™ lines. A wide variety of Moen's bathroom faucets feature M•PACT valve architecture — a ground-breaking common valve design that means changing out a faucet takes just a few stress-free minutes. Simply unscrew the handles and spout, lift them out and replace them with the new style.

In the shower, Moen offers customized options and protection against scalding with Posi-Temp®, Moentrol® and ExactTemp® valves. In particular, the ExactTemp valve features precision thermostatic control that allows consumers to dial up and maintain a consistent shower temperature day after day.

Moen research identified consumers' desire for luxury bath options, which led to the creation of the vertical spa experience. This customizable showering system offers the choice of valving, body sprays, showerheads, hand showers and tub spouts. Unlike other systems on the market, Moen's vertical spa features both half-inch and three-quarter-inch piping that allows homeowners to create the ultimate custom shower experience.

Durability is of utmost importance for homeowners. In the past, chrome was the only finish

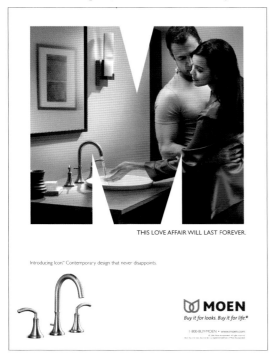

THIS LOVE AFFAIR WILL LAST FOREVER.

Introducing Icon™ Contemporary design that never disappoints.

MOEN
Buy it for looks. Buy it for life®

1 800 BUY MOEN • www.moen.com

that could truly be called long lasting, but Moen's LifeShine technology protects a wide selection of other finishes — including copper, stainless, brushed nickel and others — from tarnishing, flaking and corrosion.

Moen's product innovations also extend to water filtration. Responding to consumer concerns regarding the quality of drinking water, Moen introduced the first filtering faucet, the PureTouch, to provide better tasting water with reduced lead, chlorine and harmful cysts. The PureTouch line includes the pullout and fixed-spout faucets and the PureTouch AquaSuite® filtered water

dispenser, which provides an under-counter filter with a designer spout that installs next to the existing faucet in the kitchen or bath.

RECENT DEVELOPMENTS

For homeowners with discriminating tastes, Moen launched the ShowHouse by Moen brand offering high-end, luxury faucets and accessories for the kitchen, bath and powder room. Available in plumbing boutiques and showrooms across Canada, ShowHouse products blend cutting-edge designs and finishes with Moen quality and durability.

ShowHouse kitchen designs range from the clean, modern lines of Woodmere™, Felicity™ and Savvy™ to the more traditional Waterhill™ bridge faucet. Each collection offers select additional conveniences such as pause buttons, single-hole mounts, reversible taps, matching bar faucets and a wide selection of popular finishes.

In the bath and powder room, ShowHouse offers several distinct collections. Designs include the nature-inspired look of Bamboo™ and Organic™, the old Hollywood glamour of Très Chic™ and the rustic country style of Mannerly™, among others. Each collection features coordinating accessories. For the bath, a variety of showering, vertical spa and Roman Tub options are also available.

Moen's patented Immersion™ Rainshower Technology reinvented today's most popular style of showerhead to create a truly powerful, rain-drenched showering experience. Unlike other models currently available, Moen's design features self-pressurizing technology and precisely engineered, individual spray channels. These channels, when combined with the specific number and size of the spray nozzles, provide increased force, superior flow and optimized coverage. An added benefit of the self-pressurizing design is that it relies on its own internal pressure and is less susceptible to low home water pressure.

Moen's expertise in filtering faucets spilled over into the new ChoiceFlo™ filtration system that supplies both filtered and non-filtered water from individual channels on a single spout. Available on popular Moen kitchen faucet styles, ChoiceFlo's under-the-sink carbon filter combines contaminant reduction, superior flow rate and filter life to offer homeowners improved filtration value in the kitchen.

In 2006, Moen introduced the industry's first-ever hot-cold outdoor sill faucet, eliminating the need to go indoors to fetch hot water to fill the kids' wading pool, wash up after gardening or give the family dog a bath.

PROMOTION

Not only is Moen the number one brand of faucets sold in Canada, Moen also ranks first in consumer unaided awareness and intent to purchase. A combination of national television and magazine advertising targeted to the home enthusiast and DIY supports and promotes the strong image. Moen

also provides informative product packaging and point-of-sale displays, as well as an aggressive public relations campaign to keep its products and brand foremost in the minds of consumers.

Moen's Web site, www.moen.ca, provides visitors with helpful product and design trends information, a virtual design centre, a virtual showering experience and a convenient local retailer/wholesaler locator.

BRAND VALUES

"Buy it for looks . . . Buy it for life" says it all. Moen's tagline is the epitome of what consumers want — and expect — when they choose faucets, sinks, showering products and bath accessories. People know that Moen is synonymous with great looking and long lasting plumbing products. Moen's lifetime warranty guarantees that the company will replace any part for the life of the product.

THINGS YOU DIDN'T KNOW ABOUT MOEN

○ Before he retired in January 1982, Al Moen had acquired more than 75 patents, some of them in fields totally unrelated to plumbing.

○ The Moen single-handle faucet was chosen by the world's leading designers as one of the 100 best designed, mass produced products, ranking above Henry Ford's Model T and Ben Franklin's stove.

○ Al Moen only wanted the title "Inventor" on his business cards.

○ Moen's M•PACT valve system was one of the first in the industry to offer the ability to change out the trim from above the sink and in front of the shower wall.

THE MARKET

When Monster invented online recruiting in 1994, its founder knew the company was onto something big.

Having worked in a recruitment advertising agency, he saw the pain IT clients faced during the time it took to find qualified staff. He also knew how important it was for people to find the right job — not just in terms of salary and financial security, but also in the sense of pride and accomplishment it provided.

More importantly, if companies were challenged finding qualified candidates during the dot-com boom of the '90s, what would happen when baby boomers would begin to retire in 2008 and in their

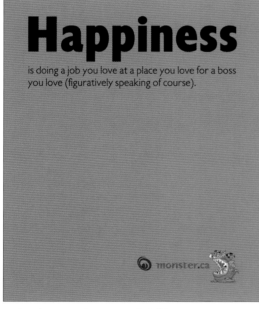

wake, leave a shortage of skilled workers across all industries.

Further, with the balance of power shifting from employers to qualified candidates, how would organizations compete for skilled labour and convince workers that switching to their companies represents the best possible choice and smartest career move?

Monster recognized early on that connecting employers with the right candidates in innovative, new ways was critically important and that the Web presented unique opportunities not possible with traditional, help-wanted newspaper advertising.

Monster also predicted that the Web would one day become the preferred source for finding a new job. And in 2005, the Internet did become

the first stop for job-hunters — surpassing both word-of-mouth referrals and newspaper advertising in Canada.

ACHIEVEMENTS

Since its modest beginnings as a simple online job board, Monster has become the world's largest career Web site and online recruitment partner with tailored language sites in 24 countries. Over 200,000 companies have posted jobs and 61 million job seekers have searched for jobs on the company's worldwide Web sites since its inception.

In Canada, Monster has also earned top ranking, boasting the highest consumer brand recognition, monthly visitors, job seeker resumes and overall growth. Moreover, of the 25 million Canadians that have Internet access, 74 percent have used Monster's Web site.

Job seekers turn to Monster.ca as much for the sheer volume of Canadian job opportunities that are advertised each month as they do for the exceptional speed and ease-of-use with which they can apply for jobs online. They can also conveniently add their profile information and resumes to a searchable, online database that can be accessed by employers and recruiters, and stay up to date via automatic e-mail alerts that notify them when a new job matching their interests is added to the Web site. The Canadian site also contains a wealth of employment-related articles, career tips and resume writing services in both English and French.

With a solid background in traditional recruitment and having invented its online counterpart, Monster has also extended equally important benefits to employers. In addition to enabling employers to get their job opportunities in front of a critical mass of job seekers 24/7, the company's B2B solutions streamline many time-consuming recruitment activities. This includes screening and comparing resumes to determine the

most qualified candidates, automating correspondence with applicants and co-workers, and writing compelling job descriptions and corporate profile pages that entice job seekers to apply.

Since opening its doors to the Canadian market, Monster has helped more than 11,000 Canadian companies to reduce their time- and cost-to-hire and fill their talent supply chain. Some of the country's biggest brands have chosen Monster Canada as their strategic, online recruitment partner, including CIBC, McDonalds, 3M, Future Shop, Deloitte, IBM, Rona and FedEx.

By bringing the reach and immediacy of the Web to recruiting, Monster has empowered both employers and job seekers alike.

HISTORY

- **1994:** Monster launches the world's first online job board in the U.S.
- **1997:** Monster opens its first international operation in Canada with a Web site in English and French. Monster Canada becomes the model for all future international markets. Later that year, Monster is acquired by TMP Worldwide.
- **1998:** As a result of further strategic acquisitions, TMP becomes one of the largest recruitment agencies in the world.

- **1999:** Monster becomes the first online recruitment brand to advertise on television with its "When I Grow Up" campaign. It is the only commercial included in *Time* magazine's list of "Best Television in 1999."
- **2000-2004:** Monster Canada becomes a strategic career partner for the Canadian Olympics Committee and sponsors the 2000, 2002 and 2004 Olympic Games in Sydney, Salt Lake City and Athens.
- **2004:** Monster acquires Tickle.com.
- **2005:** Monster becomes the number-one online recruitment Web site in Canada with the highest consumer awareness, monthly visitors and overall growth (Ipsos Reid).
- **2006:** Monster introduces the first national index to measure online employment demand in Canada.

THE PRODUCT

Monster's long-standing recruitment heritage, combined with its unique consultative approach and technology expertise, has enabled the company to develop sophisticated solutions that can be tailored to each customer's needs and used to streamline many time-consuming, recruitment tasks.

More than 12 years of industry best practices have been integrated into Monster's products and services — from online job postings and resume database access to developing and hosting a career Web site for its customers that leverages the same advanced functionality of Monster's own Web site — to ensure employers get maximum results from their online recruitment campaign.

Consultants are also available to train recruiters and HR staff on how to effectively use Monster's

online tools and reach the most qualified candidates as quickly as possible. Customers can also choose to outsource a wide variety of online recruitment tasks to Monster's consultants in order to reduce their time- and cost-to-hire. In either case, customers are provided with a performance report at the end of their campaign,

along with recommendations for how to improve their future recruiting efforts.

RECENT DEVELOPMENTS

In January 2006, Monster Canada demonstrated its thought leadership with the introduction of Monster Employment Index Canada — the first national index to measure online employment demand in Canada. Building on its tremendous success in the U.S. and Europe, the index measures online job demand by indexing the volume of advertised jobs. These include newly created and unfilled jobs in Canada, as reflected in the number of help-wanted ads that are posted online each month.

For the first time labour market watchers, financial analysts and government agencies could tap into forward-looking trends based on real-time data when evaluating the health of the Canadian economy and developing employment-related policies, such as which industries to invest in and which require additional workforce training.

Making insights into employment demand available to key stakeholders at no charge was yet another example of Monster Canada's ongoing commitment to bringing Canadian employers and job seekers together.

PROMOTION

In 2005, Monster Canada did more than just launch its most successful marketing campaign in its history. It touched a nerve with Canadians and generated the kind of buzz most U.S. companies only dream about.

A survey the company conducted early in the year revealed that the relationship Canadians have with their boss is the most important criteria for evaluating their level of job satisfaction. Monster responded by releasing a viral email campaign asking people to rate their bosses.

The online poll generated more than 100,000 responses and one clear message: Canadian bosses

are halfway to perfection. The key areas for improvement included "acknowledging their mistakes," "being a born leader" and "helping employees reach their full potential." Building on this theme, Monster developed two TV campaigns and a series of newspaper ads that reinforced the importance of having a great boss with the slogan: "A great boss makes all the difference. Find yours today at Monster.ca."

The campaign demonstrated that Monster's brand is built upon listening to the needs of the marketplace and responding to the issues that are of utmost importance to Canadians.

BRAND VALUES

Monster strives to be the world's most valued career partner, both to workers and employers. The company is deeply committed to exceeding customer expectations and has succeeded in doing so for more than 12 years by continuously challenging the status quo, reinventing the way it does business and delivering on what it says it will do. In Canada, Monster will continue to innovate in its effort to bring Canadians together to advance their lives — while setting an example and remaining an inspiration for its worldwide operations.

THINGS YOU DIDN'T KNOW ABOUT MONSTER

○ The idea to recruit employees online was conceived in a dream after Monster's founder was challenged by a client to come up with a "monster of an idea" for finding qualified IT staff.

○ "Trumpasaurus" is the name of the company's memorable green and purple mascot.

○ Monster was the 454th commercial Web site in the world.

○ Monster.com was the 17th-most visited property on the Internet in 2005.

○ Canada is Monster's fastest-growing international market.

Your Pet, Our Passion.®

THE MARKET

Cats are mischievous, reserved and dignified. Their air of independent sophistication makes them seem aloof, but every cat lover knows just how deep and glorious a cat's love can be.

Dogs are the friends we can only aspire to be. They always run to greet us; they always patiently wait for us to return. And they always love us unconditionally.

Each year, more Canadians invite cats and dogs in their homes. About six out of ten households in Canada now include an animal companion. There are more than 12.7 million pets in Canada: 8 million cats and 4.7 million dogs. The number of both cats and dogs has seen double-digit growth since 1992. And the pet product industry has kept pace with this growing population: we spend about $1.2 billion on our animal friends each year — more than we spend on other consumer packaged-goods categories such as soda, snacks, baby food and wine.

In a frantic, impersonal world, our pets have become increasingly important in our lives.

Given this profound connection, we increasingly demand the best when it comes to feeding these important family members.

Purina understands and celebrates the loving bond between people and their pets and makes it the inspiration behind every Purina product. As a result, only high-quality ingredients and tasty, flavourful and nourishing formulas

are included in Purina's family of brands. Always building on its history of excellence, Purina is a market leader.

ACHIEVEMENTS

Purina has established its reputation as a leader in the pet food market through a long term commitment to excellence, innovation and research.

Helping dogs and cats live long, healthy lives is Purina's first priority.

Purina was the first pet food company to conduct a lifelong study on dogs. The Purina Life Span Study found that feeding dogs to maintain ideal body weight could help delay the visible signs of aging and extend life by up to 15 percent — nearly two years for the Labrador Retrievers in this study. The company also developed a weight-management tracking tool for veterinarians and created dog foods with high protein levels to maintain lean body mass for dogs on a weight loss program.

In the field of cat nutrition, Purina was the first pet food company to offer formulas to help control hairballs, increase nutrient absorption and manage feline diabetes. Purina also launched both dry and wet cat foods to help maintain urinary tract health.

HISTORY

The history of Purina is filled with twists and turns and an occasional fork in the road. The one thread running through the company's

ongoing evolution is the ability to adapt to changing circumstances.

In 1894, William Danforth helped found Purina as a storefront that sold feed in St. Louis, Missouri. With a growing supply of high quality grain products, Danforth's company expanded its reach, selling a whole-wheat breakfast cereal to St. Louis grocers under the Purina brand. The company slogan "where Purity is paramount" was an inspiration for quality nutrition.

A well-known Dr. Ralston then entered the scene and by 1902, added his good name to the company's enterprises. The Ralston Purina name served the company through the World Wars, the Great Depression, technological changes and its evolution into a company focused on pet care products.

In Canada, Purina's agricultural feed production began in 1928. By the 1960s, Purina opened a new cereal manufacturing plant. Soon after, when the potential of the pet food market emerged, Purina's factories in Canada began making dry dog and cat food.

In 2001, Nestlé S.A. acquired Ralston Purina and merged Nestlé's Friskies PetCare business with Ralston Purina to produce a pet food giant on the global scene. Nestlé's portfolio of wet products, such as FANCY FEAST® and FRISKIES® brand cat foods, complemented Ralston Purina's portfolio of dry and semi-moist products, including DOG CHOW® and PRO PLAN® brand pet foods. It was a marriage that made the resulting Purina company a true one-stop shop, with a full array of dog and cat foods, and products for discerning pet lovers.

THE PRODUCT

After more than a century in the pet food business, Purina is an expert in the field of dog and cat nutrition. The company works closely with breeders and veterinarians and does its own extensive research to make sure that the company and brands it represents, continue to provide dogs and cats with the proper balance of nutrients and taste.

Today, the Purina portfolio of products consists of over 20 brands, appealing to the varied needs of consumers and pets across the country. Most widely recognized are the PRO PLAN®, PURINA ONE®, FANCY FEAST®, FRISKIES®, DOG CHOW® and CAT CHOW® brands of dog and cat foods. Purina is also a leader in the cat box filler category with MAXX® and KITTY LITTER® brands.

The highly successful BENEFUL® brand of dog food is also part of the Purina family of products. BENEFUL, introduced to the Canadian market through the BENEFUL dry dog food products, recently added a wet dog food to its lineup. BENEFUL Prepared Meals™ has made a major impact in the pet food market in both the U.S. and Canada. In this case, product innovation and packaging innovation have created a winner in the Purina brand stable: BENEFUL Prepared Meals™ offers real ingredients you can see in clear, resealable packaging to help maintain freshness.

RECENT DEVELOPMENTS

While nutrition is important in the lives of dogs and cats, Purina understands that it is just one part of raising a healthy, happy pet. Which is why Purina is always looking for ways to help owners with pet health, behaviour and care.

Bringing home a new puppy or kitten can be exciting and overwhelming. There is much to learn and much to do. Recently, Purina launched the mypuppy.ca and mykitten.ca Web sites. With its focus on overall pet care, the puppy and kitten sites help in every stage of puppy and kitten ownership: thinking, preparing, choosing and raising a new pet. Topics range from "Are You Ready" and "First Year Puppy Costs" to "Litter Box Training" and "Teaching Your Kitten Tricks."

For dogs and cats of all ages, Purina developed the Pet Priority program. By joining Pet Priority, pet owners receive emails and newsletters featuring exclusive offers, helpful hints and expert advice, catered specifically to the life stage of their dog or cat.

PROMOTION

People who love pets love knowing that they can change their pet's health for the better. The relaunch of PURINA ONE® in 2004 was a perfect opportunity to invite dog and cat owners to use the product for 30 days. The premise: in just a few weeks they should see a difference in the health of their pets: healthy-looking skin, a shiny coat and clean teeth. It worked — and the PURINA ONE® 30 Day Performance Challenge was born.

The PURINA ONE® 30 Day Performance Challenge uses a multi-media approach to capture the attention of pet owners across the country. Pet-owning radio personalities take the challenge with their own pets, highlighting results on their radio programs. Television, print ads and a redesigned Web site demonstrate the benefits of PURINA ONE® to both dogs' and cats' health. Direct Mail samples entice consumers to pick up a bag on their next store visit, where in-store displays greet them. The campaign continues to be a very successful and visible endorsement of Purina's commitment to the health and happiness of pets throughout North America.

BRAND VALUES

The PURINA® brand name has long been associated with trust, excellent quality and good value. Consumers consider Purina to be a "family member" and feel that Purina, more than other pet food manufacturers, understands that there is more to being a pet owner than feeding.

Purina rates higher amongst their consumers than do Kraft, Pepsi, Coca-Cola, McDonald's and Bell Canada, due in part to quality of products and services, history, credibility and innovation.

In a company where employees are encouraged to bring their four-legged friends to work, enriching the quality of pet lives is paramount and passion is celebrated. It's a company culture that inspires both its employees and its customers. It's no wonder that Purina has so many loyal consumers and continues to be the brand of choice for pet lovers across the country.

THINGS YOU DIDN'T KNOW ABOUT PURINA

○ For over 35 years, Purina has honoured the special role pets play in our lives through the Purina Animal Hall of Fame™. The national awards program — one of the longest-running pet recognition programs in Canada — recognizes pets that have demonstrated exceptional bravery, loyalty and intelligence in saving a human life.

○ William Danforth created the red and white checkerboard Purina logo in memory of a large family he once saw all dressed in red-and-white checked clothes. The material identified the family everywhere they went, and Danforth felt the same pattern would build brand recognition for Purina brand products. He was right!

○ When Admiral Byrd prepared for his expedition to the South Pole, he asked Purina to develop a special formula for his sled dogs. It was so successful that he used Purina's expertise to develop food for two more dog sled expeditions.

global companies that have proven their ability to manage strategic opportunities in new environmental and social markets. RBC was also a part of the Dow Jones Sustainability World Index (sixth consecutive year) and Dow Jones Sustainability North America Index recognizing financial, social and environmental leaders, as well as the Climate Leadership Index.

Based on our 2005 submission to the Carbon Disclosure Project (CDP), RBC was among 60 large companies worldwide recognized as leaders in understanding and addressing a breadth of climate change issues.

In addition, RBC Centura won the North Carolina International Community and Economic Development Award (NC Department of Commerce) in recognition of community impact, executive leadership and commitment, corporate mission statement and values and employee participation.

THE MARKET

Royal Bank of Canada (TSX, NYSE: RY), and its subsidiaries operate under the master brand name of RBC. As measured by assets and market capitalization, RBC is Canada's largest bank and one of North America's leading diversified financial services companies.

RBC provides personal and commercial banking, wealth management services, insurance, corporate and investment banking on a global basis. The corporate support team enables business growth with expert professional advice and state-of-the-art processes and technology. RBC employs approximately 70,000 full and part-time employees who serve more than 14 million personal, business and public sector clients throughout offices in North America and some 30 countries around the world.

ACHIEVEMENTS

In Canada, RBC has strong market positions in all of its businesses. In personal and business banking, it ranks first or second in most retail products. In wealth management, RBC has the leading full-service brokerage operation (by assets), the top mutual fund provider among Canadian banks and the second-largest self-directed broker (by assets).

RBC is the largest Canadian bank-owned insurer, one of the top 10 Canadian life insurance producers and a leader in travel insurance, creditor products and individual disability insurance. In corporate and investment banking, it continues to be the top-ranked securities underwriter and the leading mergers and acquisitions advisor.

RBC was named "Canada's Most Respected Corporation" for 2005 in an annual survey conducted by Ipsos Reid for KPMG. This marked the fourth year in a row the company has received this honour and the sixth time in the past 11 years.

RBC was ranked Canada's Most Valuable Brand in 2004 and 2005 by Brand Finance, a UK-based company. The survey uses publicly available sales, market-share and advertising data to estimate brand royalty rates for each of Canada's largest industry sectors. Market surveys, consumer research and company filings are used to determine the company's brand strength, consumer awareness, retail presence and marketing spending. Brand Finance found the RBC brand to have a value of $4.5 billion.

In 2005, RBC was also the first Canadian bank to be named to the Global 100 Most Sustainable Corporations in the World ranking, recognizing

HISTORY

As early as 1875, the *Halifax Chronicle* saw vast potential in the upstart Merchants' Bank of Halifax (renamed The Royal Bank of Canada in 1901) and publicly noted the bank's impressive ability to remain "always moving, alive and active." Willing to test the outer limits of the Canadian banking consensus, Royal Bank's evolution from a small

regional bank into a national institution is attributed to the strength of its people and to its bold strategies tempered by the required caution.

The history of Royal Bank closely parallels the evolution of Canada from growth to maturity. Whether opening a branch at the "end of steel" in support of emerging communities alongside Canada's fledgling national railway, or aggressively pursuing new e-commerce delivery channels, Royal Bank has always anticipated and responded to the needs of Canadians.

THE PRODUCT

RBC's domestic delivery network includes 1,104 branches and 3,906 automated banking machines, 437 investment retirement planners, 1,063 financial planners, 371 insurance agents and 975 mortgage specialists. Currently, 3.5 million people do business with RBC online, while 2.5 million clients do business over the telephone.

In the United States, RBC provides personal and commercial banking, insurance, full-service brokerage and corporate and investment banking services to about 1.5 million clients through RBC Centura, RBC Insurance, RBC Dain Rauscher and RBC Capital Markets. RBC Dain Rauscher is the eighth-largest full-service brokerage in the United States, based on number of financial consultants. RBC Centura is the 50th-largest bank in the United States, based on assets, and is focused on meeting the personal banking needs of businesses, business owners and professionals.

Internationally, the company has a strong retail banking network in the Caribbean and a

presence in niche markets. In Europe, South America and the Middle East, private banking, international estate planning and wealth management services are tailored for high-net-worth individuals, sophisticated investors and corporate and institutional clients. Investment banking, trading, capital markets and reinsurance are also offered to corporate, institutional and business clients. In a Euromoney survey released in January 2005, the Global Private Banking division ranked as the number one provider of trust services in the United Kingdom and number six worldwide. RBC

also ranked as the number-three private bank in Brazil and number four in the Americas.

In the Asia-Pacific region and Australia, RBC provides corporate and investment banking, trade finance and correspondent banking to corporate clients, reinsurance to institutional and business clients and private banking services to individual clients.

RECENT DEVELOPMENTS

In 2005, RBC Insurance opened its first new concept multi-line insurance outlets located adjacent to RBC Royal Bank branches in Canada, where rules prohibit most types of insurance from being sold in bank branches.

The company also announced the creation of a joint venture, RBC Dexia Investor Services, which ranks among the world's top ten global custodians.

In November 2005, RBC acquired Abacus Financial Services limited, significantly strengthening the Global Private Banking operations in the British Isles marketplace, providing a greater presence in Europe.

In 2005, RBC also expanded in the Americas, by opening representative offices in Porto Alegre, Brazil and San Francisco.

In early 2006, RBC opened a Royal Bank of Canada branch in Beijing, marking the first foreign bank to be located on Financial Street, the hub of Beijing's financial district.

The Carolina Hurricanes won the Stanley Cup for the 2005–2006 National Hockey League season in their home arena, the RBC Center in Raleigh, NC.

PROMOTION

RBC's advertising in all markets expresses the same, important message: it all starts with our clients. This is expressed across Canada with client-focused campaigns — using "First For You" and "Je," in English and French language media, respectively. The US and international market uses similar client-focused positioning in its marketing communications.

BRAND VALUES

RBC is committed to make a lasting social impact through inspired, responsible giving and by building strong partnerships with the charitable sector and communities. RBC has been a strong supporter of amateur athletics, including a relationship with the Canadian Olympic team that spans 59 years. RBC recently renewed it's partnership as a Premiere National Partner of the Vancouver 2010 Olympic and Paralympic Winter Games.

RBC believes in building prosperity by supporting a broad range of causes and is a leading corporate donor in North America. In 2005, more than $65 million found its way to community causes worldwide, through donations of more than $40.6 million, and an additional $25 million in the sponsorship of community events and national organizations. RBC employees and pensioners also make an enormous contribution as volunteers, sharing their financial and business knowledge, time and enthusiasm with thousands of community groups.

"Always earning the right to be our clients' first choice" is a corporate vision driven by every employee's understanding that their role is to enable its clients' success.

The values held by employees that contribute to this success include service, teamwork, responsibility, diversity and integrity.

THINGS YOU DIDN'T KNOW ABOUT RBC

○ In 1947, RBC made its first contribution supporting athletes to help get the Canadian Team to the Olympic Winter Games in St. Moritz, Switzerland. This marked the beginning of a relationship that continues today.

○ In 1900, Royal Bank employed a staff of 245 and operated 40 branches. The average price on the stock market for Royal Bank shares was $177.50 per share.

○ Royal Bank was the first Canadian bank to install a computer, an IBM 1401 in 1961.

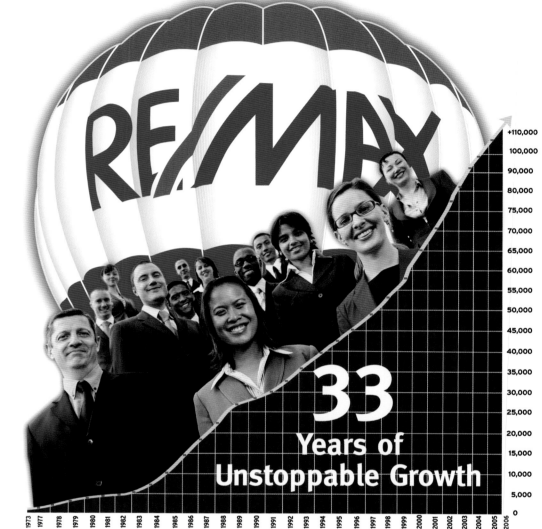

33
Years of
Unstoppable Growth

THE MARKET

Canada's resale housing market will set new records in 2006 after setting the fifth consecutive annual record in 2005 at 483,250 units. Activity is then projected to ease somewhat in 2007. Rising interest rates have done little to cool resale housing transactions this year.

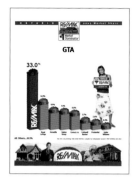

The Realtor® population has followed the same boom, with 83,000 Realtors® in Canada. RE/MAX, with three independently owned regions in Canada, has 20 percent of the Realtor® population generating a 35 percent market share. With more than twice the market share of the nearest competitor, RE/MAX is number one in the vast majority of markets across Canada with a combined sales volume of over $82 billion.

ACHIEVEMENTS

RE/MAX has grown every month since its inception over 30 years ago. RE/MAX became the number one residential real estate network in Canada in 1987 only seven years after they started. RE/MAX is a leading industry force in the United States and many other regions around the world. The most significant growth for RE/MAX in recent years has occurred outside the United States, with expansion into Europe, Africa, Asia, Australia, the Caribbean, Central America, Mexico, New Zealand and South America. RE/MAX takes proven techniques and adapts them to local markets, thereby developing a series of tools that real estate professionals find invaluable.

The first 10 years consisted of steady incremental growth; RE/MAX began to exhibit signs that a powerful momentum was forming. In 1983, the network had just less than 5,000 agents. Ten years later, RE/MAX had seven times that number with 35,000 agents, making it one of the largest real estate networks in the world. By 1998, RE/MAX had more than 50,000 agents and began to open offices in a few overseas countries. During the next five year interval, RE/MAX reached just under 90,000 agents with offices in 45 countries. In 2006, that number soared to 114,000 agents in more than 60 countries with over 16,000 agents across Canada.

As the system has grown, so has agent productivity.

HISTORY

RE/MAX is the result of the determination of founders Dave and Gail Liniger. Back in 1973 in Denver, Colorado, Dave and Gail set out to create a real estate company that only attracted the top professionals in the business. As salespeople themselves, the Linigers knew that the traditional real estate business model needed to be reinvented in the interests of the agents. There was an enduring brand idea in the concept of attracting only the salespeople who were truly Above the Crowd!® Traditional real estate companies were full of non-producing part-time agents who only paid fees when they sold something. These agents drew down both the morale and the resources in an office. Dave Liniger revolutionized the commission model so that top people would share their expenses and keep their commissions. The industry scoffed at him and tried to run him out of the business.

As the RE/MAX balloon took flight, so did the journey of the most successful real estate brand on the planet. Today, RE/MAX consists of a higher concentration of top people than any other real estate company. Although RE/MAX averages more designations and experience than agents from other companies, the strength of our brand is productivity and professionalism. A RE/MAX agent is three times more productive than the average agent.

Dave Liniger adopted the philosophy that "One log makes a lousy fire." RE/MAX now has offices in more than 60 countries. As people move from

city to city and country to country around the world, they look for the RE/MAX balloon. RE/MAX agents refer customers to each other around the world and tap into the network to help a client get the service they need wherever they need it.

THE PRODUCT

As a franchise organization, RE/MAX provides its brokers and agents with the industry's leading tools to grow their respective businesses. RE/MAX provides its franchisees with world-class marketing and events, technology, educational training and coaching and franchise support programs.

RE/MAX agents provide exemplary customer service and the combined experience of all of their real estate transactions. With every change in the market comes the need to modify the selling and negotiating strategy. RE/MAX franchise owners typically have a high volume of transactions in their offices. This provides the capital to support leading-edge office systems and support staff to facilitate a smooth and accurate transaction for the consumer.

RECENT DEVELOPMENTS

RE/MAX has launched an integrated educational program for agents at all different stages of their careers. The key difference in the RE/MAX educational program is the high level of agent mentoring available in the local offices. New agents are invited to "RE/MAX and You," an overview of the benefits within RE/MAX. SUCCEED is a customized in-office mentoring program for new agents and agents who want to refresh certain key skills. Top Producer panels are an opportunity for agents to share best practices with peers. RE/MAX also offers an exclusive in-office mentoring program on client relationships and lead management authoured by Brian Buffini & Company. And for more in-depth personal coaching for all levels of experience RE/MAX has a preferred relationship with John Ferber and an ongoing relationship with Richard Robbins and Brian Buffini.

RE/MAX has also launched a comprehensive new Web-marketing strategy. As the industry has resisted to responding to consumers' expectations on the Web, RE/MAX has launched a three-part initiative.

The first part involves offering better-quality information to buyers on the Web in a format that they enjoy using. Property searches on remax.ca now show complete property addresses and descriptions, additional photos, features and taxes, and they can be plotted or found using Google Earth. Consumers can zoom around and see neighbourhood amenities, density and proximity to parks, schools and a host of other areas of interest.

The second part involves leading-edge response technology. Today's Web consumers expect lightning-fast response times from agents who are not often in front of a computer. RE/MAX tracks all Web inquiries and automatically responds to every inquiry while simultaneously copying the

RE/MAX® Around the World.

agent. RE/MAX offers a state-of-the-art call centre for consumers who want to obtain more information immediately. RE/MAX has also implemented a follow-up lead response system for the agent and office to track the progress of business generated from the Web.

For the third part of this initiative, RE/MAX has developed a leading-edge search marketing program with Google. Without search marketing, the RE/MAX brand attracts the most consumer traffic in the industry. RE/MAX is sponsoring specific local key word searches to generate additional traffic.

PROMOTION

RE/MAX deploys a unique combination of advertising and promotional programs to enhance its dominant brand-name awareness and to attract buyers to the inventory it has to sell. In

addition to traditional consumer advertising — television, radio, print and outdoor — RE/MAX has developed a dominant consumer-event strategy and a dominant Web strategy. RE/MAX has also developed the highest level of journalistic integrity and as a consequence generates positive real estate editorial in the major media. RE/MAX is also a leader in community-cause marketing, raising considerable donations for children's hospitals and breast cancer care and research.

RE/MAX in Canada dominates paid media share of voice with 68 percent, with the nearest competitor at 27 percent. RE/MAX dominates the positive public relations share of voice with 64 percent and its nearest competitor 30 percent. RE/MAX was chosen by consumers to be "#1 on

the Web" versus other real estate companies and was also chosen by consumers to be the "Best Firm to List With" by a margin of 3:1.

RE/MAX is the first to deploy a comprehensive consumer-event strategy in high profile home shows. As presenting sponsor of the Metro, Fall, Ottawa and National Home Shows, RE/MAX educates consumers on which renovations add to the resale value of their properties and how to prioritize their renovations. When selling, RE/MAX will maximize the resale value of your property.

RE/MAX advertising differentiates RE/MAX agents as having the selling experience to get the results consumers want. RE/MAX agents understand the features and renovations that drive the value of a property; they understand how comparable properties stack up and the current market conditions that affect buying and selling.

BRAND VALUES

RE/MAX seeks to add professionalism to the real estate experience regardless of location or type of real estate transaction. The RE/MAX business model ensures that only fully committed, full-time professionals belong to RE/MAX. Having the most productive agents in the industry delivers the consumer benefit of getting the results they need. RE/MAX is an exemplary community citizen and ensures charitable donations are raised and returned to the markets they operate in. RE/MAX is not a publicly traded company. It has been built on and is the result of sweat equity.

THINGS YOU DIDN'T KNOW ABOUT RE/MAX

○ RE/MAX became number one in Canada just seven years after it started.

○ RE/MAX opened the doors to women wanting to forge a career in real estate.

○ RE/MAX generates a higher annual dollar volume in sales than Wal-Mart.

○ RE/MAX has the largest balloon fleet in the world.

ROGERS™

THE MARKET

Rogers Communications is a diversified public Canadian communications and media company and its market is as wide-ranging as the products and services that it provides. Rogers Wireless is Canada's largest wireless voice and data communications services provider and the country's only carrier operating on the world standard GSM/GPRS technology platform; Rogers Cable is Canada's largest cable television provider offering cable television, high-speed Internet access, telephony and data networking services and video retailing; and Rogers Media is Canada's premier collection of category-leading media assets with businesses in radio, television broadcasting, television shopping, publishing and sports entertainment through the Toronto Blue Jays.

Rogers also holds other interests, including an investment in a pay-per-view movie service as well as investments in several specialty television channels.

ACHIEVEMENTS

Rogers is a Canadian success story. As a premier Canadian integrated communications company, Rogers has a long history of pioneering new technologies, bringing new services to market in ways

uniquely Canadian and adding choice, value and convenience to people's lives.

Rogers is constantly seeking to improve people's lives by offering them new and innovative ways of staying informed, in touch and entertained. The company is inspired by its customers and driven by innovation. This core belief is the foundation upon which Rogers has built a unique and vibrant mix of cable, wireless, Internet, telephony and media offerings that touch the lives of Canadians every day, year after year. Rogers products share not just a common heritage, but a common brand as well — the Rogers brand — a brand which has come to stand for innovation and value in Canadian communications, entertainment and information.

HISTORY

Rogers Communications Inc. holds a proud and lengthy heritage of active progression within the media industry.

Rogers' roots within this business reach back to 1924. It was then that 24-year-old radio enthusiast and electrical engineer Edward S. "Ted" Rogers Sr. invented the world's first functional alternating current radio tube. This groundbreaking achievement

revolutionized radio communication. The medium itself was a scant two decades old. During these twenty years, radio receivers were powered by three separate batteries. The batteries would require recharging, tended to leak acid which would burn rugs and also required a spaghetti-like mass of wires to connect to the sets. While radio was becoming accepted as an everyday item in households, its progress was being hampered due to the disadvantages of the batteries.

Ted Rogers Sr. changed all that. In August 1924, he perfected his experimental "15-S" a/c tube, which went on to become the commercial Rogers Type 32. Listeners could now power their radios from their home electricity and the problems with the batteries became a thing of the past. Rogers also invented the 'Rogers Batteryless Radio' to use his tubes and introduced this remarkable product to the world at the 1925 Canadian National Exhibition (CNE) in Toronto.

The success of the world's first all-electric radio prompted Rogers Sr. to expand into broadcasting, and in February 1927 his radio station CFRB (Canada's First Rogers Batteryless) took to the air-

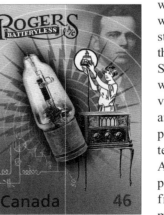

waves. By 1933, CFRB was the most powerful station in Canada, with the broadest range. Rogers Sr. also predicted the worldwide onset of television as early as 1934, and conducted the first public demonstration of television in Toronto in August 1933. Rogers partnered with a radio firm in Chicago, while maintaining his Toronto operations, and almost immediately Rogers-Majestic was the largest radio manufacturer in the country. Rogers not only survived the Great Depression of the 1930s, but was also able to keep people actively employed. Tragically, Ted Rogers Sr. passed away in 1939 due to illness. His companies and assets were disposed of, though the Rogers-Majestic brand continued until 1964.

However, his legacy continued. Ted Rogers Jr. entered broadcast media in 1960 with the purchase

of CHFI-FM. CHFI stands as the first FM station in Canada, first going on the air in 1957. FM was experiencing mediocre popularity, due in large part to the bulk and expense of FM radios. Ted Rogers partnered with Westinghouse to create a stylish and affordable FM set — with CHFI's station marker of 98.1 clearly identified with a red dot on the dial. The sets were marketed through department stores in Toronto, displayed at the Canadian National Exhibition and also given away to advertising agencies and through listener call-in contests. Each of these radios became a miniature billboard for CHFI and the audience rapidly grew.

Ted Rogers founded sister station CHFI-AM in August 1962. Today, this operates as 680News, Canada's all-news station.

While vacationing with his wife in 1967, Ted Rogers read a book about cable television. On his return, he promptly obtained a license to own a cable company, then within six months acquired Bramalea Telecable in Brampton, Ontario. Rogers Cable was now in operation, with its first 300 subscribers. Rogers introduced cable television converters to the Toronto market in 1972 — expanding from 12 channels to an unheard of 19. Under the guidance and leadership of Mr. Rogers, the cable company quickly grew, acquiring additional systems through 1979 and 1980. Rogers was now the largest cable operation in Canada.

Always seeking to provide Canadians with the best in communications, Ted Rogers created Cantel in 1983, with cellular service going live on July 1, 1985. This was the first national wireless telephone company in Canada. Today, cell phones are such an essential part of modern life that it's hard to imagine life without them. Rogers embraced the Internet age with gusto during the fall of 1994 with the launch of CableLink, the first high-speed Internet over cable access in North America. Now Canadians could surf the Web like never before, at record-breaking speed. Today, CableLink is Rogers Yahoo!, and subscribers to this premium service still enjoy the best the Internet has to offer — at top speed.

Other innovations that Rogers Cable has brought forward to Canada are fiber-optic cable, digital television, pay-per-view events and video-on-demand.

In 1994, Rogers expanded into print media with the acquisition of Maclean-Hunter Limited and today publishes an extensive number of titles to serve the varied interests of a broad readership. In 2000, Rogers acquired the Toronto Blue Jays Baseball Club, and subsequently their home stadium with the purchase of the Rogers Centre in 2004.

For over 75 years, Rogers has forged a path of invention and innovation. The commitment of the entrepreneurial spirit driving the company benefits Canadians first, yet also permits the global community to progress as new and exciting methods of communication are brought forward. The company's information, communication and entertainment products continually improve as bold new ideas are brought to light with Rogers' tradition of innovation and tireless effort.

THE PRODUCT

The Rogers Group of Companies offers a broad range of products and services through each of its subsidiary organizations.

Rogers Wireless is Canada's largest wireless voice and data communications services provider with more than 5.7 million customers and offices in Canadian cities across the country. Rogers Wireless, which operates Canada's largest integrated wireless voice and data network providing advanced voice and wireless data solutions to customers from coast to coast, is Canada's only carrier operating on the GSM/GPRS technology platform, the world standard for wireless communications technology. Rogers Wireless also operates a seamless integrated Time Division Multiple Access (TDMA) and analog cellular network. The company offers its services under the Rogers and Fido brands.

Rogers Cable is Canada's largest cable provider, servicing 3.3 million homes in Ontario,

New Brunswick and Newfoundland. Rogers Cable pioneered high-speed Internet access with the first commercial launch in North America in 1995 and now approximately 29 percent of homes serviced are Internet customers. Rogers Cable offers an extensive array of high-definition TV programming, a suite of "Rogers on Demand" services, including video on demand (VOD), subscription VOD, personal video recorders and timeshifting channels, as well as an extensive lineup of digital, multicultural and sports programming. Rogers Cable also owns and operates over 290 Rogers Video stores.

On July 1, 2005, Rogers Cable introduced Rogers Home Phone, a local residential service using advanced broadband Internet Protocol ("IP") multimedia network. Rogers Home Phone is a reliable, fully featured cable telephone service that allows consumers who switch their telephone service to Rogers to keep their existing phone numbers and receive popular calling features such as enhanced 911 emergency service, directory assistance, voicemail, call display and call waiting.

Rogers Media operates a portfolio of broadcasting, publishing and sports entertainment assets. Rogers Broadcasting has 46 AM and FM radio stations across Canada. Television properties include Toronto multicultural television broadcasters OMNI.1 and OMNI.2, a televised and electronic shopping service, The Shopping Channel, Canada's five nationally available Rogers Sportsnet channels including Rogers Sportsnet HD, and the management of two digital television services. Rogers Publishing produces many well-known consumer magazines such as *Maclean's*, *Chatelaine*, *Flare*, *L'actualité* and *Canadian Business* and is the leading publisher of a number of industry,

medical and financial publications. Sports entertainment assets include the Toronto Blue Jays baseball team and Rogers Centre, Canada's largest sports and entertainment facility.

Rogers Telecom Holdings Inc. (formerly Call-Net Enterprises Inc.) was acquired by Rogers Communications Inc. on July 1, 2005, and through its wholly owned subsidiary Rogers Telecom Inc. (formerly Sprint Canada Inc.) is a leading Canadian integrated communications solutions provider of home phone, wireless, long distance and IP services to households and local, long distance, toll-free, enhanced voice, data and IP services to businesses across Canada. Rogers Telecom owns and operates an extensive national fibre network, has over 150 co-locations in major urban areas across Canada including 33 municipalities and maintains network facilities in the U.S. and the U.K.

RECENT DEVELOPMENTS

Rogers is a company constantly on the move. Here are some of the most recent developments across the Rogers Group of Companies.
• In July of 2005 Rogers acquired Call-Net Enterprises.
• In the fall of 2004, Rogers Wireless seized a unique opportunity to acquire Microcell, then Canada's fourth-largest wireless communications provider. As a result of this acquisition, Rogers Wireless became Canada's largest wireless provider.
• Rogers Wireless recently became a wholly owned subsidiary of Rogers Communications Inc. after previously being publicly traded.
• Rogers Wireless successfully completed the deployment of EDGE technology across the entire Rogers Wireless GSM/GPRS network.
• Rogers Communications recently purchased Toronto Skydome, home of the Toronto Blue Jays baseball club and Canada's largest entertainment venue, and renamed it Rogers Centre.

Rogers Cable began offering customers in Ontario an all-digital channel lineup with all analog channels now fully digitized to offer picture and sound in digital format, to customers who have a Rogers Digital Cable terminal or Personal Video Recorder.
• Rogers Cable launched Rogers Yahoo! Hi-Speed Internet services and completed the transition of its entire residential Internet customer base to the new platform.
• The Rogers Media Radio Group was recently awarded licences for three new FM radio stations in Halifax, Moncton and Saint John, which were launched in October of 2005.
• Rogers Media Publishing Group recently launched *LouLou*, its newest magazine and brand label which has received an enthusiastic reception from consumers with its unique woman's shopping perspective on Canadian fashion and beauty.
• Rogers Media recently increased its ownership of sports television station Rogers Sportsnet to 100 percent.
• In the summer of 2004, Rogers Cable launched Rogers Yahoo!, a powerful new Internet experience which combines Rogers' broadband Internet access with one of the industry's leading Internet content and services of Yahoo! It's Canada's ultimate broadband Internet experience, offering a variety of access speeds, and all of the protection, control, services and storage our customer's desire.

PROMOTION

All of the Rogers companies have recently been rebranded under the name Rogers. The goal of Rogers as a corporation is to build a stronger presence with a single brand promoted across all our companies. The Rogers brand promise is that everything the company does helps its customers keep in touch with what matters most to them. This ensures that the entire suite of Rogers products and services is relevant to its customers' lives.

The launch of the company's e-commerce Web site, rogers.com, offers a wide variety of Rogers products and services and also provides customers with self-service options. Customers can now conveniently purchase everything

from Rogers Wireless phones and service plans to Rogers Cable and Rogers Hi-Speed Internet cable service, Rogers Home Phone service, Rogers Media magazines and even Blue Jays merchandise from one convenient site. Purchases can be added to an existing cable or wireless bill at check-out or payment by credit card can be made at the customer's option. Customers can also receive their bills electronically through the site as well as performing routine service transactions such as notifying us of their change of address, change of payment instructions or requesting a change in their service.

Rogers Video stores across the country provide customers with a retail presence that offers a wide range of Rogers' products and services. While renting the latest movie release or purchasing the most recent copy of *Maclean's* or *Chatelaine*, customers can also sign up for Rogers Cable, Wireless or Hi-Speed Internet plans.

In addition, the Rogers unified brand allows the company to offer special rates for special customers. By bundling services, Rogers offers its customers greater simplicity and convenience, as well as excellent value.

BRAND VALUES

"The quality of our brand is determined by the promises made and the promises kept."
— Ted Rogers

Canadians rely on the Rogers brand for quality products and services and the company strives to provide them with the very best options for all their communications, entertainment and information needs. Two timeless guiding principles support this promise: respect and innovation.

Since everything the company does at Rogers is inspired by its customers, Rogers values respect. And Rogers shows it by being driven to ensure that it proactively anticipates customers' needs and wants. Rogers also values innovation — which is why the company invests in new ideas and has the courage to be ahead of others.

Rogers is committed to providing the very best in customer service care and has a number of facilities in place that allow it to ensure its customers receive the help they need. At Rogers the belief is that customer service is a critical priority, and it begins with superb technology. The Rogers Network Management Centre is one of the most advanced facilities of its kind in the world. Through a combined centre in Toronto, the entire Rogers network, cable and wireless, is monitored with the latest diagnostic tools, enabling the company to deliver the highest levels of reliability. Professional technicians supported by sophisticated software tools ensure that problems are rapidly pinpointed and repaired and potential problems are often identified ahead of time, pre-empting customer inconveniences.

In addition, Rogers recognizes that its success is based on the success of its customers, employees and their communities. In return, Rogers strives to play an active and constructive role in the community.

The very nature of the company's business provides a powerful platform from which to serve its communities. The company is a major supporter of Canada's independent television and film producers through a variety of funds. And, through its 31 community television stations, Rogers Television produces over 12,000 original hours of local

programming annually, offering its communities a fresh, diverse and locally focused television alternative.

The Jays Care Foundation is dedicated to supporting programs, groups and activities that enhance the quality of life for children and youth. Since its inception, the Foundation has contributed financially over $1 million to worthwhile programs such as Field of Dreams, the Boys and Girls Clubs and many more. The Jays Care Foundation also hosts a series of innovative fundraising programs at the newly named Rogers Centre in Toronto to benefit a wide variety of local charities.

For more than 20 years, the Rogers PUMPKIN PATROL — the red Rogers Cable vans — has worked with police and emergency services to keep kids safe on Halloween. And Rogers became the first in Canada to launch a nationwide wireless phone-recycling program, Phones for Food, which collects used wireless phones to generate funds for food banks across Canada while helping to preserve the environment.

Rogers is very proud both of its tradition of support to the community and its ongoing commitment to its customers. In the words of president and CEO Ted Rogers, for Rogers, "The best is yet to come."

THINGS YOU DIDN'T KNOW ABOUT ROGERS COMMUNICATIONS

○ In 1925, Mr. Edward S. Rogers Sr. invented the world's first alternating current (AC) radio tube, which enabled radios to be powered by ordinary household current. This was a dramatic breakthrough in technology and it became the key factor in popularizing radio reception. After this invention, radios became far more commonplace.

○ In 1959 Ted Rogers partnered with publisher John Bassett and media personality Joel Aldred to successfully win a license for the creation of the first private television station in Toronto — CFTO.

○ In 1960, Ted Rogers acquired CHFI-FM, the first FM radio station in Canada.

○ During the 1970s, Rogers Cable TV became Canada's most innovative cable company. In 1974, it became the first cable company to expand past 12 channels and the cable company specialized in adding more programming choice, particularly with multicultural television.

○ In 1985, Rogers launched the first cellular telephone company in Canada, called Rogers Cantel Mobile Communications, now Rogers Wireless.

RONA⟍

The How-To People.

THE MARKET
It isn't by coincidence that RONA has become the largest Canadian distributor and retailer of hardware, home renovation and gardening products. The company's phenomenal growth is directly related to the meticulous execution of a multi-format strategy that has seen RONA blend Main Street entrepreneurialism with the marketing muscle of a major corporate chain.

The offshoot of this vision and strategy is that RONA and its affiliated dealer network are able to be "specialists" to consumers, from Atlantic Canada to Vancouver Island, at over 600 points of sale. The store formats, which cover 13 million square feet of retail space, are tailored to the consumer market and preferences: RONA's traditional hardware, home centre, building supply banner stores and large surface stores.

RONA's multi-banner strategy and the implementation of its robust business model have positioned it to meet the growing demand for hardware and construction products that is being bolstered by several factors. These include low interest rates, a healthy economy, record new housing starts, resales of existing homes, the aging of baby boomers and their houses and the changing needs of this segment of the population.

ACHIEVEMENTS
When RONA posted $5 billion in sales in 2005, it marked the 15th consecutive year of record results for the company whose slogan is *The How-to People*. RONA's president & CEO Robert Dutton projects network retail sales will reach $7 billion by the end of 2007, further consolidating RONA's industry leading status.

How does RONA do it? By relying on its four major growth drivers: acquiring businesses, recruiting independent dealer-owners, building new stores and improving its organic growth. It has combined this with store-format diversity and the dedication of some 24,000 employees to customer service, which Mr. Dutton describes as being "in our DNA."

RONA's achievements extend beyond the business component. Staunchly Canadian and profoundly people and community-oriented, RONA established a foundation in 1998 that has donated over $1.2 million to nonprofit organizations across Canada. A large share of the money has gone to assist young people between the ages of 12 and 30 who have dropped out of school or are in need of training to overcome illiteracy.

HISTORY
Fulfilling the needs of the independent dealer has been the guiding principle of RONA since its founding in 1939, when a small group of Quebec-based dealers banded together to form Les Marchands en Quincaillerie Ltée (Hardware Merchants Ltd). Two members of this group, Rolland Dansereau and Napoléon Piotte, were at the helm of RONA.

In 1960s, the affiliate stores began operating under the name Ro-Na — it went through other name variations before becoming RONA Inc. in 1998 — and in the decades to come, the brand became synonymous with great value, superior service and excellent assortment in hardware and home-improvement products.

Throughout the '80s and early '90s, RONA continued to broaden its product selection to meet the growing demands of consumers. The early '90s also marked the arrival of RONA's first big-box stores, a category that currently represents almost half of the company network in terms of revenues and employees.

The start of the new millennium was also the dawn of RONA's emergence as the industry leader. Between 2000 and 2005, the company completed four major acquisitions — Cashway, Revy/Lansing, Réno-Dépôt and TOTEM — adding $2.2 billion in sales, 11,000 employees and $70 million in synergies in the process.

RONA's national expansion was fueled by a bold move the company made in a historic initial public offering in 2002. The IPO raised $150.1 million, validating RONA's multi-format strategy.

THE PRODUCT
The purchasing power of RONA and the implementation of its Optimum Selection system provides dealers and by extension, consumers, with access to an inventory of more than 100,000 products, 90 percent of which are from Canadian-based suppliers. Whether it's a painting or planting

project, building a deck or firing up the barbecue, redoing the décor or merely changing a lightbulb, consumers can obtain whatever they need on a "Run to Rona."

This ever expanding line of high quality, affordable name-brand and private-label products is made available through a network of seven distribution centres across the country. The sophisticated distribution process enables RONA to match the right products with the market for which they are intended.

"As Canada's leading home improvement retailer, what our brands represent in the minds of our consumers is a priority," relates Michael Brossard, RONA's senior vice-president, Marketing. "RONA's marketing program gives it four databases, each providing a window on who are its customers and what they want."

In keeping with this priority, RONA partners with companies that are leaders in their business sectors to provide consumers with the best and latest products available on the market. Combined with its increasingly popular Private Label, of which there are currently more than 2,000 items, RONA is able to offer the right product at the right price.

Product is only a part of the equation. As Mr. Brossard remarks, "We are your complete service provider," and in fulfilling that promise, RONA employees are technically trained through the RONA Academy so that they can provide the most courteous, helpful and product knowledgeable service across the country.

RECENT DEVELOPMENTS

RONA has attained the dominant position in its sector by being active, aggressive, dynamic and visionary — and it continues to do so, at every level of its operation.

Corporate: Following its purchase of TOTEM, the legendary 16-year building supply chain in Alberta, RONA gained a firm foothold in Atlantic Canada – where it previously had limited market share — with the acquisition of Chester Dawe Ltd. RONA also recently announced it will invest some $400 million over the next two years to build 40 new points of sale, including some in the successful 40,000–52,000-square-foot "Proximity" format. It is also spending $40 million in 2006 to renovate dozens of corporate stores.

RONA is also imminently introducing a service program offering time-strapped consumers the installation of doors and windows,

kitchen cabinets and flooring. And summer 2006 marks the debut of a new national team known as RONA Pro Services, a program designed to streamline services to the trades and building maintenance professionals.

Community: RONA is the title sponsor of the RONA MS Bike Tour, which is the largest cycling series run by a not-for-profit organization in Canada with 21 events from coast-to-coast. Since RONA began its sponsorship, funds raised from the event have increased from $4.9 million in 2003 to $6.5 million in 2005. RONA recently signed a $600,000 national partnership agreement with the Red Cross to help Canadian families be evacuated from their homes when disasters occur. All of RONA's stores across the country are participating in the project. Elsewhere, RONA's funding to 100 prospective Canadian Olympic athletes, in conjunction with the 2010 "Own the Podium" program, is about to be activated.

PROMOTION

Total unaided awareness of the RONA brand, which currently stands at 87 percent in Quebec, 69 percent in the West and 60 percent in Ontario, is continually rising, attributable in large measure to strong promotional efforts.

At the forefront of such marketing initiatives is RONA's national flyer distribution campaign. Reaching over 6 million Canadian households in a given week, 40 times a year, it delivers equal marketing punch for the largest big-box or smallest independently owned RONA affiliate. In tandem with the flyer blitz, RONA conducts extensive television advertising throughout the year. The company has been hailed for the innovativeness and cleverness of its commercials, notably "The How-to People" series.

Integration of the Air Miles™ program across the RONA network

has contributed to raising the brand-awareness profile, as almost 3 million RONA customers are using the program. The introduction of a RONA gift card last October was another promotional coup.

The RONA brand derives considerable visibility and exposure across the country from major sponsorships with the Canadian Football League and its eight-year partnership agreement with the 2010 Olympic and Paralympic Winter Games VANOC, which includes an extensive athletes' funding program.

BRAND VALUES

RONA's brand values are intrinsically linked:
- An unconditional commitment to customer service
- Team unity in providing the most enjoyable store experience possible
- The utmost respect toward employees, customers, shareholders and business partners
- Partnering with people and businesses that share our belief in working toward the common good
- Encouraging initiative and fostering a sense of responsibility in every employee
- Enabling employees to grow with the company

THINGS YOU DIDN'T KNOW ABOUT RONA

- ○ RONA holds 15 percent of the Canadian hardware-renovation market.
- ○ 85 percent of the Canadian population lives less than 30 minutes from a RONA store.
- ○ RONA's Web site on the Internet receives an average of 800,000 visits per month.
- ○ In 2004 and 2005, 56 dealers crossed over to the RONA banner, representing almost $300 million in retail sales.
- ○ RONA's CEO Robert Dutton grew up helping his father run the family RONA banner store on Montreal's north shore. He became president and CEO of RONA in 1992 at the age of 37.

ROYAL DOULTON

ENGLAND

HISTORY

Royal Doulton has been producing ceramics and tableware for nearly 200 years. In 1815, the company founder, John Doulton, began making practical and decorative stoneware in Lambeth, today a suburb in the south of London, England.

His son, Henry Doulton, built up the business, relocating it 60 years later to Stoke-on-Trent, the hub of the potteries industry in England. By 1901, Doulton's achievements had caught the eye of King Edward VII, who permitted the company to add "Royal" to its name and the company was awarded the Royal Warrant. In 1887, Queen Victoria knighted Henry Doulton for his contributions to art and industry, making him the first English potter to receive this honour.

By the 1930s, the business expanded into the manufacture of tableware and figurines. The company opened its subsidiary office in Toronto in 1956. Today, Royal Doulton Canada is a leading member of the Canadian gift and tableware industry with 230 employees in its sales, marketing, distribution and retail operations.

In 1966, Royal Doulton was awarded the Queen's Award for Technical Achievement, the first china manufacturer to be honoured with this award.

In 1993, Royal Doulton became a publicly traded company listed on the London Stock Exchange. Today, Royal Doulton is part of the Waterford Wedgwood Group.

THE MARKET

Pottery and ceramics are a strong indicator of the art and lifestyle of any given age. It's no wonder that archeologists rely on shards of pottery fragments to establish the level of sophistication of past civilizations.

Today's consumers are more demanding and discriminating than ever before. The increasing trend to home entertaining has been matched by the introduction of contemporary tableware that combines fabulous style with easy-care function. And as modern life cuts into traditional family mealtime with a reliance on fast food and microwaved entrees, the industry has responded by extending informal tableware ranges designed for hectic days and nights.

Despite market fragmentation, ceramic giftware has enjoyed considerable growth. It exemplifies the best in home decoration and gift giving for consumers who value the qualities of heritage and craftsmanship. Ceramic giftware not only offers real, long-lasting value for the money — but can also be a long term investment opportunity for collectors.

ACHIEVEMENTS

Royal Doulton is one of the world's largest manufacturers and distributors in the premium ceramic tableware and giftware market. Its illustrious brand names include Minton, Royal Albert and its core Royal Doulton brand.

With 200 years of heritage, Royal Doulton is a thriving global organization, with over $200 million in worldwide annual sales. It employs approximately 2,800 people in its production sites, sales, marketing and distribution operations and retail shops around the world. Approximately half of its sales are generated outside of the UK home market.

The company's Hotel and Airlines division is also one of the world's foremost suppliers of bone china to the international airlines industry and hospitality sector. Royal Doulton Canada supplies custom designed tableware to Air Canada for its first-class service. Royal Doulton Canada has a long-

standing partnership with Four Seasons Hotel properties around the world and has been chosen by the Department of External Affairs to supply bone china tableware in its Canadian Embassies around the world.

In total, Royal Doulton offers a range of 6,000 different items across a broad range of product categories.

THE PRODUCT

Each of the company's principal brands — Royal Doulton, Minton and Royal Albert — enjoys a long association of royal patronage and holds at least one Royal Warrant. They are also trademark registered.

There is an incredibly rich archive of designs from the long histories of each of the brands. The Royal Doulton Pattern Books, for example, include over 10,000 hand-painted watercolours illustrating the talent of artists employed over the years. It provides an invaluable historical record of decorative ceramic styles — from the exquisitely gilded and delicately hand-painted tableware of the Victorian and Edwardian eras to the bright and bold angular design of the 1930s Art Deco. The collection is also an inspirational source for the company's current Design Studio.

Ongoing research determines the colour and style trends that modern consumers will embrace

— wherever they may be in the global community. Local market product development is a vital part of the company's design process.

The Royal Doulton brand provides a wide range of domestic tableware in bone china and fine china. Styles range from simple white casual designs to ornately decorated formal designs. The brand is also renowned for its collectible range of Pretty Lady figurines, character jugs and crystal stemware and giftware.

For the younger generation, Royal Doulton also produces nurseryware and collectibles, and many of these ranges are also of interest to the adult collector. Its most popular collection is "Bunnykins," first launched in the 1930s and still the ceramic keepsake gift of choice for a new baby. More recent additions of licensed ranges such as Brambly Hedge and The Disney Collection including Winnie the Pooh have broadened the offering to include classic children's themes.

Royal Albert, which traces its origins back to 1896, has become an internationally recognized

brand, offering domestic tableware and gift accessories. Its leading design, Old Country Roses, is quintessentially English and perfectly expresses the brand positioning of "A Passion for Florals."

Equally famous, with an illustrious heritage dating back to 1793, is the Minton brand, best known for its most popular pattern, Haddon Hall, which is particularly loved by the Japanese market. Minton is also renowned for its intricate gold patterns featuring traditional labour-intensive techniques, where one plate can cost over $1,000. The skilled artists in the Minton Studio also undertake special commissions. In addition to company-owned brands, Royal Doulton Canada has special marketing relationships with such prestigious brands as Royal Crown Derby.

Royal Doulton is noted for its high standard of working practices and technology throughout the international china industry. As a testament to its ongoing commitment to quality and improvement, Royal Doulton Canada has been ISO 9001 registered since 1997.

Royal Doulton Canada distributes its domestic products through leading department stores, national chains, independent Retail specialty stores and its own chain of 13 Royal Doulton corporate stores across Canada.

RECENT DEVELOPMENTS

Royal Doulton is undergoing an important period of change in its long history. A three-brand master strategy, in addition to New Retail Merchandising systems, an updated online selling Internet site, improved product packaging, point-of-sale and designer endorsement have all been identified as key to the branded development.

In 2004, a license agreement was set up with Zandra Rhodes, a UK fashion designer icon, to act as a spokesperson for Royal Albert and to create a new range entitled "My Favourite Things." Julien Macdonald, the young fashion designer, has created innovative glassware and tableware designs for the Royal Doulton brand. In 2006, an exciting new collaboration with renowned chef Gordon Ramsay will launch an outstanding new collection of tableware and glassware.

The Licensing Division, created in the UK in the mid 1990s, has propelled the three brands into new product sectors such as textiles, children's clothing and giftware, silverware, fine art prints, teas, gift accessories and jewellery.

PROMOTION

Marketing and promotional activities continue to be key components in the developments of the company's brands and their communication vehicles. New logos, updated packaging and in-store promotional material clearly communicate the brand personalities and messages.

Royal Doulton has high brand awareness and perception and a significant share of the Canadian tableware and giftware market. The company continues to employ a wide variety of traditional marketing and promotional activities ranging from in-store consumer promotions, consumer and trade show participation, special artist signing events and targeted consumer advertising in bridal and lifestyle magazines.

A significant focus of the public relations activity is dedicated to the corporate support of the fight against breast cancer. Through the sale of an annual Royal Doulton "Pretty Lady" figurine over the past number of years, Royal Doulton Canada has contributed over $300,000 to the Canadian Cancer Society to help cancer research and support programs.

BRAND VALUES

Royal Doulton has continued to focus on what it does best — produce outstanding tableware and giftware collections. With emphasis on excellent design coupled with attention to the practicalities of modern living, Royal Doulton products are stylish, functional and user friendly.

Around the globe, Royal Doulton is valued for its sense of heritage and quality. As one of the

oldest and best recognized chinaware brands in the world, Royal Doulton has earned itself a reputation for excellence, quality and distinctiveness of design — values which it intends to build on in order to take the brand forward.

Royal Doulton has an international reach far beyond its English roots and products. To sustain its position, the emphasis for future brand growth centres on its ability to focus on the consumer, to understand its buyers and then to produce products that suit individual tastes and needs.

Royal Doulton identifies its core brand values as integrity, innovation, creativity, craftsmanship and decorative skills.

www.royaldoulton.com

THINGS YOU DIDN'T KNOW ABOUT ROYAL DOULTON

○ The largest and most expensive figure made by Royal Doulton takes more than 160 hours to paint and costs in excess of $40,000.

○ Royal Doulton was the first china to enter space. China plates were carried on the inaugural flight of the space shuttle *Columbia* in 1984.

○ Royal Doulton's Royal Albert design "Old Country Roses" has become the world's best selling bone china pattern, with more than 150 million pieces sold since its introduction in 1962.

○ Royal Doulton terracotta tiles and ornamental architectural details have been used on the facades of many buildings around the world, including several buildings in Canada — among them the Hotel Vancouver, the Southam Building in Montreal, the Bloor-Gladstone Library in Toronto and St. John's Church in Saskatoon.

that was easy.®   rien de plus simple.ᴹᴰ

THE MARKET

If you've ever had to forage around for a pen, ransack desk drawers in search of notepaper or run out of ink toner midway through printing an important presentation, you'll agree that there are countless advantages to having a STAPLES Business Depot store in your neighbourhood. As Canada's largest distributor of office supplies, business machines, office furnishings and business services, the company is a proven leader in providing definitive solutions that help small business and home office customers run their operations as efficiently and inexpensively as possible.

ACHIEVEMENTS

Just mention the name STAPLES Business Depot (SBD), or Bureau en Gros (BEG), as the company is known in the province of Quebec, to any Canadian — from the smallest town to the largest city — and you'll see evidence of instant recognition. In only fifteen years, the company has gained a solid reputation as a groundbreaking retailer with an exceptional record of fiscal outperformance, while building a platform of philanthropic initiatives — from helping to promote environmental awareness, to supporting enrichment programs in local communities.

Each SBD/BEG store contributes regularly to both national and local organizations, donating funds from an annually allotted community marketing budget of over $2,000. Stores offer support to many worthwhile community initiatives — Boys & Girls Clubs, local libraries, Junior Achievement programs.

In addition, the company is a key sponsor of Special Olympics Canada, with contributions constituting 15 percent of Special Olympics Canada's annual operating income. Each year, SBD/BEG runs the "Give A Dollar. Share A Dream" program, which raises money to help send Special Olympics Canada's athletes to the National and World Games. In the past year alone, over $485,000 was raised through this program.

SBD/BEG also works to promote children's literacy and raise money to support Canadian schools by organizing a National Writing Challenge for elementary children from every province. Students are invited to submit short stories based on annual themes. The winning stories of 101 children are published in a short story book sold in every store, with net proceeds donated to schools.

When it comes to protecting and preserving our country's natural resources, SBD/BEG demonstrates solid commitment through its business practises. Customers will find nearly 2,800 products featuring recycled content. As part of its recycling initiative, SBD/BEG operates a program that recycles mobile electronics — cell phones, PDAs, pagers, chargers — through Collective Good, an electronics recycler. Proceeds from collected items that have been refurbished are donated to Special Olympics Canada. As well, the company promotes Recycle For Education, an inkjet and toner cartridge recycling program that helps provide additional funds for Canadian schools through proceeds collected. SBD/BEG was able to donate over $225,000 last year — this year, a goal of over $400,000 is expected to be met before the close of 2006.

With an ongoing commitment to energy conservation issues, SBD/BEG invests in green technologies, incorporating them into all their store and distribution centre designs and are currently exploring the use of renewable power sources such as wind and solar energy.

HISTORY

As former president of Beaver Lumber, Jack Bingleman knew intuitively that it was only a matter of time before big-box stores would become permanent fixtures on the Canadian retail landscape. Embarking on a journey inspired by his vision to develop a retail force that would revolutionize the way people viewed the office supply industry in Canada, Jack met with Tom Stemberg, founder of a wildly successful office supply superstore south of the border, Staples, Inc., to discuss his plans to launch a similar operation in Canada. In 1991, with Staples, Inc. sharing 16 percent interest and signing on to acquire outstanding shares within five years, Jack founded The Business Depot Ltd., Canada's first low-cost office supply superstore.

The first store opened its doors on October 15, 1991, in Vaughan, a municipality north of Toronto, Ontario. Canadians were more than ready to take advantage of the irresistible combination of large product assortment and low pricing. The concept was such a roaring success that rapid growth evolved naturally. Bingleman's goal had been to open twenty-six stores within five years; naysayers considered such a plan far too optimistic. Plunging ahead, expansion progressed — the original goal far surpassed when over sixty stores were successfully operating before the fifth year had ended. Suitably impressed, Staples, Inc. decided to increase their initial investment ahead of schedule, acquiring the remaining interest in

Business Depot a full two years before the originally agreed-upon five-year period. By January 1999, Business Depot had achieved a milestone of $1 billion in sales. The new millennium rolled in with a name change in the works, and in July 2001, The Business Depot Ltd. became STAPLES® Business Depot™. A year later, the 200th store was opened in Ottawa, Ontario. Today, SBD/BEG operates over 265 stores, with growth plans in the range of 300 to 350 more to come.

The force that drives the numbers is also a distinguishing factor in setting SBD/BEG apart from other retailers: its exceptional family of associates. Skilled at attracting talented individuals motivated by a desire to contribute and outperform, the company strives to provide an environment that encourages and rewards the pursuit of excellence. Associates are proud to be members of a company that does not just talk the talk.

SBD's popularity with the public stems from its goal to create a shopping experience for customers that is as easy and as pleasant as possible. Current president Steve Matyas believes that SBD/BEG manages to distinguish itself from competitors through a process of ongoing innovations. "Part of the innovation ties back into listening to your customers, and giving them exactly what they want," he states. With a foundation built on the vision statement, "To be the best provider of business solutions in every Canadian market," and living true to their key success strategy, "Great Service Every Day, In Every Way!" it's no surprise that SBD/BEG are destined to go down in Canadian history as trailblazers in the office supply retail industry.

THE PRODUCT

No matter which office product you're looking for, you'll find it at SBD/BEG. Stores are easy to locate in every major city across the country, as well as in many smaller cities and towns. Along with everyday low prices on more than 7,000 office products and business services, SBD/BEG offers an in-stock guarantee on a broad selection of ink and toner cartridges. Polite, knowledgeable

associates are trained to help every customer shop in an atmosphere of optimum efficiency and ease.

A typical store is about 20,000 to 25,000 square feet and, in addition to the enormous range of items, most stores operate Copy & Print Centres that provide a huge selection of competitively priced business services. In the spirit of giving customers

exactly what they want, stores offer a build-to-order computer service, and conveniences such as catalogue and secure online shopping accompanied by free next day delivery on local orders over $50.

A large segment of the company's future growth is designated to feature the new Barrington format — smaller replicas of typical store layouts. Averaging about 15,000 square feet, Barrington's more compact design will allow the company the flexibility to expand into smaller markets around the country.

RECENT DEVELOPMENTS

In September of 2005, SBD/BEG launched a new print centre concept in Montreal, called dossier. After opening four test locations in Montreal's downtown core, dossier was quickly realized as representing an entirely new generation of quick-print and high-efficiency business services. Providing customers with the use of on-site workstations and state-of-the-art technical equipment, graphic design studios and a wide variety of high-quality services, dossier's state-of-the-art digital workflow processes provide mobile professionals and mid-size businesses with a whole new world of full-service, high quality

production with quick turnaround times, from locations that are convenient to access.

As a customer-centric organization, SBD/BEG is extremely disciplined when following through on customer requests. Thanks to recurrent encounters with customer advisory panels, SBD soon discovered that many customers were frustrated with the long waiting periods associated with their rebate program. In response, the Easy Online Rebate Program was developed, where customers register online by submitting information from their receipts. In only a few weeks, the rebate is processed and the customer receives a cheque. They can even track the process online.

In recent months, BEG opened a new 104,000 square foot distribution centre in Laval, Quebec, with the goal of improving delivery service for Quebec-based customers.

PROMOTION

SBD/BEG injects humour into their commercials in an effort to connect with customers while reinforcing the company's accessible and people-friendly brand personality. In 2003, SBD/BEG took a fresh look at how the brand was being presented in stores, in promotions and in all internal communications. The result was the launch of a national advertising campaign supporting a new brand promise: SBD/BEG makes buying office products EASY. This brand positioning and tag line — "That was EASY" in English markets or "SIMPLE" in French markets — has been featured prominently in print, online and radio advertising,

on store signage and in catalogues and on the company Web site.

To reinforce the tag line's burgeoning popularity, the company developed an actual Easy Button that, when pressed, declares "That was EASY!" A popular fixture on many desktops across the country, this amusing novelty item also serves a charitable purpose: one dollar from every sale is donated to Special Olympics Canada.

BRAND VALUES

As pioneers of the office supply superstore industry in Canada, SBD/BEG changed the way people thought about and purchased office products. The company's mission — to slash the cost and hassle of buying office supplies — held a message that small businesses could identify with. Today, all across Canada, the SBD/BEG name is synonymous with unbeatable low prices and great selection — and making shopping for office products easy. In a fast-paced society, SBD/BEG offers customers the flexibility to shop as they choose: by walking into a store, calling or faxing in, or logging on. In a nutshell . . . STAPLES Business Depot / Bureau en Gros: That was EASY!

THINGS YOU DIDN'T KNOW ABOUT SBD/BEG

- ○ SBD/BEG employs more than 13,500 Canadians.

- ○ During our Back to School season, we sell enough chairs to comfortably seat every person living in the province of P.E.I.

- ○ Our current president, Steve Matyas, also holds the title of STAPLES Business Depot's very first employee, hired by Jack Bingleman.

- ○ In one season, you could trail the correction tape we've sold up and down Mount Everest 297 times!

THE MARKET

Digital information is the currency of today's global economy. Individuals and enterprises rely on it to govern nations, conduct business transactions and make personal decisions. However, data — whether personal or business — is always at risk. Increasingly, sophisticated criminal elements are now behind many of today's cyber attacks and unlike the hackers of the past, they are much more interested in anonymity than in notoriety. Today's threats are silent and highly targeted. What these criminals are searching for is personal and financial information — and they are looking to use it for serious financial gain. We have moved past the days where data backup and clustering technologies were sufficient to protect the data center and where antivirus software and a firewall were all that was required to protect the desktop computer.

IT professionals and consumers alike must protect their physical systems, operating environments and applications. They must protect a broad range of information types — from email to business documents to digital photos to audio and video files. And they must expand their focus to protect the interactions themselves — the connections . . . the collaborative environments . . . and the movement of data while in use.

In other words, users must protect their infrastructure, their information and their interactions. That means creating a trusted environment — one free of risks to security, availability, compliance and performance.

ACHIEVEMENTS

Since its merger with VERITAS Software in 2005, Symantec has become the fourth-largest independent software company in the world. Today the company has 260 patents in technologies addressing security, systems management and storage needs.

Symantec's wide range of security and availability products for enterprises has enabled it to conduct business with 99 percent of the companies listed on the 2005 Fortune 1000 list. Moreover, in its 2006 fiscal year, Symantec shipped almost 23 million boxes of software, in addition to the tens of millions of electronic transactions that were conducted with customers and partners worldwide. In addition, in May 2006, Symantec's consumer business achieved a remarkable milestone of 200 million Norton products sold around the globe.

Symantec has recently been recognized for its accomplishments by many industry experts. In 2003 Symantec was added to the S&P 500 Index. In 2005, *Fortune* magazine ranked Symantec on several exclusive lists, including: The Fastest Growing Companies List, the Fortunes 1000, America's Most Admired Companies and the 100 Best Companies To Work For In America. In April 2005, *Fortune* magazine also named Symantec a Blue Ribbon Company, a designation reserved for corporations that achieve recognition on four or more of *Fortune*'s exclusive trademarked lists. Furthermore, in 2005 and 2006, Symantec was listed in the Leaders Quadrant in the following Gartner Magic Quadrants: personal firewall, email archiving, managed security services, combined SRM and SAN management software, enterprise backup/restore, email security boundary and J2EE application server management. Gartner has also recognized Symantec as a global market-share leader in the following categories: antivirus software, core storage management software, distributed systems backup/recovery software, overall systems backup/recovery software, as well as personal firewall software.

HISTORY

In 1982, Dr. Gary Hendrix, a linguistics and technology expert, created Symantec while he was working on a revolutionary PC software program that would unite database power with natural language ease of use.

From these beginnings Symantec has leveraged its innovation in software development and marketing savvy to become a global leader in the security and availability spaces. A carefully thought-out strategy of innovative software development and timely and forward-looking mergers and acquisitions have helped create what is now one of the largest and most successful software companies in the world.

Following the first key merger in 1984 with C&E Software, Symantec formed Turner Hall Publishing in 1985 to apply its technical and marketing prowess to find and develop additional PC software products. In that same year the company released the Q&A software program and it soon became the company's flagship product.

On June 23, 1989, Symantec became a publicly traded company on the NASDAQ stock exchange under the symbol SYMC.

Anticipating the need to manage security on networked computers, Symantec released the first virus protection software for the Macintosh in 1989 and in 1990, the company combined with Peter Norton Computing, Inc. to continue development of PC-based utility and security software. The result of this collaboration — Norton AntiVirus — quickly became Symantec's top-selling product and the world's most trusted antivirus solution.

Since 1999, Symantec has been led by current CEO John W. Thompson. Under Thompson's leadership, Symantec has grown from a small consumer software publisher to the market leader for security and availability solutions to help customers manage their rapidly growing digital assets.

Recognizing the growing importance of information and the need to protect it, Thompson has spearheaded company efforts to solidify and expand its industry-leading security products. This has been achieved by developing additional software solutions and acquiring 40 companies, including: AXENT Technologies, PowerQuest Corporation, ON Technology, Brightmail and Sygate.

The 2005 merger of Symantec with VERITAS Software (an industry leader in backup and data-protection software) helped establish Symantec as an IT industry powerhouse that ranks as the fourth-largest independent software company in the world.

THE PRODUCT

Symantec protects a wide range of customers — from consumers to small and mid-sized businesses to large enterprises and government organizations.

Symantec's Norton brand of consumer security solutions delivers Internet security and problem-solving capabilities to individual users, home offices and small businesses. The Norton brand of products is a market leader in desktop protection,

with integrated products that work seamlessly to protect customers' computers from virus outbreaks and malicious attacks.

For the enterprise and mid-market, Symantec offers products for backup and recovery of data and systems, optimizing storage resource utilization, simplifying administration of heterogeneous environments and providing continuous availability of mission-critical applications and data. The company provides enterprise security solutions for all network tiers: the gateway, the server and the client level — including desktop computers, laptops and handheld devices.

RECENT DEVELOPMENTS

Today, Symantec is one of the fastest growing software companies in North America. Symantec is currently reshaping the competitive landscape and is uniquely positioned to drive industry convergence across the major security and availability segments of the market.

The new, post-VERITAS–merger Symantec will provide enterprise customers with a more effective way to protect their infrastructure, information and interactions. Symantec can now deliver security and availability solutions across all platforms and to customers of all sizes.

PROMOTION

Norton's new consumer message is built around freedom, because that is what customers value most about their computers and the Internet. Symantec's value proposition describes the functional and emotional benefits customers enjoy when we keep the Norton promise: "Use Norton products and services to enjoy your freedom to work and play in the connected world — protected from fear, frustration, loss and chaos."

Symantec's consumer marketing efforts have traditionally focused on promoting its flagship products, Norton AntiVirus and Norton Internet Security. Historically, Symantec has run its very successful "Back to School" and "Tax Time" promotions at retail stores across North America. However, more recently, Symantec has partnered with other companies in order to create some very exciting and compelling marketing campaigns. For Symantec's annual "Tax Time" promotion it has partnered with Intuit in Canada. This has enabled Symantec to bundle security software with tax software and reach a new set of customers. In 2005 Symantec partnered with Warner Brothers on its "Security Begins with Symantec" promotion. This promotion tied into the *Batman Begins* movie and offered customers the chance to win exciting prizes such as a trip to the movie's world premier. And in 2006 Symantec partnered with Sony Pictures on its "Protect Your Secrets" promotion which leveraged the movie *The Da Vinci Code*. This promotion featured eye-catching point-of-purchase displays, online banner ads, high-impact print ads, as well as the opportunity for customers to win a trip to Paris and the code to $100,000. These marketing partnerships have allowed Symantec to provide an exciting and creative draw for customers, while achieving greater mind share and more touch points at retail stores.

Symantec's enterprise marketing efforts are centered on educating partners and customers.

Symantec has a wide range of educational resources, such as: Webcasts, online courses, articles, podcasts, white papers, seminars and events. The recently launched "Symantec Yellow Books" are a great educational tool, as they provide technical know-how to IT professionals in Symantec's customer and partner communities — and to the technical marketplace in general. Written to show how to solve real-world business and technical problems using Symantec solutions, these books include best-practice recommendations as well as detailed information on installation, configuration and product integration.

Symantec Vision, the company's annual premiere global enterprise customer and partner showcase, provides Symantec's enterprise stakeholders with an opportunity to make a direct and compelling connection with the Symantec brand. Attendees have access to a myriad of workshops, seminars and forums that provides them with a 360-degree understanding and appreciation of how Symantec can help provide them with the protection they need to be able to do business with confidence. Symantec Vision is replicated, on a smaller scale, in countries around the world — helping ensure that the company engages its enterprise customers and partners wherever they may be.

BRAND VALUES

The company's commitment to its brand and values over its 20-plus-year history has been at the heart of its business success. Symantec believes that people should be able to work and play freely in a connected world. The brand is more than a logo or color scheme — it is the combined behaviours, actions and talent of Symantec's greatest asset — its people. That's why people turn to Symantec to protect their connected experiences and why the company can confidently state that it protects more people from more online threats than anyone else in the world.

THE MARKET

Texas Instruments virtually invented the semiconductor industry. When a TI engineer named Jack Kilby demonstrated the first integrated circuit to his colleagues in September 1958, he helped launch an industry that has now topped $235 billion in annual revenue worldwide.

Today semiconductors literally surround us. They're not only in our computers and cell phones and automobiles, but also in our washers and dryers and airplanes and MP3 players and televisions. Digital signal processing and analog technologies are the semiconductor engines of modern electronics and TI has clearly established itself as the world leader in both.

TI designs and manufactures semiconductors for wireless telephones, digital cameras, digital audio products, medical devices and many other products. In fact TI envisions a world in which every phone call and every Internet connection, every digital photograph, song and TV broadcast are touched by the power of TI's digital signal processing and analog technologies.

That dream is coming true. TI is making it happen right now.

ACHIEVEMENTS

Since its earliest days using technology to locate hidden reservoirs of oil in Depression-era Texas, TI has rung up a distinguished and impressive history of achievements, including the first commercial silicon transistors, the first integrated circuit and the first electronic handheld calculator.

TI innovation has empowered countless inventions that touch the lives of just about everyone, from an executive wirelessly checking e-mail at Toronto Pearson Airport to a teenager jamming to an MP3 song on a Tokyo subway to a photographer capturing digital pictures of a Brazilian sunrise.

Today's TI engineers and technicians produce semiconductors in clean rooms that protect chips from even the tiniest motes of dust. Those semiconductors can then perform real-time processing of incredibly complex data — like the ultrasound image of a child in its mother's womb or the subtleties of the slow movement of a Mozart symphony.

And TI's technology is everywhere — in homes and offices and pockets and purses. In cell phones, cable modems, home theaters, digital cameras, cars and much more. TI calculators are a staple in classrooms, the company's award-winning DLP® technology is revolutionizing high-definition TV and engineers are using TI technology to develop everything from the latest satellites bound for Mars to a vision system that will allow blind people to see.

With 35,000 employees worldwide and $12.3 billion in revenue in 2005, TI is known worldwide for combining real-world know-how with high-tech savvy.

HISTORY

TI began in 1930 as a company called Geophysical Service Inc. pioneering a type of oil exploration that applied revolutionary signal processing technology. The young company's seismic field crews led a nomadic life, traveling the flooded jungles of Sumatra, the swamps of Louisiana, the waterways bordering the North Pole and the wind-blown, sun blistered plains of West Texas. The entrepreneurial spirit, vision and innovation that served the company so well in exploration built a solid foundation for today's Texas Instruments.

THE PRODUCT

TI is a world leader in designing and manufacturing semiconductor chips. Among the most complex products human beings have ever produced, these tiny chips typically contain electrical pathways connecting millions of transistors and other electronic components.

Working around the clock, TI employees use exacting processes to create layer upon layer of circuit patterns on thin, round wafers of silicon. Then those employees establish microscopic metal interconnections that run both along and between the chips' layers, resulting in three-dimensional circuitry that can perform up to 8 billion instructions per second.

Perhaps best of all, economies of scale enable TI to sell many of its chips at a price that puts advanced technology — in the form of cell phones, electronic toys and smart appliances — within the reach of nearly everyone.

RECENT DEVELOPMENTS

TI's nonstop innovations and advances in technology and business strategies keep the company at the forefront of its industry, providing its customers with leading-edge technology. Among TI's most recent developments:

• In June 2006, TI unveiled details of a 45 nanometer semiconductor manufacturing process that will double the number of chips produced on each silicon wafer, increase processing performance and reduce power consumption.

• In May 2006, TI completed construction of its next major semiconductor manufacturing plant. Located just north of Dallas, the facility will house some of the world's most advanced 300 mm semiconductor manufacturing capabilities.

• In January 2006, TI completed its acquisition of Chipcon, a leading company in the design of short-range, low-power wireless radio-frequency transceiver devices. The move expanded TI's high-performance analog portfolio and enables TI to provide customers with industry-leading ZigBee™ compliant solutions and a broad range of proprietary radio frequency integrated circuits that make innovative low-power wireless applications possible.

• TI is regularly introducing additions to its new DaVinci™ technology family of devices. Optimized for digital video systems, DaVinci technology enables breakthrough innovation in digital media devices for the hand, home and car.

PROMOTION

TI's semiconductor devices generally perform their technological prowess without calling attention to themselves or to TI. They're key components of products bearing the names of Nokia, Apple and many other leading companies.

TI's DLP technology is one case in which the company has implemented a consumer communications campaign. Makers of HDTVs and projectors emblazon the DLP logo on their products

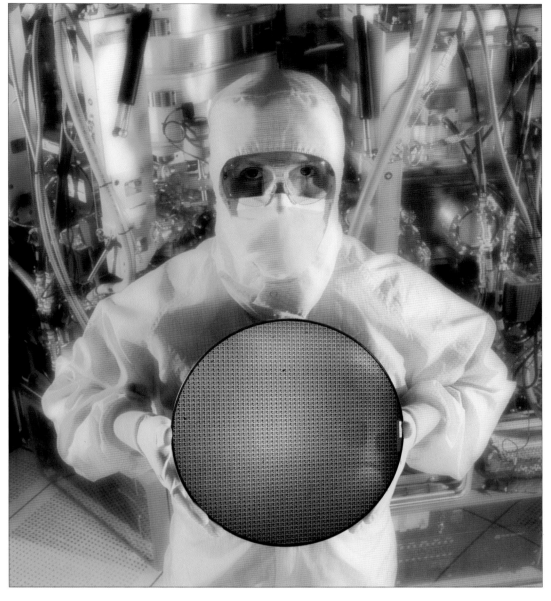

as proof of those products' excellence and TI has supported the branding of DLP technology through a two year old campaign designed to reach consumers via TV, radio and the Web. The TV ads have focused on reaching sports enthusiasts and other key consumer audiences. Meantime, online education has appeared on a variety of sites, including home entertainment blogs.

TI's DLP Products group is also sponsoring Hall of Fame Racing in the NASCAR Nextel Cup Series. NASCAR is America's fastest growing sport and racing fans have good reason to embrace HDTV, since all races are broadcast in high definition.

In addition, TI takes a targeted approach to promoting many of its products through an array of technology publications and Web sites that cater to electronics design engineers, who are crucial decision makers in designing TI technology into a wide variety of electronic products.

BRAND VALUES

Texas Instruments has been making a positive impact on technology and the world for more than 75 years. The company's ingenuity takes the ideas of TI customers further, continually helping to create products that make lives better.

In the face of growing pressure to get to market faster and cheaper, companies regularly turn to TI to solve the challenges that stand between their ideas and reality. Only TI

has the breadth and depth — with the manufacturing capabilities, worldwide local presence and proven track record — to turn great concepts into remarkable things time and time again.

TI is inventive. TI is essential to the people it supports. But what's truly amazing is the positive impact that TI makes on technology and on the lives of people all around the world every day.

THINGS YOU DIDN'T KNOW ABOUT TEXAS INSTRUMENTS

TI's record of creativity and risk-taking has been sprinkled with industry firsts and far-reaching inventions:

○ TI has earned more than 15,000 patents over the years — testimony to the innovative, bright minds that keep the company at the technological vanguard.

○ More than half of all cell phones sold worldwide use TI semiconductor technology.

○ TI invented the commercial transistor radio in 1954 and the handheld calculator in 1967.

○ TI's Jack Kilby won the Nobel Prize in physics in 2000 for his part in inventing the integrated circuit.

○ TI's DLP technology has earned the company two Emmy Awards for its television applications, and DLP Cinema® technology produces 35 trillion colors on movie theater screens.

Tim Hortons

THE MARKET

When the first Tim Hortons® store opened in Hamilton, Ontario, Canada in 1964, dining out was viewed as an occasional treat. Throughout the last 42 years, the pace of life and demand for on-the-go service has increased. Quick, friendly service at the drive thru or in-store, combined with fresh, consistent offerings at a great value has made Tim Hortons a welcome addition to communities across Canada and the United States. Today, customers look for restaurants in convenient locations with diverse menu choices. Tim Hortons is proud to deliver — providing fresh coffee, baked goods and options at breakfast, lunch and dinner.

ACHIEVEMENTS

In 2004, Tim Hortons celebrated its 40th anniversary in Canada. Tim Hortons' commitment to top quality, always fresh product, great service and community leadership has allowed it to grow into Canada's largest quick service restaurant. In 2006, Tim Hortons is offering its always fresh coffee, baked goods and home-style lunches at more than 2,600 locations across Canada and over 290 restaurants in the United States.

Tim Hortons has received many awards of recognition including: Canada's Best Managed Brand, *Canadian Business Magazine*, 2004; Marketer of the Year, *Marketing Magazine*, 2004;

Company of the Year, *Report On Business Magazine*, 2002 and was listed as one of Canada's Top 100 Employers for five consecutive years.

HISTORY

The Tim Hortons chain was founded in Hamilton, Ontario, Canada in 1964 by National Hockey League All-Star defenseman Tim Horton. In 1967, Horton partnered with franchisee and then operator of three Tim Hortons restaurants, Ron Joyce. Together they opened 37 new restaurants over the next seven years. Following Tim Horton's tragic death in 1974, Mr. Joyce continued to expand the chain, becoming its sole owner in 1975.

In the early 1990s, Tim Hortons and Wendy's® entered into a partnership to develop combination restaurants containing Wendy's and Tim Hortons under the same roof. On December 29, 1995, The TDL Group Corp., the licensing company for Tim Hortons franchises, completed a merger with Wendy's International, Inc., creating one great company with two quality brands. The merger

gave new focus and impetus to the expansion of the Tim Hortons concept in key markets in Canada and the United States.

Throughout the last 10 years, the Tim Hortons chain has continued to enhance its growth opportunities while maintaining its core commitment to top quality, always fresh product, value and exceptional service. Most standard Tim Hortons locations are open 24 hours. Customers can dine-in, take-out or use convenient drive-thrus, catering to consumers on-the-go. The chain's "We Fit Anywhere" strategy has allowed for expansion in a number of nontraditional locations such as gas stations, convenience stores, universities, hospitals, office buildings and airports.

THE PRODUCT

The first Tim Hortons restaurant offered only two products — coffee and donuts. The selection of donuts was highlighted by two original Tim Hortons creations, the Apple Fritter and the Dutchie.

Tim Hortons' menu has constantly evolved to meet ever-changing consumer tastes, and growing demand for fresh, diverse menu choices throughout the day. In 1976, the chain introduced the phenomenally successful Timbit® (bite-sized donut hole). The chain's growth in the '80s brought a series of product introductions including muffins, croissants, cookies, soups and chili. With an increased focus on a balanced diet in the '90s, healthier options were introduced, including an all-star line-up of six "Tim's Own"® sandwiches and a variety of bagels. Tim Hortons also added a number of new beverage options including flavoured cappuccino, Café Mocha and Iced Cappuccino. In recent years, Tim Hortons has continued to introduce new product innovations to the menu, including the Cinnamon Roll, Hot Smoothee and Yogurt & Berries.

Tim Hortons' biggest drawing card remains its legendary coffee. The premium blend is also available in tins, as are Tim Hortons hot chocolate and flavoured cappuccinos, allowing customers to enjoy these great tasting products at home.

RECENT DEVELOPMENTS

In March 2006, Tim Hortons reached another milestone with the initial public offering of the company. Trading commenced on the Toronto Stock Exchange and New York Stock Exchange on March 24 under the symbol THI.

PROMOTION

The marketing program at Tim Hortons is designed to create and extend the brand image as "your neighbourhood Tim's," offering quality products at reasonable prices. Despite becoming one of the most recognizable brands in Canada,

the company maintains its focus on the franchisees and customers who helped make it the success it is today. Letters and stories from loyal customers have served as inspiration for many of Tim Hortons most popular promotional efforts. For example, the "True Stories" television commercials are created from outstanding customer testimonials and feature the true-life experiences of customers' interaction with Tim Hortons.

In 1986, another customer-driven promotion began — Roll Up The Rim To Win®. Designed as a fun and interactive way to thank Tim Hortons' loyal customers, the annual promotion gives away millions of prizes each year and has become a "rite of spring" for loyal customers.

Tim Hortons' franchisees believe in building long-term relationships with customers by giving back to the communities that support them. Regional marketing groups support locally targeted initiatives, including the "Smile Cookie" program, which raises money for hundreds of local charities and non-profit organizations. In addition, Tim Hortons is a major supporter of minor sports. Over 120,000 Timbit youth athletes between the ages of four and eight can be found in arenas and sports fields throughout North America.

Tim Hortons has also taken a leadership role in promoting environmental awareness. Through educating customers and offering eco-friendly choices, the company is committed to keeping streets clean and the environment healthy.

Whether it's in the marketplace or in the neighbourhood, Tim Hortons considers itself a member of the community and makes caring for customers a priority.

BRAND VALUES

Rooted to the caring and unpretentious style that has propelled the chain to where it is today, Tim Hortons is committed to providing the same great value, fresh product and friendly service that were instilled by company founders. Tim Hortons considers itself a member of the communities in which it operates. Committed to its customers, Tim Hortons consistently supports local, regional and national nonprofit initiatives.

Our most notable community outreach project is the Tim Horton Children's Foundation. Founded in 1974, the Tim Horton Children's Foundation is an independent non-profit charitable organization that selects local children age nine to twelve who could otherwise not afford it to attend various programs throughout the year, including a 10-day residence camp experience. The camp experience is designed to give children confidence in their abilities, pride in their accomplishments and the chance to gain a positive view of the world and their future in it. In 2005, more than 11,000 kids attended one of the six Foundation camps, located in Kananaskis, Alberta; Parry Sound, Ontario; St. George, Ontario; Quyon, Quebec; Tatmagouche, Nova Scotia; and Campbellsville, Kentucky. Every spring, Tim Hortons and its franchisees demonstrate their commitment to the Tim Horton Children's Foundation through participation in Camp Day, the one day a year where every penny from coffee sales is donated to the Foundation.

THINGS YOU DIDN'T KNOW ABOUT TIM HORTONS

○ Tim Hortons "Always Fresh" promise guarantees a fresh cup of coffee every time. If it's not served within 20 minutes of being brewed, it's not served at all.

○ Since 1974, the Tim Horton Children's Foundation has sent over 83,000 economically disadvantaged children on the camping adventure of a lifetime. It is largely supported by Camp Day — the one day a year when all Tim Hortons store owners donate 100 percent of their coffee sales to the Foundation.

○ Tim Hortons' Sustainable Coffee Partnership Program was recently launched in Guatemala. Committed to improving the living conditions of coffee farmers and their families, the program teaches farmers about proper coffee growing techniques and helps improve living conditions by establishing new infrastructure and opportunities.

TSX group

THE MARKET

Toronto Stock Exchange (TSX) is a national icon in Canada, respected as a symbol of quality, integrity and financial leadership in the capital markets.

TSX has carved out a niche as a nimble and innovative competitor adept at bringing breakthroughs to the market. TSX Group, which brings Toronto Stock Exchange together with TSX Venture Exchange, Natural Gas Exchange and a 45 percent interest in the fixed-income market CanDeal, is characterized by efficient operations and original products that help ensure equity financing remains an affordable option for small and mid-sized companies as well as the corporate giants listed on it.

Since becoming a publicly listed company in 2002, TSX Group has entered a new phase in its development as a growth company. It is expanding its trading expertise into new asset classes, extending its geographic reach and accelerating its innovations.

ACHIEVEMENTS

Toronto Stock Exchange became an aggressive, agile contender because it has been competing with two of the world's dominant exchanges for years. Many of Canada's largest corporations reinforce key business relationships with American customers by electing to raise capital by interlisting on U.S. exchanges. Now U.S. firms are listing in Canada to take advantage of TSX Group's innovative, tax-efficient products and its specialization in small and mid-cap company finance. As a consequence of the interconnected economies, Canadian stock exchanges have competed successfully with U.S. exchanges for listings and trading volumes for years. TSX Group recognizes this as a powerful competitive tool that brings efficiencies essential to the success of Canadian capital markets. As exchange consolidation continues globally, TSX Group will capitalize on its strengths in resource financing, in small and mid-cap companies and in product innovation to capitalize on Canada's unique strengths.

TSX Group prides itself on its history of innovation and on the variety of technology, product and exchange improvements it has pioneered for its customers.

Toronto Stock Exchange became, in 1977, the first stock market in the world to introduce electronic trading. Twenty years later the Exchange's trading floor closed, and all trading went electronic. As the latest market innovation, algorithmic trading, is adopted by traders, TSX Group's technology remains at the leading edge.

TSX has also been a product innovator. It began trading the world's first Exchange Traded Fund (ETF), called TIPS, in March 1990. Three years later, a U.S. stock exchange introduced the first American ETF.

Income trusts are a more recent innovation that TSX helped develop into a popular investment tool for income-seeking investors. Structured products are the newest category of investments that TSX is helping to develop to meet investors' growing demand for income investments.

A spirit of innovation is also evident at the corporate level. Since 2001, when Toronto Stock Exchange acquired the venture exchange, it has established TSX Venture as a national market for emerging growth companies. TSX Venture is a unique market that has developed several of its own innovations to serve the economically important public venture capital market. Among them are its Capital Pool Company (CPC) listing technique and the NEX market that provides emerging companies with a place to regroup and reorganize.

TSX Group also took a decisive step forward when it became the first exchange operator in North American to sell its shares to the public. Its shares began trading on its senior exchange in 2002 under the symbol "X". Since then it has ranked among some of the top exchanges in the world in terms of performance.

HISTORY

On July 26, 1852, a group of Toronto businessmen met to form an association of brokers to encourage the trading of company shares. Several of the original listings on Toronto Stock Exchange were mining companies.

TSX Group's two stock exchanges, TSX, the senior market for larger established companies, and TSX Venture Exchange, for emerging companies with high growth potential, are the world leaders in resource finance. In 2005, TSX Group helped mining companies raise $4.8 billion in new equity capital, more than 40 percent of all mine equity financing raised globally. TSX Group has similar strength in the energy sector. More oil and gas companies are listed on its exchanges than on any other exchange or exchange group.

The most dramatic changes in the Exchange's long history occurred in the last decade. The tradition of the Exchange as a mutual company owned by its members began coming to an end when it became a for-profit company in 2000. Canada's five smaller regional stock exchanges had begun consolidating in 1999, and TSX acquired the newly amalgamated venture exchange in 2001. TSX

Venture's head office remained in Calgary. The following year TSX Group completed the transformation by carrying out an initial public offering and listing its shares on its senior exchange.

It began expanding its trading expertise into other types of asset classes including fixed-income and energy. The company has also begun diversifying into other international markets with a new focus on Canada's closest neighbour and its largest trading partner, the United States.

THE PRODUCT

Electronic exchanges like TSX Group's provide fast, fair and efficient markets. But trading transactions that are initiated and concluded inside computers are virtually invisible. Recognizing that investors tend to associate a stock market with the activities of a frenetic trading floor, the TSX Group Broadcast Centre was created. The Centre has become a popular hub of capital markets activity for Bay Street. Its broadcast wall of stock ticker screens is now a familiar image that reinforces Toronto Stock Exchange's position at the heart of the country's capital markets.

TSX Group is, by nature, a technology company whose business expertise is operating an open, transparent and fair electronic market. About two-fifths of its employees are IT professionals and it invests in continuous upgrades of its world-class trading system. Since its new trading engine went into operation in 2001, during a period when algorithmic trading prompted huge order volume increases, its trading availability has exceeded 99.9 percent reliability.

Robust technology also contributes to the company's ability to deliver a range of new products and services, including the addition of the FIX trading protocol, and two trading enhancements, TSXPress™ and ATX™. TSX Group is also preparing to launch its next-generation trading platform.

TSX Group also sells many data products. In addition to traditional data packages that include

various levels of pricing and index data, it also provides corporate data and disclosure data. Other recent product introductions include: Compliance Alerts Reporting System (CARS™), a product that helps compliance officers monitor trading infractions and TSXconnect®, which serves investor relations needs.

RECENT DEVELOPMENTS

The flagship composite indexes of both of TSX Group's stock exchanges have recorded exceptional performances since 2000. That, combined with the Canadian dollar's resurgence, has attracted growing numbers of international investors. Rising resource prices contributed to the gains, but Canadian equities have outperformed the U.S. markets in other sectors as well. All but two of the 10 TSX composite index sectors — health care and information technology — significantly outperformed their S&P 500 counterparts in the United States during the six-year period ended December 31, 2005.

TSX Group diversified its trading asset base when it acquired Natural Gas Exchange (NGX), a Calgary-based energy exchange that trades natural gas and electricity, in 2004. NGX has been expanding in the United States and has helped TSX Group accrue expertise in derivatives trading.

The company has also announced plans to enter derivatives trading no later than 2009 when regulatory restrictions expire and is now preparing for that initiative.

PROMOTION

Although Toronto Stock Exchange has a 154-year history as a leader in Canada's capital markets, the TSX brand is new.

By adopting the TSX brand image, with its distinctive upward-sloping curve on the X as its new symbol, TSX Group ended potential confusion with other international exchanges such as the Tokyo and Taiwan stock exchanges. And it signalled its intent to enter the international market.

BRAND VALUES

TSX Group is a customer-focused company that works closely with stakeholders to provide capital market leadership and serve the needs of the broad stakeholder group that depends on it.

As a technology company whose service is depended upon to deliver the highest levels of reliability, it must also be innovative and responsive to customer needs. Toronto Stock Exchange and TSX Venture Exchange deliver a variety of innovations. Whether they are new products like ETFs and income trusts for investors, or services for companies like TSX Venture's CPCs and NEX, TSX Group's innovations make the capital markets, stronger and the Canadian economy more competitive.

TSX Group is a respected leader in the capital markets, and it fulfills its responsibilities effectively.

Excellence is required, integrity is essential and TSX Group delivers nothing less.

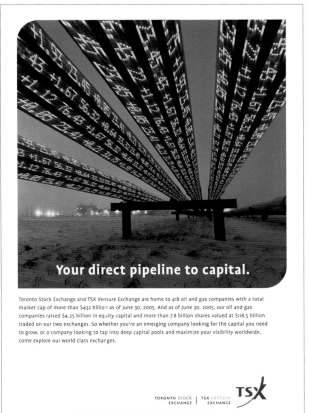

United Way
Centraide

THE MARKET

The United Way-Centraide Movement (UW-C) in Canada is made up of 124 autonomous, volunteer-based UWs-Cs located in ten provinces and two territories and a national organization, United Way of Canada-Centraide Canada (UWC-CC). Its mission is "to improve lives and build community by engaging individuals and mobilizing collective action." UWC-CC acts as a voice for its members within the Canadian voluntary sector and internationally and provides leadership, programs and services to its members. The national organization also maintains a close relationship with United Way of America, United Way International (UWI) and through UWI, with other UW organizations around the world.

Next to governments, the UW-C Movement is the largest funder of the voluntary sector and social services in Canada. Each year, UWs-Cs raise upwards of $430 million, the vast majority of which is reinvested in local communities to support programs and services directed at improving the social conditions of Canadians. The UW-C Movement employs approximately 900 staff and engages tens of thousands of volunteers in various capacities.

ACHIEVEMENTS

UW-C achievements are measured by the communities they strengthened, the people they touched, the resources they mobilized and the productive partnerships they forged. UW-C is about attracting or engaging people who want to achieve lasting impact in their community in order to meet the needs of individuals whose lives are changed as a result of its work. There are many examples of UW-C achievements in communities across Canada. To know more about your community UW-C, visit www.unitedway.ca.

As a collective, the achievements of the UW-C will lead to improved social conditions for individuals and families across Canada. This is best highlighted by pan-Canadian initiatives. For example, 211 is a free, easy-to-remember three digit

phone number to non-emergency human services that is located in five centres and growing. There are plans for a national roll-out, with the goal of extending 211 to all Canadians by 2011.

UWC-CC is also leading a national children's initiative focused on improving the well being of children and families and ensuring that all children in Canada have the opportunity to succeed. Finally, Action for Neighbourhood Change is a unique learning initiative that is exploring and assessing approaches to locally driven neighbourhood revitalization in order to enhance the capacity of individuals and families to build and sustain strong, healthy communities.

HISTORY

The UW-C Movement was born out of a "community collective" philosophy which began in Denver in 1887 and spread to Canada prior to the 1920s. This was a turbulent time in world history. Canada was enmeshed in the Great War to end all wars and the first threads of our social safety net were still almost 30 years away. Individuals and families were reliant upon their own ingenuity and the generosity of their neighbours and community. It is in this environment that UW-C first emerged. In 1917 in Montreal and Toronto, charities started community collectives to raise funds to strengthen their communities.

Additional community collectives sprang up across Canada over time. Known originally as Red Feather, Community Chest and the United Appeal, it was not until the 1970s that these organizations took the name of United Way and Centraide (in 1973 and 1975, respectively). A national office was first established in 1939. Today, there are 124 UWs-Cs across Canada, with a presence from coast to coast.

In the 20th century, UW-C gained a reputation as a premier umbrella fund-raiser and became particularly active in workplaces due to a partnership with the Canadian Labour Congress and agreements with corporations and all orders of government. Each year, millions of dollars have been raised and reinvested in communities through funding of voluntary, not-for-profit, human and social service organizations.

Today UW-C is a catalyst for community action — bringing people and resources together to create positive change in communities across Canada.

THE PRODUCT

UWs-Cs have the dual strengths of being locally driven and nationally connected. This unique feature allows them to remain responsive and accountable to local communities while drawing on the strength of a pan-Canadian Movement.

UW-C recognizes and appreciates the significant role they have, as community organizations and as a Movement, to be a catalyst for effective community action. UW-C is committed to bringing citizens together to identify and realize a vision of better lives, improved conditions and stronger communities for everyone.

Achieving the vision requires input and involvement from people across all parts of our communities. Whether they participate by volunteering, contributing financially or providing knowledge and expertise, people are seeing the powerful results — the impact — of collective action.

By providing safe, healthy environments for children and youth — opening doors for their lifelong success. By supporting people's efforts to escape poverty, live independently and overcome challenges — building self-reliance and capacity to give back. By building safer, more welcoming and economically strong neighbourhoods — creating a vibrant community that can better respond to challenges now and in the future.

In 2005, Canadians invested over $430 million in the UW-C Movement.

RECENT DEVELOPMENTS

UWs-Cs are keenly aware that the environment in which we operate is always changing. Public policy, demographic and social trends, technological innovations, economic changes, and shifts in individual and corporate values and expectations have all experienced major change in recent years.

With significant changes in their local environments, and with the issues facing their communities becoming more and more complex, communities across Canada were looking for leadership. UWs-Cs challenged themselves to respond and united behind a common mission, aspirations

and values and a commitment to "achieving community impact through community building."

By bringing together a broad cross section of society to identify, track and address community issues, to raise and leverage funds and to engage individuals through volunteering, UW-C mobilizes communities into action. Integral to their community building efforts is the belief that all communities have assets which need to be identified and built upon and that societal issues must be dealt with holistically and at their root.

PROMOTION

Campaign achievement is demonstrated through the strong commitment of our UWs-Cs who marshal local, provincial and national media channels; through corporate and union workplace campaign support; from individuals who provide support financially and/or through time; and through cross promotion and sponsorship partnerships — all of which support the annual fall UW-C campaign and year-round awareness of creating community impact through community building efforts.

As part of the partnership between UWC-CC and the Canadian Labour Congress, unions encourage their members to work with and volunteer for UWs-Cs and community agencies all year long. Many unions get directly involved in workplace campaigns, promoting member donation and volunteer activities during campaign.

The "Thanks a Million" national award of UWC-CC recognizes the corporations and unions that have facilitated their employees or members raising $1 million or more for UWs-Cs across the country. An advertisement is generally run in a nationally distributed newspaper, which offers further recognition to the UW-C Movement.

With the continued rapid evolution of technology, UWC-CC has updated its public Web site at www.unitedway.ca. The Web site acts as a portal for Canadian citizens to connect to their community UW-C. It also serves as a valuable marketing tool as it can be viewed and accessed by virtually anyone.

National initiatives and partnerships such as Action for Neighbourhood Change and 211 have received attention from various constituents through different local and national networks.

BRAND VALUES

Organizations that are successful in this turbulent, complex and fast-moving environment share common characteristics. First, they have a clear mission and brand position. Second, they work differently, investing heavily in knowledge and knowledge management and redesigning their processes. Third, they boast strong leadership and a laser-like focus. Fourth, they deliver against their clear mission and objectives.

UWs-Cs are doing just that. In May 2003, the UW-C Movement adopted a Movement-wide mission: "To improve lives and build community by engaging individuals and mobilizing collective action," as well as aspirations and values to support this mission.

The goal of the UW-C Movement is to achieve community impact through community building. Community impact has been described as "cumulative, lasting, measurable change that improves

lives, builds resilient communities and mobilizes collective action."

Through Interbrand research conducted in the United States, the calculated brand value of $34.7 billion U.S. would place it in the top ten of the world's most valuable brands.

Photos: cscottrobinsonphoto.com

THINGS YOU DIDN'T KNOW ABOUT UNITED WAYS – CENTRAIDES IN CANADA

○ Day of Caring® is a UW-C program that connects organizations and employees to spend a day working directly with the agencies and programs that help people in the community.

○ The number of Canadians with access to 211 grew in 2005 from 3.2 million to 4.6 million or from 10 to 15 percent of the total population.

○ UW-C–funded union counselling courses train union members to link other members in need with the agencies and services their donations have supported through the annual campaign.

○ UW-C Leadership Development Services delivers training to voluntary boards to strengthen their governance and accountability.

The Weather Network | Météo Média

theweathernetwork.com ■ meteomedia.com

THE MARKET

Canadians have a favourite topic of conversation — the weather. The Weather Network and its French language counterpart, MétéoMédia, have been providing weather-related information to Canadians since 1988. In the beginning, it was strictly the television services that Canadians relied upon. With the explosion of technology, The Weather Network and MétéoMédia are now available not only on cable, satellite and telco services, but also through online services, wireless communications and major newspapers across the country. The forecasts go beyond providing Canadians with information to plan their daily activities. The Weather Network Commercial Services division offers complete weather solutions to market segments such as transportation, energy, municipalities and media. The Weather Network and MétéoMédia, owned and operated by Pelmorex Media Inc., will continue to keep pace with the growth of technology and reach Canadians anywhere, anytime, anyhow.

Weather is a universal topic, and there are many weather sources, but Pelmorex has been able to stand out from the competition. The company has become the undisputed leader of weather-related information services in Canada. All they do is weather, and it has been a winning formula. Their goal is very clear; they do not aim to be the biggest in the communications sector but rather the best weather-related information services company in Canada. The Weather Network and MétéoMédia follow these guiding principles to accomplish their goal of being

the very best in the weather category: focus, competitive advantage, teamwork, win-win relationships and control over its destiny. By continuing to focus on its unique integration of creativity, science and technology, Pelmorex plans to lead the weather business in Canada for many years to come.

ACHIEVEMENTS

Pelmorex aims to be the best employer in the broadcast industry with the philosophy that it is the people behind the brand that make things happen.

Recognized as a leader for employment equity and diversity, Pelmorex was named one of Canada's top employers in 2003. In a *Maclean's* cover story on Canada's Top Employers, the magazine had this to say about Pelmorex: "The federal government ranks the operator of TV's weather channels tops in its industry for employment equity."

Pelmorex also received the Vision Award in 2003 for Excellence in Employment Equity by the federal Ministry of Labour.

MétéoMédia has won seven awards at the International Weather Festival (now known as le forum international de la météo). Patrick DeBellefeuille, on-camera presenter with MétéoMédia, was the first Canadian to have won the grand prize twice.

HISTORY

In the fall of 1988, English and French language weather services, The Weather Network and MétéoMédia, launched in Canada. One year later, Pelmorex was founded by Pierre Morrissette, chairman, president, CEO and controlling shareholder. Pelmorex acquired The Weather Network and MétéoMédia in 1993. In 1995, the growing company launched its highly successful Web sites, theweathernetwork.com and meteomedia.com. The following year, The Weather Channel based in Atlanta, Georgia was brought on board as a strategic minority shareholder. In 1997, The Weather Network moved to the Greater Toronto Area from Montreal to be in its largest market.

The number of employees has more than doubled since the acquisition of the networks, jumping from 125 to over 300. When the services launched, many Canadians didn't believe there was a market for a 24-hour weather service. Today The Weather Network and MétéoMédia are the leaders in the Canadian weather-related information services business and among Canada's most popular media services.

THE PRODUCT

One of the core strengths of The Weather Network and MétéoMédia is product and service innovation. Consumers and clients receive added value through the ongoing development of in-house meteorological and weather-related content. The company operates one of Canada's most elaborate and dynamic database businesses. This is all made possible by the over 40 employees dedicated to developing software. More than 30 meteorologists are on staff, making Pelmorex the largest employer of meteorologists in the Canadian private sector.

Innovative product and service development contributes to the overall success of the three main business divisions: Television, Interactive Services and Commercial Services.

The specialty television networks, The Weather Network and MétéoMédia, are among the most frequently consulted and widely distributed specialty networks, with over 10 million households relying on their services and 99 percent of cable,

satellite and telco subscribers receiving them. The Weather Network also has one of the highest levels of viewer satisfaction and has consistently been voted number one for best forecasts on television.

What makes the networks so unique is their ability to be national yet simultaneously deliver local forecasts to over 1,100 communities across Canada. This is accomplished by using Pelmorex's patented PMX technology that sends a different alpha-numeric forecast to each cable system across the country. Each cable system receives only the forecast for its area. The technology is very useful for advertisers who want to reach local markets and send a targeted message to each area. The Local Forecast, available every ten minutes on the tens, is one of the most popular pieces of programming on the networks.

Interactive Services includes the theweathernetwork.com, meteomedia.com and farmzone.com (the latter Web site designed to meet the weather needs of the Canadian agricultural industry). With about 7 million unique users and about 100 million page views each month, the Web sites consistently rank among Canada's top Web sites. In addition, over 50,000 portals and other Web sites link to theweathernetwork.com and

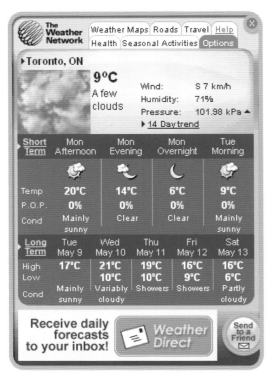

meteomedia.com for weather content. Interactive Services also offers weather tools that make accessing weather information even more convenient. For example, over 1 million Canadians use WeatherEye, a desktop weather application; over 240,000 Canadians receive their forecast by e-mail with WeatherDirect; and almost 120,000 text weather messages per month are accessed via cell phones and other wireless devices.

Commercial Services provides complete weather solutions for a variety of industries and sectors — Transportation, Energy, Municipalities, Retail and Media. As Canada's largest independent meteorological company, The Weather Network Commercial Services Division has the infrastructure and resources to service the most demanding operations with timely, dependable and cost-effective solutions

enabling clients and their organizations to stay one step ahead of the weather. Pelmorex recently acquired the operations of World Weatherwatch, a well-established Canadian weather service provider.

RECENT DEVELOPMENTS

The Weather Network's recent move to a state-of-the-art media centre in Oakville, Ontario demonstrates its ongoing growth. The newly built 60,000 square foot facility is nearly twice the size of its previous home. "Our new headquarters reflects our growth and the move allows us to take advantage of the latest broadcasting and meteorological technologies. We are state-of-the-art in every respect and well positioned for growth," said Pierre Morrissette, president and CEO of Pelmorex.

PROMOTION

The ever popular, award-winning billboard campaign that launched in 1999 took The Weather Network brand to the next level in terms of brand awareness. The billboards debuted one day after a record snowfall in Toronto. Headlines like "Told You So" and "You're Welcome" with

arrows pointing towards the sky instantly got noticed. The campaign made headlines on television and newspapers and won numerous advertising awards.

The combination of out of home, radio, print, online and television advertising, as well as effective cross-promotional activities across all Pelmorex properties have all contributed to The Weather Network's success as one of Canada's most recognizable media brands.

BRAND VALUES

Being the very best at meeting the weather information needs of Canadians whose activities are dependent on weather is the foundation of The Weather Network and MétéoMédia brand. This is based on delivering the most updated, accurate, reliable, convenient, immediate and accessible weather information in Canada. Offering weather information anywhere, anytime and anyhow is critical for the brand to continue to dominate the Canadian weather information services business.

THINGS YOU DIDN'T KNOW ABOUT THE WEATHER NETWORK AND MÉTÉOMÉDIA

○ The Weather Network and MétéoMédia were the first Canadian services to deliver an hourly forecast, 7 day outlook, 14 day trend and seasonal forecasts on television and online.

○ The Weather Network and MétéoMédia issue approximately 33,000 forecasts each day. That is over 12 million forecasts each year and about three forecasts per minute.

○ Nearly 190,000 feet of cable were used in The Weather Network's state-of-the-art media facility.

○ On-camera presenters broadcast from virtual studios using chroma-key technology. The presenter is in a green room, and the camera takes a picture of everything that is green and replaces it with the map viewers see at home.

Yellow Pages™

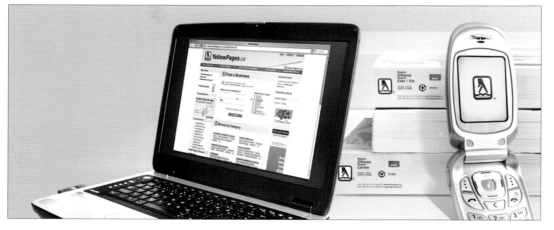

THE MARKET

Yellow Pages Group is Canada's largest telephone directories publisher. Its national platform of print and online directories affords it a unique geographic positioning for a media company in Canada. Yellow Pages Group is the incumbent directory publisher in Quebec, Ontario, Alberta, British Columbia and the Territories, and in Atlantic Canada through Aliant ActiMedia.

The company owns and manages Yellow Pages.ca™ and Canada411.ca*, Canada's most visited online directories, as well as CanadaPlus .ca™, a network of seven local city sites. Yellow Pages Group offers deep online local content on a national basis.

With its strong nationwide sales force that maintains long-standing relationships with over 381,000 advertisers, Yellow Pages Group is ideally positioned to gather content that is not only thorough and detailed, but also up-to-date and relevant to today's Canadian consumers.

ACHIEVEMENTS

The year 2003 marked the rebirth of two of the most well-known brands in Canada — the Yellow Pages™ brand and the Walking Fingers Design™ brand. The company's first step was to re-think what the brands meant to users and how their positioning could differentiate them in the marketplace. After extensive market research, a mass advertising campaign was launched. The company invested heavily in its products, notably by redesigning the directory covers to better reflect its new positioning.

In 2005, the company redesigned its brand and corporate logos to reflect its more modern, innovative and youthful products as well as its leadership in the Canadian directory market. The company also expanded the definition of the brand notion to include online and wireless formats.

Concurrent with the modernization of the brand, Yellow Pages Group enlarged its marketing strategies to include B2B initiatives such

as the creation of an online Advertiser Center and e-Newsletter.

Today, Yellow Pages Group is one of Canada's leading media companies. Since the Yellow Pages Group IPO, the company has achieved industry-leading levels of organic growth and operating margins. Yellow Pages Group continues to have great momentum in its operating and financial metrics and believes that with its strong national platform, it is well positioned for the future.

HISTORY

Yellow Pages Group is in many ways a new and rejuvenated company with a 100-year-old history.

The company published its first directory in 1908 and operated as a division of Bell Canada until 1971, when it was incorporated as Tele-Direct (Publications) Inc. At that time, the company published directories that covered nearly all of Ontario and Quebec, following the local telephone service footprint, and the markets of Yukon, Northwest Territories and Nunavut.

In 1999, Tele-Direct (Publications) Inc. changed its name to Bell ActiMedia Inc. and repositioned itself as a multimedia company. Yellow Pages Group was formed in 2002, with the acquisition of the directory publishing operations of Bell Canada by Kohlberg Kravis Roberts & Co. (KKR) and Ontario Teachers' Merchant Bank.

On May 15, 2003, Yellow Pages Group concluded the purchase of the CanadaPlus.ca city sites network from Bell Canada's Sympatico Portal Division. In 2005, Yellow Pages Group launched the TorontoPlus.ca™ city site, completing its nationwide city sites presence.

On August 1, 2003, Yellow Pages Group, through Yellow Pages Income Fund, completed the largest income trust's IPO in Canadian history. By 2004, the company had completed its transition to a stand-alone publicly traded entity while laying the foundation for a new future.

On May 25, 2005, Yellow Pages Group completed the purchase of Advertising Directory Solutions Holdings Inc. (ADS), creating a national platform for its print and online directories.

THE PRODUCT

Yellow Pages Group publishes more than 330 Yellow Pages™ and residential directories annually. The Yellow Pages™ directories are present in markets that cover 93 percent of the Canadian population. That means that virtually every household and business in these markets receives a Yellow Pages™ directory.

Yellow Pages Group is the exclusive owner of the Yellow Pages™, Pages Jaunes™ and Walking Fingers Design™ trademarks in Canada.

In addition to its print products, Yellow Pages Group operates leading online directories, YellowPages.ca™ (Find a business), Canada411.ca* (Find a person), and CanadaPlus.ca™, a network of local city sites including MontrealPlus.ca™, QuebecPlus.ca™, TorontoPlus.ca™, CalgaryPlus.ca™, EdmontonPlus.ca™, OttawaPlus.ca™ and Vancouver Plus.ca™. These sites attract approximately 7.5 million unique visitors per month, making the network the sixth most visited by online Canadians.

In 2006, Yellow Pages Group started extending its product line, as a complement to its traditional Yellow Pages™ directory advertising offering. The company entered into a partnership with Transcontinental Media to

develop specialized guides that contain both editorial content and directory information for a specific topic. The first guides on home improvement were launched in Toronto and Montreal in 2006.

RECENT DEVELOPMENTS

Yellow Pages Group is focused on extending the directory category by developing new products beyond the print book. The company seeks to offer the public seamless solutions that do not distinguish between print, online and wireless formats. The goal is to incite people to turn to one of Yellow Pages Group directories, in any of its formats, whenever they are looking for a product, service, business or person. This objective also leads to a broader visibility for advertisers and greater content for users.

The new YellowPages.ca™ search engine is a prime example of this. In 2006, Yellow Pages Group launched this unique, keyword searchable online search platform that allows users to submit unstructured queries and obtain structured results. The new YellowPages.ca™ Web site has become a "find engine" that will enable the company to

consolidate its leadership position in the area of local search.

The WebNumber™ service also demonstrates the company's commitment to offer broad visibility to advertisers. Launched in May 2005, this

service provides a free Web site to every business in Canada that has a Yellow Pages™ listing. The Internet address for these sites comprises the merchant's telephone number, followed by "yellowpages.ca" or "yp.ca."

Another new product being piloted is HelloYellow™, a voice-activated telephone directory assistance service that allows users to conduct a business category search by phone.

PROMOTION

Yellow Pages Group advertising and promotions are aligned with the objective of expanding the directory category. Recent campaigns were intended to further rejuvenate the brand and increase the top-of-mind awareness of the company's online properties.

The way Yellow Pages Group has been doing this is by combining the usual gamut of media — TV and radio spots, out-of-home and street advertising — with some truly unexpected guerrilla tactics and stunts. Initiatives that have been getting lots of attention at airports include the "Sleeping Dummy" media — a mannequin that resembles a woman sleeping on a bench. Above her is a Yellow Pages.ca™ ad that reads "www.5 star hotel within 5 km.ca," suggesting that she should have used the directory to find a hotel.

Other innovative airport tactics have included the use of suitcases,

luggage trolleys and electronic display boards to deliver unexpected and memorable messages.

It is not just at airports where Yellow Pages Group has been getting creative, though. It is also at home, bridal and maternity shows. Essentially, Yellow Pages Group wants to be involved in every business search in a remarkable way.

BRAND VALUES

Yellow Pages™ directories are more than search engines. They are "find engines." They are not used as entertainment or for casual surfing, but are instead perceived as a singular resource to find something. And finding ultimately connects buyers and sellers.

Consumers have come to rely on Yellow Pages™ directories to help them make clever buying decisions. That is because they know they are efficient and easy to use, and they trust that they will help them find exactly what they are looking for — every time.

The Yellow Pages™ brand is constantly evolving to serve new audiences in new ways. The Web site offerings play a pivotal role in that evolution. Directory users get excited by next-generation products. But they need a reason to believe — and that reason lies in the insight that Yellow Pages™ directories play a different role than other search engines. So they must continually entice audiences emotionally, push them towards new products and ultimately link the

products, the experience and the value with the Yellow Pages™ brand essence of "fuelling clever buying decisions."

* Canada411 is a trademark of Stentor Resources Centre Inc., used under license.

THINGS YOU DIDN'T KNOW ABOUT YELLOW PAGES™ DIRECTORIES

- More Canadians than ever refer to directories — 76 percent have used an online or print directory in the past month.
- Sixty-six percent of users make a purchase after using a directory.
- Fifty-four percent of the purchasers are new customers for the advertiser.
- Yellow Pages Group network of Web sites reaches 35 percent of all online Canadians every month.
- On average, every dollar spent in advertising in a Yellow Pages™ directory generates $26 in revenue for the advertiser.

BRAND GUARDIANS

Aeroplan

PAUL GILBERT
Vice President, Marketing

Paul Gilbert leads the marketing team responsible for planning and execution of all marketing programs, outbound channels, Customer Relationship Management and brand management. His team led the successful Aeroplan re-branding program in 2004 — launching Aeroplan's first comprehensive member card re-issue and its first national TV campaign.

Paul holds an Honours BFA from Mount Allison University and has 26 years of experience on the agency side of marketing as a creative practitioner, executive/owner and brand consultant. He is active in the arts community as a member of the Communications Committee of the Art Gallery of Ontario and the Writer's Trust. He and his wife Nancy are Founding Sponsors of The Atlantic Ballet Theatre of Canada. In addition, Paul is a member of the Canadian Marketing Association and a juror for the Canadian Marketing Hall of Fame.

Air Canada

LOUISE MCKENVEN
Senior Director, Product Design

Louise is responsible for overseeing Air Canada products including Maple Leaf Lounges, cabin interior makeovers and introduction of new aircrafts such as the B-777, in-flight entertainment systems and content management as well as Concierge Services and the corporate brand identity. Her knowledge in brand strategy and customer experience since joining Air Canada's Marketing area in 1985 has been further enriched with four years of experience as head of Marketing for the Star Alliance Network based in Frankfurt.

AIM Trimark Investments

PHILIP TAYLOR
Senior Managing Director
Philip Taylor assumed responsibility for AMVESCAP's North American retail business in April, 2006. Mr. Taylor had served as chief executive officer of AIM Trimark Investments in Canada since January 2002 and has been a member of the Executive Management Committee of AMVESCAP since January 2003. He joined AMVESCAP's Canadian business in 1999 as senior vice president of operations and client services and later became executive vice president and chief operating officer. Mr. Taylor received a Bachelor of Commerce (Honors) from Carleton University and an MBA from the Schulich School of Business at York University.

KARLA CONGSON
Vice President, Marketing Communications
Karla Congson is the Vice President of Marketing Communications at AIM Trimark. Her primary responsibility is the strategic leadership of communication efforts ranging from investor brand advertising, to advisor collateral, to the production of the annual report.

Ms. Congson joined AIM Trimark in 2003. She brings 12 years of marketing communications experience, most recently as a strategic planner at Publicis, where she provided brand strategy expertise to a number of Fortune 500 clients. Prior to that, she worked at Foote, Cone and Belding on clients such as Tropicana, TD Bank, Mead Johnson, Tetley Tea and Corby Distilleries.

Benjamin Moore

Thomas J. Stack
Vice-President, Sales & Marketing
Benjamin Moore & Co., Limited
Thomas oversees the implementation of the following strategic initiatives: Retail and Commercial Development, Customer Management, Brand Marketing and Sales Training. He is also responsible for overall Sales and Marketing Leadership: Direction, Alignment and Motivation.

Before joining Benjamin Moore in 1995, Thomas was Director of Marketing for Tupperware Canada.

Thomas J. Stack
Vice-président des ventes et du marketing
Benjamin Moore & Cie Limitee
Thomas supervise la mise en oeuvre des initiatives stratégiques suivantes : le développement du commerce de détail, la gestion de la clientèle, la commercialisation de la marque et la formation en vente. Il est aussi responsable du leadership global pour les ventes et le marketing : direction, alignement et motivation.

Avant de se joindre à Benjamin Moore en 1995, Thomas était Directeur du marketing pour Tupperware Canada.

Buckley's

KIRONMOY DATTA
Senior Brand Manager, Buckley's, Otrivin and Delsym

Kironmoy began his career in sales at Sony of Canada in 1990. After completing his MBA, he went on to join Procter & Gamble Canada, where he worked in brand management on Folgers Coffee and Pampers Diapers. He then joined Pillsbury Canada as a Marketing Manager on the Old El Paso brand. After Pillsbury was purchased by General Mills, he worked on other brands, including Betty Crocker Potatoes and Hamburger Helper. He joined Novartis Consumer Healthcare in 2005 as a Senior Brand Manager. In his current role, he is responsible for marketing and development of the Buckley's brand in both Canada and the United States.

Calgary Stampede

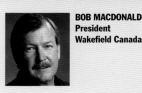

Vern Kimball
Chief Executive Officer
Calgary Exhibition & Stampede

Vern Kimball has led the Calgary Exhibition & Stampede since 2004. Prior to this, he served 10 years as Chief Financial Officer for the organization and has held various leadership positions within the organization, including significant roles in Food Services, Sales and Facilities, marketing and long-range planning.

Vern attended the University of Calgary for his Bachelor of Arts, and then later his MBA.

Vern contributes his time and energy to a number of community organizations: he is a member of the Rotary Club of Calgary, serves as a member of the United Way Cabinet, is an advisory committee member to the Faculty of Communication and Culture at the University of Calgary, and is a Director of the Calgary Philharmonic Society.

Canfor

TIM MOSLEY
Brand Manager
Canfor, Wood Products Division

Tim Mosley joined Canfor in 2002 and is responsible for the creation and development of the Canfor Wood Products brands for domestic and overseas markets. Tim oversees all aspects of brand communication, research, strategic development and PR for the Canfor product brands. Tim launched the Jadestar brand into Japan, creating the largest lumber brand in that market. During the last five years Tim has helped develop a stronger image for the Canfor brands, including the house brand name. Prior to Canfor, Tim managed brands for Nestlé UK and Reckitt Benckiser UK, working in various categories including confectionery, food, household cleaning products and pharmaceuticals. The brands Tim has been responsible for include Smarties, Quality Street, Airwick and Lemsip.

Castrol

BOB MACDONALD
President
Wakefield Canada Inc.

As the sales and marketing drivers of Castrol products in Canada, Wakefield's people are ambassadors who focus on the brand and support it with exemplary customer service. Created through Bob MacDonald's leadership, Wakefield represents "a global first" for Castrol and a new way of doing business in the Canadian marketplace. Bob had retired in 2004 as Chief Operating Officer of BP Lubricants in North America, after 30+ years with Castrol in Canada and the United States. It is Bob's remarkable "people come first" tutelage that adds such potency to the Castrol brand. Wakefield is providing the added value that comes with product expertise, proactive customer relationship building and the core need to be results oriented from the customer's viewpoint. It's a new Canadian success story.

Cirque du Soleil

MARIO D'AMICO
Vice-President of Marketing
As Cirque du Soleil's Vice-President of Marketing, Mario D'Amico is responsible for brand development, sponsorships, the Web site, graphic design, public relations and the worldwide marketing of Cirque's shows and other products. A graduate of McGill University, he has over 20 years of marketing experience in the food sector and the advertising industry.

JOANNE FILLION
Senior Brand Director
Since 2000, Joanne Fillion has been Cirque du Soleil's Senior Brand Director. Her mandate includes managing the positioning of Cirque du Soleil in every region where it is active and developing new show brands, along with related communications. As guardian of Cirque du Soleil's brand image, Joanne has in-depth knowledge of a brand's impact and value.

CN Tower

LISA TOMPKINS
Director of Marketing and Communications

Lisa Tompkins has over 25 years experience in the entertainment and leisure/tourism industry, and currently directs the marketing and communication efforts at the world's tallest building — the CN Tower in Toronto, Canada. Prior to joining the Tower in 1993, she did a variety of work in theatre and event management.

Lisa is a graduate of Queen's University in Kingston, ON, Canada, and holds a bachelor's degree in Drama and English.

She serves on a number of Boards, including Communities In Bloom, a national initiative promoting beautification and civic pride, and its subsidiary WinterLights, which encourages communities to develop and promote festive celebrations and events throughout the winter months across Canada.

Crown Royal

HASAN IMAM
Vice President Marketing
Diageo Canada Inc.
Hasan's career spans over thirty years, twenty-five of which are in the beverage alcohol business with a five-year stint in the Tobacco business (Philip Morris). He worked in many functions including Market Research, Finance & Corporate Planning before becoming a Marketing Executive. In his current role, Hasan is responsible for providing leadership to the Diageo Marketing organization in the areas of Consumer Insights, Communication, Research, Strategic Planning and Innovation. Hasan is an Engineer complemented with an MBA in Finance & Operations Research.

MICHELE D'ANGELO
Category Director Brown Spirits
Diageo Canada Inc.
Michele's extensive background in the beverage alcohol industry began in the Research & Development area with Gilbey Canada Inc. She then moved into Sales and Marketing and specialized in public relations, sponsorship, event management and on premise. In her current role as Category Director at Diageo Canada, she is responsible for overseeing all marketing strategy and communication in Canada for Johnnie Walker, Captain Morgan and of course, Crown Royal. Michele is a graduate of the University of Guelph.

Esso

SIMON SMITH
Vice-President & General Manager, Fuels Marketing, Imperial Oil
Simon Smith has been responsible for the marketing of all Esso-branded products and services in Canada since 2001. Previously, he spent four years with ExxonMobil in Europe as marketing manager for France, then retail sales manager for all of Europe. Earlier in his career at Imperial, Simon held managerial roles in the industrial & wholesale, corporate planning and supply departments, after having served as the retail sales manager for Quebec, and automotive sales manager for Saskatchewan. He joined Imperial in 1982 after graduating from the University of Toronto with an MBA in Marketing.

ALEX ROTH
North America Brand Manager, Imperial Oil / ExxonMobil
Alex Roth oversees the presentation of the Esso, Exxon and Mobil brands to retail customers in Canada and the United States, with specific responsibility for marketing communications, customer research and brand offer development. Alex has spent many years in marketing at Imperial, including working in the areas of sponsorships, credit-card marketing and customer research. He joined Imperial in 1981 after earning a degree in Computer Science from York University in Toronto.

Fido

KARIM SALABI
Vice President, Marketing
Karim joined Fido in 1999 as Director, Corporate Strategy and Planning, and most recently held the position of Director, Marketing, Market and Customer Management, where he was the driving force behind the industry-leading customer loyalty program, the Fido Rewards Program. Karim is responsible for leading product commercialization, pricing, segment management, consumer loyalty and knowledge, marketing communications and branding, roaming services and international marketing activities for the company.

Karim holds a Bachelor of Arts Degree in Economics and a Master's Degree in Strategy and Marketing, both from McGill University.

PATRICK HADSIPANTELIS
Director, Marketing and Branding
Patrick has over 14 years of experience in consumer marketing, consumer long distance, market and campaign management, advertising and direct marketing.

Patrick joined Fido (then Microcel) in 1999 as Director, Marketing Communications and Branding. He is responsible for all national marketing communications, including advertising, direct marketing, Internet, POP and merchandising. In addition, he manages the Fido brand and its sub-brands, develops positioning strategies and ensures internal and external consistency.

He graduated from the Écoles des hautes études commerciales (Université de Montréal) with a Bachelor's degree in Business Administration.

Ford

DAVID GREENBERG
Vice President of General Marketing
Ford Motor Company of Canada Limted

David Greenberg is the Vice President of General Marketing at Ford Motor Company of Canada Limited.

David began his career in Ford Division Marketing and Sales in 1986 and by 1997, he joined Lincoln-Mercury Division as Brand and Advanced Product Strategy Manager.

As General Manager of Mazda Motor Corporation's Global Marketing Division based in Japan, David held worldwide responsibilities for Mazda's Product Marketing, Brand Strategies, Sales Planning, and Accessories Marketing and Development efforts.

In December 2003, David was named Group Product Marketing Manager, Ford North American Product Marketing.

He earned his M.B.A. from Duke University.

Hbc

DEBBIE EDWARDS
Senior Vice President of Marketing and Olympics
Hudson's Bay Company

Debbie has held a broad range of retail executive positions spanning over an illustrious 30-year career in retail with Hudson's Bay and Zellers. She has held roles in Store Operations, Marketing, Merchandising, Real Estate and Logistics.

In her current position as Senior Vice President of Marketing and Olympics, Debbie is responsible for all HBC Marketing, CRM and Business Intelligence. She also heads up the Olympics project, which includes outfitting Canada's Olympic Team through to 2012 as well as product design, development and sourcing for all HBC stores. She is also in charge of HBC's licensing agreement with COC and Vanoc.

The Heart & Stroke Foundation

SALLY BROWN
Executive Director, CEO

Sally Brown joined the Heart and Stroke Foundation of Canada in October of 2001 as executive director and CEO. She was previously with the Association of Universities and Colleges of Canada (AUCC), where she spent 10 years, first as vice-president, external relations and then as senior vice-president. Prior to AUCC, she was a special advisor in the prime minister's office. Sally is proud to lead an organization whose brand enjoys such a powerful reputation as a leader in heart disease and stroke research, with a strong track record of success. Over the past few years, the Foundation has undergone a revitalization of its brand, with its ten provinces working closely together to achieve consistency in communication and design that will go far in optimizing its presence and effectiveness as a champion of heart disease and stroke prevention.

111

BRAND GUARDIANS, *continued*

Hunter Douglas Inc.

MARV HOPKINS
President & Chief Executive
Officer

During his 20 years at Hunter Douglas Inc., President and CEO Marv Hopkins has led the transformation of window coverings from a commodity into a fashion statement. In doing so, he has galvanized the industry and propelled the company to the leadership position it enjoys today as North America's top manufacturer and marketer of custom window fashions, with 9,000 employees and 40 operations.

According to Hopkins, the Hunter Douglas brand is a treasured asset that has been built by a steadfast commitment to well-designed, innovative products supported by quality custom manufacturing, reliable and responsive service, consistent, tasteful marketing, and enduring customer relationships.

Hopkins is a graduate of the United States Air Force Academy. Prior to joining Hunter Douglas, he was a Division President at Lenox Inc.

Intel

ERIC KIM
Senior Vice-President and
General Manager

Eric Kim is Senior Vice-President and General Manager of Intel Corporation's Sales and Marketing Group. He also serves as Intel's Chief Marketing Officer. Mr. Kim is responsible for all sales and marketing operations worldwide. Prior to joining Intel in November 2004, Mr. Kim was an executive vice president at Samsung Electronics Co., Ltd. He was responsible for global marketing and new business development and helped make Samsung a leading worldwide consumer brand. Kim holds a bachelor's degree in physics from Harvey Mudd College, a master's in engineering systems from UCLA, and an MBA from Harvard Business School.

Jaguar Canada

GARY S. MOYER
President
Aston Martin Jaguar
Land Rover Canada

Moyer began his career at Ford Motor Company in 1981 in the New Orleans District Sales Office working for both Ford and Lincoln Mercury divisions as an analyst. He continued his career with Ford Motor Company in various capacities, including District Sales Representative, Fleet & Leasing Sales Specialist, Market Representation Manager, Advertising Manager, General Zone Manager and Regional Operations Manager. In 1998, Moyer held the position of Global Brand Manager for Mazda Motor Corporation in Hiroshima, Japan, where he was responsible for establishing a single brand strategy for Mazda globally. Before becoming president of Jaguar Land Rover Canada, Moyer held the position of president of Land Rover Japan in Tokyo for three years. Moyer's breadth of experience spans from working closely with the retailer side of the business in various field assignments to internal tactical experience working on global brand strategy.

Land Rover

GARY S. MOYER
President
Aston Martin Jaguar
Land Rover Canada

Moyer began his career at Ford Motor Company in 1981 in the New Orleans District Sales Office working for both Ford and Lincoln Mercury divisions as an analyst. He continued his career with Ford Motor Company in various capacities, including District Sales Representative, Fleet & Leasing Sales Specialist, Market Representation Manager, Advertising Manager, General Zone Manager and Regional Operations Manager. In 1998, Moyer held the position of Global Brand Manager for Mazda Motor Corporation in Hiroshima, Japan, where he was responsible for establishing a single brand strategy for Mazda globally. Before becoming president of Jaguar Land Rover Canada, Moyer held the position of president of Land Rover Japan in Tokyo for three years. Moyer's breadth of experience spans from working closely with the retailer side of the business in various field assignments to internal tactical experience working on global brand strategy.

Lay's

DALE HOOPER
Vice President Marketing
Frito Lay Canada
Frito Lay Canada is Canada's largest manufacturer and marketer of snack foods, with brands such as Lays, Ruffles, Doritos, Tostitos and Cheetos. Frito Lay Canada has been recognized as the winner of the Donald M. Kendall Award in two of the past four years. This Award recognizes the Top Frito Lay Operating Division in the World. Dale has more than 15 years of experience in the consumer packaged goods industry. 2006 marks his eighth year with Frito Lay Canada, and previously he worked for Cadbury Chocolate Canada. Dale is a graduate of Laurentian University's Bachelor of Commerce in Sports Administration program, and is based in Frito Lay Canada's head office in Mississauga, Ontario.

DAVID COLEBROOK
Director of Marketing
Frito Lay Canada
David Colebrook began his career at Procter & Gamble as an assistant brand manager. He then moved to Frito-Lay Canada, and in the past seven years has held multiple brand and sales assignments. He is currently responsible for overseeing all brand marketing activities of the Potato Chip, Doritos, Munchies, Multipacks and Cheetos brands. David is a graduate of Wilfrid Laurier University, and has an MBA from the Kellogg-Schulich EMBA program. David is based in Frito Lay Canada's head office in Mississauga, Ontario.

M&M's Chocolate Candies

CHRISTINE PARENT-INCH
Senior Brand Manager
Effem Inc.

Christine Parent-Inch leads the M&M's brand as Senior Brand Manager at Effem Inc., in Canada, a wholley owned subsidiary of Mars Inc. Christine has worked at Effem for nine years in many capacities, initially with Research & Development as a Senior Packaging Scientist focusing on "next generation" packaging formats for several global brands. During the past two years, she has developed and executed the Canadian M&M's sharing platform, resulting in strong and consistent share growth and brand awareness. Christine earned a Bachelor of Applied Science and Engineering at the University of Toronto and is a member of the Professional Engineers of Ontario.

MasterCard Canada

TAMMY SCOTT
Vice President, Brand
Marketing

Tammy Scott's marketing expertise extends well beyond her time at MasterCard, with over 12 years of advertising and marketing experience at Rethink, AGF Funds, Arnold Advertising and Canon Canada. During this time, she excelled in brand awareness programs and was a member of an award-winning team recognized at Cannes, The London International Advertising Awards and the Clios. In her current role as MasterCard Canada's brand ambassador, Ms. Scott and her team are responsible for developing and expanding new and existing branding initiatives, creating compelling marketing programs and developing effective brand tools for MasterCard Canada.

Michelin

BIBENDUM
Visionary and Champion for
Better Mobility
Michelin World

Bibendum is Michelin's ambassador, mediator and spokesman. In 1894, the two founding brothers, André and Edouard Michelin, were visiting the Universal Exhibition in Lyon when they noticed a pile of tires on one of the stands. The overall effect was sufficiently evocative for Edouard to think that, with arms, "it would make a man". Some time afterwards, André signalled out a sketch among drawings by the artist O'Galop. They adapted it to make a figure made of tires . . . and the character was born. Right from the outset, Bibendum has been a travelling companion or friendly guide, accompanying people on the move and showing them the way, no matter how short or long the distance. A citizen of the world, he is there to assist travelers, helping humankind and the world advance in the right direction.

Moen

MIKE DENNIS
President, Moen Canada and Latin America

Mike's more than 20-year-long career in the plumbing industry began with positions at American Standard and Jacuzzi Canada. Joining Moen Canada in 1991 as Vice President Wholesale Sales, he went on to become Vice President and General Manager in 1993 and President in 1997. In 2003, Mike was also appointed President of Moen's Latin American operations.

A well-known industry leader, Mike was first elected to the Board of Directors of the Canadian Institute of Plumbing and Heating in 1995 and continues to serve as Honourary Vice Chairman. In addition, Mike has participated on the Plumbing Industry Advisory Council and the Canadian Advisory Council on Plumbing.

Monster

GABRIEL BOUCHARD
Vice President and General Manager

Gabriel Bouchard is one of Canada's leading experts on employment and recruitment trends. While vice-president of marketing at TMP Worldwide in 1996, he founded an online recruitment service, and in 1997, he launched Monster.ca in Quebec and Canada. His insights into how the Internet is reshaping Canada's employment marketplace have driven Monster.ca's rapid growth as Canada's expert in online recruiting and one of the country's most successful Internet companies. He regularly travels across Canada to speak with employers and HR professionals about current employment issues and their impact for the future of Canadian companies.

LOUIS GAGNON
Vice President of Marketing

His vast experience in marketing spans several continents where he has, among other things, launched numerous products in new and established markets, and provided consulting services. Prior to joining Monster Canada, Mr. Gagnon developed and commercialized innovative, Web-based client acquisition solutions. He has also worked in SME environments and collaborated with sales teams on several occasions. Mr. Gagnon holds a Master of Science in Business Administration from University of Montreal.

Purina

SUSAN MOLENDA
Vice President, Marketing
Nestlé Purina PetCare

Susan is responsible for overseeing a broad portfolio of pet care brands to maintain Purina's dominant position in the marketplace. She began her career with Purina in 1989 and over the past 16 years has held various roles in marketing and customer development. She now oversees the entire marketing department, sits on the executive team and is challenged to find innovative ways to support this diverse portfolio. With the acquisition by Nestlé, increased globalization and pressures to remain competitive through innovation, the role of the V.P. is ever changing and challenging. Susan is an avid pet lover and a huge supporter of the Company slogan, Your pet, Our passion.

MARY SIEMIESZ
Director, Marketing
Nestlé Purina PetCare Canada

Starting her career at Purina over 15 years ago, Mary has led the marketing team in strengthening equity and launching well-known brands such as Pro Plan, Purina ONE, Beneful, Dog Chow and Cat Chow. With a belief in well-executed campaigns and innovative communications, she is touted as a true "lead by example" presence at Purina. Mary has also been a corporate spokesperson for many years, promoting the company's message about the important role that pets play as they interact with humans. In her own life, Mary's two dog companions — Labrador Retrievers named Indy and Oakley — are constant motivators.

RBC

JIM TORRANCE
Director, Global Brand Strategy

Jim Torrance is responsible for developing the programs that help sustain and enhance the RBC brand. Over the past four years, Jim and his team have revitalized RBC's brand through a series of internal and external programs, including its successful "First for You" external advertising campaign, implementation of a global brand communications system and development of internal communications to engage employees in support of the client-focused brand strategy. In a career that spans more than 20 years in brand strategy, Jim has held progressively senior positions at some of Canada's largest and most respected companies, including Canada Trust, Imperial Oil, Warner Lambert and Loblaws.

RE/MAX

DAVID BROWN
Executive Vice President, Brand Marketing and Promotion

David is responsible for leading all of RE/MAX's brand and promotional marketing for both consumer and industry channels. He also heads up Web site strategy and special consumer and internal events. Before joining RE/MAX in 1998, David worked extensively with leading franchise organizations like McDonald's and General Motors. He is a graduate of University of Toronto.

Rogers Communications, Inc.

STEPHEN GRAHAM
Executive VP, Corporate Marketing and Convergence

Early in his career, Stephen Graham was recruited to Coca-Cola Canada, where he helped boost Coke's market share by appealing to younger customers. At 32, he became President of Scali McCabe (now Lowe Roche) which won accolades as Agency of the Year. As AT&T's U.S. vice-president of worldwide marketing communications, Stephen was named number one on *Advertising Age*'s 1999 Power 50 list. In 2002, he joined CIBC as EVP and successfully reinvigorated its retail branches and advertising. Stephen moved to Rogers Communications early in 2006.

THOMAS A. TURNER
Vice President, Convergence

Thomas A. Turner is responsible for insuring that Rogers provides a consistent and supported customer experience and that a strategy of convergence and integration is implemented throughout the Rogers Group of Companies. Tom is also responsible for the management of the E-Commerce organization at Rogers.

Tom has been with the Rogers Group of Companies for 13 years. During his 9 year tenure at Rogers AT&T Wireless, Tom held various senior management roles in Finance, Sales, Marketing and Customer Care.

RONA

MICHAEL BROSSARD
Senior Vice-President, Marketing and Development
RONA Inc.

Michael Brossard has been working in marketing for 29 years. Over the years, he has established a solid reputation as a brand builder with Culinar, Delisle, TQS as well as Bauer Nike Hockey. Michael also worked on numerous projects in the United States and Europe, which allowed him to have an international perspective on the advertising market.

For the past five years, he has occupied senior marketing positions at RONA. In May 2005, he was promoted to Senior Vice-President, Marketing and Development and is now responsible for RONA's main marketing plan throughout Canada. Michael is the one who orchestrated RONA's acquisition of the Olympics Rings Rights for the next four Olympic Games, including Vancouver 2010.

Royal Doulton

MICHAEL PEARL
Vice President, Sales & Marketing

Prior to joining Royal Doulton Canada as Vice President of Sales & Marketing in 2006, Michael worked in various senior marketing, sales, and new product development positions in the confectionery and bakery industries. Michael's confectionery career began in 1983 with Cadbury. He moved to Topps Canada as General Manager. As Director of New Product Development at Canada Bread, he launched products which won both the Canadian Grand Prix New Product Award for bakery innovation and the Sial D'Or award for most unique bakery product in the world in 1995. Michael has also worked as a consultant in strategic consumer research management.

BRAND GUARDIANS, *continued*

STAPLES Business Depot

STEVE MATYAS
President
STAPLES Business Depot

Steve's retail career began with Shoppers Drug Mart Ltd. His hands-on approach to store operations came to the attention of Jack Bingleman, who founded the office supplies superstore industry in Canada in 1991. He joined the start-up company as its first employee and quickly advanced to Vice-President, Sales and Operations. In August 2000, Steve became President, with sales now exceeding $2 billion, and with Staples brand positioning a prime force contributing to that growth. As part of the parent company's senior leadership team, Steve brings a strong focus on innovation to global strategies.

Symantec

James A. Rose
Vice President
Brand and Global
Marketing Communications

Jim is responsible for leading the branding and marketing communications for the world's fourth-largest software company. Believing that the primary purpose of a brand is to enable company strategy, Jim strives to ensure that every element of the company is "on brand."

Prior to joining Symantec in 2005 Jim was responsible for the Branding and Marketing Communications efforts of the IBM Software Group and the Citibank Internet Payments Division. He also spent a number of years as an advertising agency Account Executive, where he managed accounts such as AT&T Network Systems, Compaq Computer, Xerox and Lear Jet.

Texas Instruments

Jan Spence
Brand Director

Jan Spence directs all branding activities for Texas Instruments, overseeing brand positioning and evolution of both the TI brand and product brands within the company, directly impacting marketing, communications and advertising of the multibillion-dollar global semiconductor company. Jan has been with TI for more than 20 years, serving in various marketing and technical positions. Prior to taking on the lead brand role for TI, she was communication manager for the company's successful DLP Products® division, serving the HDTV and digital cinema markets. She joined DLP Products in 1996 at its commercial inception to develop and eventually oversee all customer and consumer communications. She was responsible for leading TI's first consumer advertising in almost 30 years. Jan began her career with TI as a programmer and has served in sales roles throughout the organization.

Tim Hortons

CATHY WHELAN MOLLOY
Vice-President, Brand
Marketing and
Merchandising

A graduate of Carleton University, Cathy Whelan Molloy brought five years of extensive retail and packaged goods advertising agency experience to The TDL Group in 1993 when she joined the company as a Regional Marketing Manager. Cathy was promoted to Brand Manager in 1995 and moved to the position of Director, Brand Advertising & U.S. Marketing in 1997. It was in this role that she developed the strategic positioning for the brand's launch in the United States. In 2000, Cathy was promoted to her current role, Vice-President, Brand Marketing and Merchandising, where she is accountable for developing the strategic direction and creative execution of the brand vision across all consumer touch points. Under Cathy's leadership, Tim Hortons has achieved a number of marketing accolades, including "Marketer of the Year," *Marketing Magazine*, 2005.

TSX Group

DAVID ABLETT
Vice President, Public and
Corporate Affairs

David is responsible for formulating TSX Group's corporate communications for one of Canada's exceptional brands. He helped TSX Group introduce and refine brand strategy as it transformed into a publicly traded for-profit company. Prior to joining TSX Group, David executed plans involving communications strategy and brand development at two leading banks, as well as the Privy Council Office of the Canadian government. A former Editorial Page Editor and National Newspaper Award winner at the *Vancouver Sun*, and Senior Assistant Secretary to the Cabinet in the Privy Council Office, he received his MS in Journalism from Columbia University, New York, and was named Pulitzer Traveling Scholar.

STEVE KEE
Director, Media &
Marketing

Steve's responsibilities for corporate communications reflect his long career at TSX Group. Most recently his management has been extended to brand and marketing functions, where he is responsible for the maintenance of brand standards and consistency across the company. Prior to joining Toronto Stock Exchange, Steve was a member of senior management at Canada's first all-news radio network. He graduated with honours from Humber College Radio Broadcasting Program and completed the leadership development program at Wharton Business School.

United Way of Canada-Centraide Canada

Al Hatton
President and Chief
Executive Officer

Al Hatton is President and Chief Executive Officer of United Way of Canada-Centraide Canada, a national organization that provides leadership and programs and services to its 124 member United Ways-Centraides in Canada. Mr. Hatton was the former Executive Director of the Coalition of National Voluntary Organizations. He was Executive Director for the YMCA in Montreal and National Director of Job Generation and Director of External Relations for YMCA Canada. He is a founding member of the Voluntary Sector Roundtable and now serves as a member of the Voluntary Sector Forum. Mr. Hatton also served in various volunteer positions including Youth Services Bureau of Ottawa and Canadian Council of International Co-operation. He was also a member of different task forces including Citizenship and Immigration Canada, Employment and Immigration Canada, and Human Resource Development Canada.

Weather Network and MétéoMédia

PIERRE MORRISSETTE
President and CEO,
Pelmorex Media Inc.

Pierre Morrissette is the controlling shareholder, President and CEO of Pelmorex Media Inc., a communications company which he founded in 1989. The company's core business is weather-related information services distributed nationally through its specialty television networks, The Weather Network and MétéoMédia, and its Web sites, theweathernetwork.com and meteomedia.com. The television networks, which rank among Canada's most widely distributed and watched television networks, are available in over 10 million homes across Canada. The Web sites are among the leading content sites in Canada. The company employs over 300 people.

Yellow Pages Group

Geneviève LeBrun
Vice President, Marketing
Yellow Pages Group

Over the last 10 years at Yellow Pages Group, Geneviève LeBrun has played a key role in positioning the company as a market leader while overseeing the national marketing programs and product development. She contributed to the sale of the company from Bell Canada in 2002, and then became one of the key players behind the renaissance of the Yellow Pages™ brand. In 2003, she actively participated in the company's initial public offering, and in the acquisition of SuperPages® in 2005. Following this acquisition, she helped re-introduce the Yellow Pages™ brand in Western Canada. Since June 2006, she is the Vice President, Marketing of Trader Corporation, a Canadian leader in print and online vertical media where she will work on modernizing the brand portfolio for the automotive, real estate and generalist verticals. She holds a Bachelor of Commerce and an M. Sc. in Marketing from HEC (Montréal).